PUBLIC SCHOOL EDUCATION

First published 1872
This edition published by Lector House in 2024

ISBN: 978-93-6138-109-6

Lector House LLP
Registered Office: H. No. 96, Block C, Tomar Colony,
Burari, Delhi – 110084, India
info@lectorhouse.com
www.lectorhouse.com

PUBLIC SCHOOL EDUCATION

MICHAEL MÜLLER

2024

LECTOR HOUSE LLP

PUBLIC SCHOOL EDUCATION

BY

MICHAEL MÜLLER, C.S.S.R.,

Priest of the Congregation of the Most Holy Redeemer.

CONTENTS

Chapter *Page*

I. Introductory. 1

II. Education—Its Object and Necessity. .5

III. Origin of the Public School System. 13

IV. Exposé of the Public School System.. 27

V. Evil Consequences of the Public School System on the Male Portion of Society. 30

VI. Evil Consequences of the Public School System on the Female Portion of Society. 32

VII. What is it to be a Mother?. 40

VIII. Evil Consequences of the Public School System Continued. 47

IX. The State.—Its Usurpation of the Individual Rights.—Its Incompetency to Educate. 51

X. The State a Robber.—Violation of our Constitution and Common Law. 60

XI. Remedy for the Diabolical Spirit and the Crimes in our Country. 69

XII. The Denominational System alone Satisfies the Wants of All, and can save the Republic.. 84

XIII. The Catholic Priest on the Public School System. 106

XIV. Answers to Objections. 121

XV. Zeal of the Priest for the Catholic Education of our Children. 133

CHAPTER I.

INTRODUCTORY.

American fellow-citizens—America is my home! I have no other country. After my God and my religion, my country is the dearest object of my life! I love my country as dearly as any one else can. It is this love that makes my heart bleed when I call to mind the actual state of society in our country, and the principles that prevail everywhere. It is indeed but too true that we live in a most anti-Christian age; principles are disregarded, and iniquity is held in veneration. We see nothing but confusion in religion, in government, in the family circle. Sects spring up and swarm like locusts, destroying not only revealed religion, but rejecting even the law of nature. Fraud, theft, and robbery are practised almost as a common trade. The press justifies rebellion, secret societies, and plots for the overthrow of established governments. The civil law, by granting divorce, has broken the family tie. Children are allowed to grow up in ignorance of true religious principles, and thereby become regardless of their parents. The number of apostates from Christianity is on the increase, at least in the rising generation. Current literature is penetrated with the spirit of licentiousness, from the pretentious quarterly to the arrogant and flippant daily newspaper, and the weekly and monthly publications are mostly heathen or maudlin. They express and inculcate, on the one hand, stoical, cold, and polished pride of mere intellect, or on the other, empty and wretched sentimentality. Some employ the skill of the engraver to caricature the institutions and offices of the Christian religion, and others to exhibit the grossest forms of vice, and the most distressing scenes of crime and suffering. The illustrated press has become to us what the amphitheatre was to the Romans when men were slain, women were outraged, and Christians given to the lions to please a degenerate populace. The number of the most unnatural crimes is beyond computation. A wide-spread and deep-seated dishonesty and corruption has, like some poisonous virus, inoculated the great body of our public men in national, state, and municipal positions, so much so that rascality seems to be the rule, and honesty the exception. Real statesmanship has departed from amongst us; neither the men nor the principles of the olden time exist any longer.

The shameless cynicism with which the great public plunderers of our day brazen out their infamy, is only equalled by the apathy with which the public permits these robberies, and condone for them by lavishing place and power upon the offenders. "The way of the transgressor" has ceased to be "hard"—unless he be a transgressor of very low degree—and rascality rides rampant over the land, from the halls of Congress to the lowest department of public plunder.

The poet has well said that Vice, once grown familiar to the view, after first exciting our hate, next succeeded in gaining our pity, and finally was taken into our embrace.

The familiarity of the public mind with daily and almost hourly instances of public peculation and betrayal of high trusts has created this indulgent disposition, until at last the wholesome indignation, which is the best safeguard of honesty, has been diluted into a maudlin sympathy with the malefactors. And the rankness of the growth of this evil is not more startling than its rapidity. It is a new thing—a foul fungus, suddenly forced into fetid life, out of the corruptions engendered by the war. It is "a new departure" in a wrong direction—down that smooth, broad path to the devil.

We all remember the sensation which, before the war, was ever caused by the discovery of a public defaulter, and the indignation which drove him ever forth from place and country, on his detection. Punishment sure and swift was certain to seize upon him, if he dared linger after the facts were known.

A breach of trust was not then considered a joke, nor theft elevated into the dignity of a fine art, whose most eminent professors were to be regarded with envy and admiration.

Think of the clamor which was raised over the comparatively petty peculations of Swartwout, Schuyler, Fowler, and other small sinners like them, who even found the country too hot to hold them, and died in exile, as an expiation to the public sentiment they had outraged.

Yet their frauds were as molehills to the mountains which the busy hands of our public peculators have heaped up, and are daily piling higher. Within the last ten years, where they stole cents, their successors stole by thousands and tens of thousands; and, instead of flying from punishment, flaunt their crimes and their ill-gotten wealth in the face of the community, heedless either of the arm of the law, or the more potent hiss of public scorn.

And this financial dishonesty of the times is as true of commercial as of political circles, and as patent at Washington as at New York and other cities. "Think you that those eighteen men on whom the tower of Siloam fell, were sinners above all others in Jerusalem? I tell you nay!" Think you that those six or seven on whom the axe of the public press fell, are sinners above all in New York and elsewhere? If all men that have been guilty of fraud in New York and elsewhere were to have a tower fall on them, there would be funerals enough for fifty years.

One of the saddest symptoms of degeneracy in a people is evinced by a desperate levity—a scoffing spirit such as that which inspired the French people when they denied even God, and substituted a prostitute to be their "Goddess of Reason." Much of that spirit is unhappily manifesting itself in our country.

That most fearful picture of a corrupt community drawn by Curran in his description of the public pests of his day—"remaining at the bottom like drowned bodies while soundness remained in them, but rising only as they rotted, and floating only from the buoyancy of corruption"—seems, unhappily, destined to find its parallel here, unless public virtue and public indignation should awake to condemn and chastise the corruption which is tainting and poisoning the air around us.

The judgment which overtook the men of Siloam was visited on them for sins not unlike those which seem to invite a similar judgment from offended Heaven upon our modern Siloams, and is no jesting matter. Nay, in view of the many recent terrible visitations which have fallen upon different parts of our country, many voices have already been raised proclaiming them as marks of Divine wrath against national sins, perpetrated by a people who should, by their lives, testify their sense of the blessings showered upon them in more prodigal profusion than on any other nation in the annals of mankind.

That the great body of our people are corrupt, or that they at heart approve of corruption, no one will be mad enough to maintain. But they are responsible before Heaven and to posterity for the criminal apathy they manifest in their silent sanction of the corruption and crime which are fast making the American name a synonyme for theft, for brazen impudence and unblushing rascality.

In the life of a nation, as in that of an individual, there are periods which are critical; and a restoration to health, or the certainty of speedy death, depends on the way this malady is met. The crisis which now menaces the life and health of the United States cannot be far distant; for private virtue cannot long survive the death of public honor and honesty, nor private morality fail to catch the contagion of public profligacy. If the representative men of a country, those in whom its high trusts are reposed, be corrupt and shameless, they will drag down into the same mire the morals of the people they plunder and misrepresent. Indeed we want no prophet, nor one raised from the dead, to tell us the awfully fatal results. What can be done to stem the fearful torrent of evils that flood the land? We all know that when, in 1765, the famous Stamp Act was passed in the British Parliament, on the news reaching Boston the bells were muffled, and rang a funeral peal. In New York the "Act" was carried through the streets with a death's head bearing this inscription: "The Folly of England and the Ruin of America." So great was the opposition to the "Act," that it was repealed during the spring of 1766. This shows how quickly the evils of society can be put down if people set to work in earnest.

Now we cannot expect the people to set to work in earnest about stemming the torrent of the great evils of the land, unless they are well enlightened as to the source from which they flow. This source is principally that wrong system of education introduced into this country about fifty years ago. At that time very few, perhaps, could foresee what effects it was calculated to produce. After a long trial, we can now pronounce on it with certainty by its results. The tree, no longer a sapling, can be judged by its fruits. These fruits have been so bad that it is high time to call the attention of the public to the tree.

Now in calling attention to this tree, I wish it to be once for all distinctly understood, that whatever of a seemingly or even really harsh nature I may say in this discussion on the Public Schools, is intended and directed *solely against the system*. For those who manage or officiate in them, as teachers or otherwise, I have, I trust, all the courtesy, charity, and respect due from one citizen to another. If I offend the prejudices, convictions, or susceptibilities of any on this strangely misrepresented subject, no one can more regret it than myself; I can truly say it is not intended. All I ask of my fellow-citizens is a fair discussion on this great question of education, to look at it without prejudice, without bigotry; for if prejudice and bigotry stand in our way, they will stand in the way of the glory and stability of this country, whose future God only knows. It is the duty of all citizens to labor with a good heart, a clear mind, an earnest soul, to do all they can in building up, and strengthening, and making still more glorious this great American people.

CHAPTER II.

EDUCATION—ITS OBJECT AND NECESSITY.

The question of Education is, of all others, the most important. It has for some time back received a good deal of attention in public meetings, in newspapers, and in the pulpit. In fact it has become a question of the day. On this question, however, there is unfortunately such an amount of ignorance, prejudice, and confusion of ideas, that it is almost impossible to make the public understand it. The reason of this is, because so many follow the vague views expressed on this subject in newspapers. Many a paper is undoubtedly political, and so far partisan; and as such its editor will defend and advance what he believes to be the principles of his party. But the question of education rises above party politics; yet when you read many a paper you will find that the editor appeals to the prejudice and passions of party in a way quite unworthy of an independent journalist, and of the grave subject under consideration. He advances principles which, at first sight, seem to be quite true; for instance: "Public School Education is necessary for our republican form of government, for the very life of the Republic." "It is an admitted axiom, that our form of government, more than all others, depends on the intelligence of the people." "The framers of our Constitution firmly believed that a republic form of government could not endure without intelligence and education generally diffused among the people. The State must, therefore, take all means within its power to promote and encourage popular education, and furnish this intelligence of the people through her public schools."

At first sight such principles seem to be true, and the people in general will accept them. Experience teaches that the public will accept, without question, almost any maxim or problem, provided it be formulated in such a manner as to convey some specific meaning that does not demand reflection or complex examination. For the same reason no small portion of the public will reject anything that at first sight seems to exceed the measure of their understanding. Knaves and charlatans, knowing this, impose on the public by flattering their intelligence, that they may accomplish their own ambitious and selfish ends. In this way a multitude of pernicious religious, social, and political maxims have come into vogue, especially in reference to the question of public instruction. Yet on the sound principles concerning this question of education, and on the right understanding of them, depend not only the temporal and eternal happiness of the people, but also the future maintenance and freedom, nay, even the material prosperity, of the Republic.

In the discussion of the system of education it will no longer do to use vague, unmeaning expressions, or to advance some general puzzling principles to keep the public in the dark on this important point. It is high time that the public should be thoroughly enlightened on the subject of education. Everybody is talking about education,—the advantages of education, the necessity of education; and yet almost all have come to use the word in its narrowest and most imperfect meaning, as implying mere cultivation of the intellectual faculties, and even this is done in the most superficial manner, by cramming the mind with facts, instead of making it reflect and reason. The great majority even of those who write upon the subject take no higher view.

The term *education* comprehends something more than mere instruction. One may be instructed without being educated; but he cannot be educated without being instructed. The one has a partial or limited, the other a complete or general, meaning. What, then, is the meaning of Education? Education comes from the Latin "educo," and means, according to Plato, "to give to the body and soul all the perfection of which they are susceptible"; in other words, the object of education is to render the youth of both sexes beautiful, healthful, strong, intelligent and virtuous. It is doubtless the will of the Creator that man—the masterpiece of the visible world—should be raised to that perfection of which he is capable, and for the acquisition of which he is offered the proper means. It is the soul of man which constitutes the dignity of his being, and makes him the king of the universe. Now the body is the dwelling of the soul—the palace of this noble king; the nobility of the soul must induce us to attend to its palace—to the health and strength and beauty of the body;—health, strength and beauty are the noble qualities of the body.

The noble qualities of the soul are virtue and learning. Virtue and learning are the two trees planted by God in Paradise; they are the two great luminaries created by God to give light to the world; they are the two Testaments, the Old and the New; they are the two sisters, Martha and Mary, living under one roof in great union and harmony, and mutually supporting each other.

Learning is, next to virtue, the most noble ornament and the highest improvement of the human mind. It is by learning that all the natural faculties of the mind obtain an eminent degree of perfection. The memory is exceedingly improved by appropriate exercise, and becomes, as it were, a storehouse of names, facts, entire discourses, etc., according to every one's exigency or purposes. The understanding—the light of the soul—is exceedingly improved by exercise, and by the acquisition of solid science and useful knowledge. Judgment, the most valuable of all the properties of the mind, and by which the other faculties are poised, governed and directed, is formed and perfected by experience, and regular well-digested studies and reflection; and by them it attains to true justness and taste. The mind, by the same means, acquires a steadiness, and conquers the aversion which sloth raises against the serious employments of its talents.

How much the perfection of the mind depends upon culture, appears in the difference of understanding between the savages (who, except in treachery, cunning and shape, scarce seem to differ from the apes which inhabit their forests) and the most elegant and civilized nations. A piece of ground left wild produces nothing but weeds and briers, which by culture would be covered with corn, flowers and fruit. The difference is not less between a rough mind and one that is well cultivated.

The same natural culture, indeed, suits not all persons. Geniuses must be explored, and the manner of instructing proportioned to them. But there is one thing which suits all persons, and without which knowledge is nothing but "a sounding brass and tinkling cymbal": this is the supernatural culture of the soul, or the habitual endeavor of man of rendering himself more pleasing in the sight of God by the acquisition of solid Christian virtues, in order thus to reach his last end—his eternal happiness. It is for this reason that our Saviour tells us: "What doth it profit a man if he gain the whole world, and lose his own soul? For what shall a man give in exchange for his soul?"—(Matt. xvi. 26.) It is, then, the *supernatural culture,* or the perfection of the soul, that is to be principally attended to in education.

Now what is the perfection of soul? The perfection of each being in general, is that which renders the being better and more perfect. It is clear that inferior beings cannot make superior ones better and more perfect. Now the soul, being immortal, is superior to all earthly or perishable things. These, then, cannot make the soul better and more perfect, but rather worse than she is; for he who seeks what is worse than himself, makes himself worse than he was before. Therefore the good of the soul can be only that which is better and more excellent than the soul herself is. Now God alone is this Good—He being Goodness Itself. He who possesses God may be said to possess the goodness of all other things; for whatever goodness they possess, they have from God. In the sun, for instance, you admire the light; in a flower, beauty; in bread, the savor; in the earth, its fertility; all these have their being from God. No doubt God has reserved to Himself far more than He has bestowed upon creatures; this truth admitted, it necessarily follows that he who enjoys God possesses in him all other things; and consequently the very same delight which he would have taken in other things, had he enjoyed them separately, he enjoys in God, in a far greater measure, and in a more elevated manner. For this reason, St. Francis of Assisium often used to exclaim: "My God and my All"—a saying to which he was so accustomed that he could scarcely think of anything else, and often spent whole nights in meditating on this truth.

Certainly true contentment is only that which is taken in the Creator, and not that which is taken in the creature; a contentment which no man can take from the soul, and in comparison with which all other joy is sadness, all pleasure sorrow, all sweetness bitter, all beauty ugliness, all delight affliction. It is most certain that "when face to face we shall see God as He is," we shall have most perfect joy and happiness. It follows, then, most clearly, that the nearer we approach to God in this life, the more contentment of mind and the greater happiness of soul we shall enjoy; and this contentment and joy is of the self-same nature as that which we shall have in heaven; the only difference is, that here our joy and happiness is in an incipient state, whilst there it will be brought to perfection. He, then, is a truly wise and learned, a truly well-educated, man, who here below has learned how to seek God, and to be united as much as possible with the Supreme Good of his soul. He therefore imparts a good education to the soul, who teaches her how to seek and to find her own Good.

Now what is it to teach the soul to find her own Supreme Good? It is to train, to teach, to lead the child in the way he should go, leading him in the paths of duty, first to God, and secondly to his neighbor. All not professed infidels, it appears to me, must admit this definition. But as very many believe in "Webster," or "Worcester," I give the former's definition of education: "Educate"—To instill into the mind principles of art, science, *morals*, *religion*, and behavior. According to this definition of education, morals and religion constitute essential parts of education. Indeed, the first and most important of all duties which the child must learn are his moral and religious duties; for it will, I hope, be universally admitted that man is not born into this world merely to "propagate his species, make money, enjoy the pleasures of this world, and die." If he is not born for that end, then it is most important that he be taught for what end he was born, and the way appointed by his Creator to attain that end.

Every child born into this world is given a body and soul. This soul, for which the body was created, and which will rise with it at the last day, be judged with it for the acts done in life, and be happy or unhappy with it for all eternity, is, in consequence of the "fall," turned away from God, and the body, no longer acting in obedience to right reason, seeks its own gratification, like any irrational animal. Religion (from *religio*) is the means provided by a merciful God to reunite the chain broken by the sin of our first parents, and bridge over the chasm opened between man and his divine destiny. To give this knowledge of religion is the principal purpose of education. Without this it is mere natural *instruction*, but no education at all. It would be worse than giving, as we say, "the play of Hamlet with the part of the Prince of Denmark left out."

Religion, then, forms the spirit and essence of all true education. As leaven must be diffused throughout the entire mass in order to produce its effects, so religion must be thoroughly diffused throughout the child's entire education, in order to be solid and effective. Not a moment of the hours of school should be left without religious influence. It is the constant breathing of the air that preserves our bodily life, and it is the constant dwelling in a religious atmosphere that preserves the life of the youthful soul. Here are laid the primitive principles of future character and conduct. These religious principles may be forgotten, or partially effaced, in the journey of life, but they will nevertheless endure, because they are engraved by the finger of God Himself. The poor wanderer, when the world has turned its back upon him, after having trusted to its promises only to be deceived, after having yielded to its temptations and blandishments only to be cruelly injured and mocked, may, at last, in the bitterness of his heart, "remember the days of his youth," and "return to his father's house." So long as faith remains, however great the vice or the crime, there is something to build on, and room to hope for repentance, for reformation, and final salvation. Faith or religion once gone, all is gone. Religion is the crystal vase in which education is contained, or rather the spirit which infuses and vitalizes it. Religion is the very life of society, the very soul of a Christian State.

All nations and governments know and understand that to exclude Christian education from the schools is to exclude it from their law, legislature, courts, and public and private manners. It should, then, ever be borne in mind that religion, though distinguishable, is never separable from true civil and political science and philosophy. Enlightened statesmanship will always accept and recognize religious education as a most valuable and powerful ally in the government of the State, or political society. The great Washington clearly asserts this in his farewell address to the American people: "Of the dispositions," he says, "which lead to political prosperity, religion and morality are indispensable supports. Where is the security for property or for life, if the sense of religious obligation desert the oaths which are administered in our courts of justice? And let it not be supposed that morality can be maintained without religion." Accordingly our legislatures are opened with prayer, the Bible is on the benches of our courts; it is put into the hands of jurymen, voters, and even tax-payers; indeed, from its late use and abuse, one might think that we were living under the Pentateuch, and that the whole moral law and Ten Commandments were bound to the brows of the public or State phylacteries.

Indeed, the politics of every tribe, nation, or people, will reflect in an exact degree their moral and religious convictions and education. If these are false, the political society will be violent, disorderly, and abnormal; if true, the State is calm, prosperous, strong and happy. If these propositions be true, and I claim they are as axiomatic and undeniable as any proposition in Euclid—yea more so, for they are the maxims of inspired wisdom—how immeasurably important is a true Christian education!

And if its influence is so great in determining even the political conduct of men, it is still more necessary and powerful in forming the character of true woman—the Christian wife, mother, and daughter. The influence of Christian woman on society is incalculable. Admitting it possible, for a moment, that irreligious men might construct or direct an atheistical State, yet it would be utterly vain to build up the family, the groundwork of all organized communities, without the aid of the Christian woman. She it is who, in the deep and silent recesses of the household, puts together those primitive and enduring materials, each in its place and order, on which will rest and grow, to full beauty and development, the fair proportion of every well-ordained State. This foundation is laid in the care and rearing of good and dutiful children. The task of the Christian mother may indeed be slow, and unobserved; but God makes use of the weak to confound the strong, and this is beautifully illustrated in the Christian woman, who is strong because she is weak, most influential when she is most retired, and most happy, honored, cherished and respected when she is doing the work assigned her by Divine Providence, in the bosom of her household.

It will be admitted, then, that the education of girls demands a special culture. Generally upon mothers the domestic instruction of the children, in their infancy, mainly depends. They ought, therefore, to be well instructed in the motives of religion, articles of faith, and all the practical duties and maxims of piety. Then history, geography, and some tincture of works of genius and spirit, may be joined with suitable arts and other accomplishments of their sex and condition, provided they be guided by and referred to religion, and provided books of piety and exercises of devotion always have the first place, both in their hearts and in their time.

They should, then, from their earliest years, if possible, be separated in their studies, their plays, and their going and returning from school, from children of the opposite sex. They should be placed under the *surveillance and instruction* of mature and pious women. Every possible occasion and influence should be used to instil into their young and plastic minds, by lesson and example, principles of religion and morality. Their studies should be grave and practical. Their nervous organization is naturally acute, and should be strengthened, but not stimulated, as it too often is, thereby laying the foundation for that terrible and tormenting train of neuralgic affections of after-life, debilitating mind and body.

A thorough Christian education, then, is the basis of all happiness and peace, for the family as well as for the State itself; for every State is but the union of several families. It is for this reason that we find good parents so willing to make every sacrifice for the Christian education of their children, and that all true statesmen, and all true lovers of their country, have always encouraged and advocated that kind of education which is based upon Christian principles.

Good, dutiful children are the greatest blessing for parents and for the State, whilst children without religion are the greatest misfortune, the greatest curse that can come upon parents and upon the State.

History informs us that Dion the philosopher gave a sharp reproof to Dionysius the tyrant, on account of his cruelty. Dionysius felt highly offended, and resolved to avenge himself on Dion; so he took the son of Dion prisoner, not, indeed, for the purpose of killing him, but of giving him up into the hands of a godless teacher. After the young man had been long enough under this teacher to learn from him everything that was bad and impious, Dionysius sent him back to his father. Now what object had the tyrant in acting thus? He foresaw that this corrupted son, by his impious conduct during his whole lifetime, would cause his father constant grief and sorrow, so much so that he would be for him a lifelong affliction and curse. This, the tyrant thought, was the longest and greatest revenge he could take on Dion for having censured his conduct.

Plato, a heathen philosopher, relates that when the sons of the Persian kings had reached the age of fourteen, they were given to four teachers. The first of these teachers had to instruct them in their duties towards God; the second, to be truthful under all circumstances; the third, to overcome their passions; and the fourth teacher taught them how to be valiant and intrepid men.

This truth, that good children are the greatest blessing and that bad children are the greatest affliction that can befall parents and the State, needs no further illustration. There is no father, there is no mother, there is no statesman, who is not thoroughly convinced of this truth. Can we, then, wonder that the Catholic Church has always encouraged a truly Christian education?

There is nothing in history better established than the fact that the Catholic Church has been at all times, and under the most trying circumstances, the generous fostering-mother of education. She has labored especially, with untiring care, to educate the poor, who are her favorite children. It was the Catholic Church that founded, and endowed liberally, almost all the great universities of Europe. Protestants and infidels are very apt to overlook the incalculable benefits which the

Church has conferred on mankind, and yet without her agency civilization would have been simply impossible.

The Catholic Church was, moreover, the first to establish common schools for the free education of the people. As early as A.D. 529, we find the Council of Vaison recommending the establishment of public schools. In 800, a synod at Mentz ordered that the parochial priests should have schools in the towns and villages, that "the little children of all the faithful should learn letters from them. Let them receive and teach these with the utmost charity, that they themselves may shine as the stars forever. Let them receive no remuneration from their scholars, unless what the parents, through charity, may voluntarily offer." A Council at Rome, in 836, ordained that there should be three kinds of schools throughout Christendom: episcopal, parochial in towns and villages, and others wherever there could be found place and opportunity. The Council of Lateran, in 1179, ordained the establishment of a grammar school in every cathedral for the gratuitous instruction of the poor. This ordinance was enlarged and enforced by the Council of Lyons, in 1245. In a word, from the days of Charlemagne, in the ninth century, down to those of Leo X., in the sixteenth century, free schools sprang up in rapid succession over the greater part of Europe; and, mark well, it was almost always under the shadow of her churches and her monasteries! Throughout the entire period, called, by ignorant bigotry, the "dark ages," Roman Pontiffs and Catholic Bishops assembled in council and enacted laws requiring the establishment of free schools in connection with all the cathedral and parochial churches. This is a fact so clearly proven by Catholic and Protestant historians, that to deny it would be to betray a gross ignorance of history. Even at the present day, the Papal States, with a population of only about 2,000,000, contain seven universities, with an average attendance of 660 students, whilst Prussia, with a population of 14,000,000, and so renowned for her education, has only seven! Again, in every street in Rome there are, at short distances, public primary schools for the education of the children of the middle and lower classes. Rome, with a population of only about 158,000 souls, has 372 public primary schools, with 482 teachers, and over 14,000 children attending them, whilst Berlin, with a population more than double that of Rome, has only 264 schools. Thus originated the popular or common schools, or the free education of the people, as an outgrowth of the Catholic Church.

Every one knows that to the Catholic Church is due the preservation of literature after the downfall of the Roman Empire; and all those who are versed in history must admit that the Popes, the rulers of the Church, have been the greatest promoters and protectors of literature and learned men in every age. They collected and preserved the writings of the great historians, poets, and philosophers of Greece and Rome, and they encouraged and rewarded the learned men who, by their labors, made those fountains of classical literature easily accessible to all students. What shall I say of the patronage which they accorded to painting, sculpture, architecture, music, and the other arts which raise up and refine the human soul? Even the present glorious Pontiff, Pius IX., in the midst of troubles and persecutions, has done more for education than the richest and most powerful sovereigns of the world. You will unite with me, I am sure, in praying that he may soon recover the sovereignty of Rome and the Papal States, and that he may live many years to defend, as he has done in the past, the cause of religion, truth, Christian education, and civilization in the world. But it would take a whole day to refer even briefly to all that the Catholic Church and her Supreme Pontiffs have done to dissipate ignorance, and to improve and enlighten the mind of man. I shall merely add that a Protestant writer, and an open enemy of our religion, does not hesitate to state that, acting under the guidance and protection of the Holy See, some of our religious orders, which are so often assailed and calumniated, have done more for the promotion of philosophy, theology, history, archæology, and learning in general, than all the great universities of the world, with all their wealth and patronage.

Moreover, it is a well-known fact that the Catholic Church has always fought for the liberty to educate her children not only in the necessary branches of science, but also, and above all, to teach them, at the same time, their religious duties towards God and their fellow-men. And who but an infidel can blame her for that?

Every one must know that by the united efforts of the Catholic clergy and laity, schools, colleges, seminaries, boarding-schools for ladies and boys, and other educational establishments, have been erected in almost every part of the world, and erected without a cent of public money, which was so plentifully lavished on Protestant institutions. But, without leaving this country, do we not find in the various States of the Union magnificent proofs of generous Catholic zeal in promoting everything connected with education? And have not the parochial and religious clergy in so many places made the noblest exertions to erect institutions for the instruction of their flocks? and have not the laity assisted them in a most munificent manner? All this shows their great desire to promote the growth of knowledge.

Man is born a believing creature, and cannot, if he would, destroy altogether this noble attribute of his nature. If he is not taught, or will not accept, a belief in the living and uncreated God, he will create and worship some other god in His stead. He cannot rest on *pure negation*. There never has been a real, absolute unbeliever. All the so-called unbelievers are either knaves or idiots. All the Gentile nations of the past have been religious people; all the Pagan powers of the present are also believers. There never has been a nation without faith, without an altar, without a sacrifice. Man can never, even for a single instant, escape the All-seeing Eye of God, or avoid the obligations of duty imposed on him by his Creator. The Pantheists of ancient as well as of modern times recognize this fact, although they do not discharge their religious obligations conformably to the Divine will, but make to themselves other gods instead.

As there has been a religion and a ritual among all nations, tribes and peoples, so has there been also a "hierarchy" to teach this religion, and make known its obligations. These religious obligations constituted then, and constitute even now, the basis of all popular education throughout the world—Christian, Gentile, or Pagan—there is no exception to this fact save in these *United States* of America.

CHAPTER III.

ORIGIN OF THE PUBLIC SCHOOL SYSTEM.

Strange as it may seem, it is a certain undeniable fact that there is not, on the entire continent of Europe, or in the entire world, a single country, Protestant or Catholic, that upholds the Pagan system of education which has been adopted in this free country. In all of them Catholic and Protestant children receive religious instruction, during the school-hours, from their respective pastors. The present system of the Public Schools in the United States professes to exclude all religious exercises. We are often told that this is the American system, and that it is very impertinent for foreigners to wish to bring religion into schools against the American idea. Now the assertion that the exclusion of all religion from the schools is truly American, that it is an essential part of our national system, is utterly false. So far as any system of public schools can be said to have an American idea, the idea will be found to be "education based on religious instruction."

The first schools established in the Union were religious denominational schools. These schools were supported by the churches with which they were connected, and by their patrons. Religious exercises formed a part of the daily duties of the class-room. The early founders of this Republic were not able to understand how they could bring up their children in the knowledge, love, and service of God by banishing the Bible, prayer, and religious exercises of every kind from the school. Hence religion was reverenced, and its duties attended to in all institutions of learning in the country. The American system of education, in its incipiency, and for a long while, was one founded on Bible-teaching and religious exercises. The present system is un-American, anti-American.

Now how did it happen that the primitive Christian system of education became unchristian and anti-American? To make you understand more clearly the origin of the present system of the Public Schools, I must first show you how *Secret Societies seek to spread Irreligious Education in Europe.*

These societies profess the most irreligious and anti-social doctrines. Among the chief means employed by them for pushing forward their diabolical principles is *Education without Religion*. The "International," one of the most powerful of these organizations, has lately put forward a programme, in which the following points are laid down as most necessary to be insisted upon in the agitation conducted by the socialist democratic party in Switzerland:

> ". . . *Compulsory and gratuitous education* up to the completion of the fourteenth year of each child's age. . . . Separation of the

Church from the State, *and also of the schools from the Church.*"

About three short years ago a pamphlet was published in which we find detailed the efforts made in France to spread irreligion by means of bad education. The letters of eighty of the Prelates of France are appended to the pamphlet. Alas! the sad forebodings of that noble episcopate have been too soon and too terribly fulfilled!

The following lengthy extracts are taken from the late Pastoral of the Bishops of Ireland on Christian Education:

"EFFORTS TO SPREAD IRRELIGIOUS EDUCATION IN FRANCE—DISASTROUS RESULTS IN FRANCE.

> "'I see,' says the most reverend author, 'that for some time past the most extraordinary efforts are made in France to spread impiety, immorality, the most anti-social theories, under the pretext of spreading education. No longer as formerly, it is in newspapers and books that religion, morality, and the eternal principles of good order are attacked with the most deceitful and formidable weapon of a corrupt system of education. Under cover of an excellent object—and here is the great danger, for we are deluded by this pretext—under the pretext of spreading education and waging war against ignorance, infidelity is spread, war is waged against religion; and thus, whether we will or no, we rush on to the ruin of all order, moral and social. And we, the Bishops, who are as desirous as others, and perhaps more desirous than others, to see spread far and wide the blessings of education, the education of children, female education, the education of our whole people, for this is by excellence a Christian work, we are accused of being enemies of education, because we oppose anti-Christian and anti-social education.'"

The first fact mentioned by the learned writer is the existence of schools, which are called *"professional schools for females,"* into which young girls are received at twelve years of age and upwards, for the purpose of continuing their education and learning a profession. These schools have been founded by women, free-thinkers, who formally and expressly declare it to be their object to train the youth of their own sex in rationalism and infidelity. The following incident shows the impious end for which these schools have been founded: One of the principal teachers died, and over her grave her husband pronounced these words,—"I will tell you, for it is my duty to tell you, that if this funeral is that of a free-thinker" [unaccompanied by any religious ceremony], "it is so not only by my wish, but also and chiefly because such was the desire of my dear wife." He adds that she had devoted herself to "the great work of spreading education and *morality without religion*, because she had no faith except in *learning and in justice*; she was of those who, having once seen and comprehended these truths, can have no other beacon to guide them *in life, or at the hour of death*." Round that grave, whose occupant had rejected religion and its ministrations in life and in death, stood three hundred girls, pupils of those *"professional schools,"* holding bouquets in their hands, and throwing flowers on the coffin of their mistress. The schools are of a piece with the teachers. Ten hours are spent in them, but all religious instruction is strictly forbidden, under the pretext that they are free schools, *"open to children of all persuasions, without religious distinction."* The founders of these schools propose to give to the girls intrusted to them *a moral education without ever speaking to them of religion!* And this is the system of education which people are anxious to spread throughout France, and even in this country also. But, though we hope they will not succeed, can we feel fully confident that we shall escape the contagion, when we remember that this system is no other than the *"mixed system,"* and when we bear in mind the untiring efforts which are made to develop and consolidate that system in Ireland in every branch of education, from the university, through the model-school, down to the humblest village-school? Read the description of the schools in France, of which we are speaking, and say, does it not apply to every school, even in Ireland, where the mixed principle is thoroughly carried out?

> "The printed prospectus of these schools" [continues the most reverend writer] "clearly explains the advantages of professional education, while it hides the religious danger under vague expressions of an apparent liberality, such as the following: '*The school is open to children of all persuasions, without religious distinction.*' The meaning of which words is no other than that in these schools, where children are kept from the twelfth to the eighteenth year of their age, and for ten hours every day (from eight A.M. to six P.M.), God and the Gospel shall be treated as if they never existed; not only religion shall never be mentioned, but these girls shall be taught morality independent of any dogmatic faith, any religion. . . .
>
> "The second engine used by the enemies of religion in France for the maintenance and spread of infidelity, is the Educational League. This League has been introduced from Belgium into France by the Freemasons and the 'Solidaires'—the members of an impious association, the avowed object of which is to prevent persons from receiving the sacraments, or any of the sacred rites of the Church, in life or in death. The Educational League, with a wonderful spirit of propagandism, has established throughout France libraries and courses of instruction for men and for women, and even for girls and young children. On their banner is inscribed 'Spread of Education'; but under this device is hidden the scheme of propagating irreligion. The founder of the 'League' in France[1] was a Freemason, and both his declarations and those of the organs of Freemasonry leave no doubt of the Masonic origin of the scheme, and of the spirit which animates it. Now the third article of the statutes of the 'League' declares, when speaking of the education to be given by their association, that 'neither politics

[1] Jean Macé.

> nor *religion* shall have any part in it.' And lest there should be any mistake as to the meaning of this article, one of the leading Masonic journals declares that religion is 'useless as an instrument for forming the minds of children, and that from a certain point of view it is *capable of leading them to abandon all moral principles*. It is incumbent on us, therefore,' concludes this journal, 'to *exclude* all religion. We will teach you its rights and duties in the name of liberty, of conscience, of reason, and, in fine, in the name of our society.'[2] And again: 'Freemasons must give in their adhesion *en masse* to the excellent Educational League, and the lodges must in the peace of their temples seek out the best means of making it effectual. Their influence in this way will be most useful. *The principles we profess are precisely in accord with those which inspired that project.*'[3] In April of the same year, the same organ of Freemasonry contained the following paragraph: 'We are happy to announce that the Educational League and the statue of *our brother* Voltaire meet with the greatest support in all the lodges. There could not be two subscription-lists more in harmony with each other: Voltaire, the representative of the destruction of prejudices and superstition; the Educational League, the engine for building up a new society based *solely upon learning and instruction*. Our brethren understood it so.' In fine, that there may not remain upon our minds the least doubt as to the identity of the principles of this League with those of Voltaire, we find its founder in France proposing, at a great Masonic dinner, a toast to the memory of that arch-infidel; while the newspaper from which we have quoted so largely, informs its readers that at one of the 'professional schools,' described above, the prize for good conduct (*le prix de morale*) was awarded to '*the daughters of a free-thinker, who have never attended any place of religious worship*.'"

We cannot better conclude our remarks on the efforts made in France to destroy religion in the masses by means of education, than in the following words of warning, not less applicable to good and sincere Catholics in Ireland nowadays, than to those to whom they were specially addressed:

> "Good and sincere Catholics (continues the author of the pamphlet already quoted), who, deceived by the motto of the association, have given their names to this *Educational League*, take part, without knowing it, in a Masonic institution, and in building up this new state of society, from which religion is to be banished. Well may the Bishop of Metz say: 'These persons forget that, like Proteus in the fable, Freemasonry knows how to multiply *ad infinitum* its transformations and its names. Yesterday it called itself '*Les Solidaires*,' or 'morality independent of religion,' or 'freedom of thought'; to-day it takes the title of an 'Educational League';

[2] *"La Solidarite."* (Le Monde Maconnique, October, 5866 [1866], p. 472.)
[3] *"La Solidarite."* (Le Monde Maconnique, February, 5867 [1867].)

to-morrow it will find some other name by which to deceive the simple."

The efforts to corrupt the youth of unhappy France by means of bad education in its higher branches, have been not less energetic and wide-spread. The lectures of the School of Medicine of Paris were inaugurated in 1865, amid shouts of "*Materialism forever,*"[4] and on the thirtieth of December a candidate for degrees was permitted by the Medical Faculty to advance the following revolutionary doctrine, grounded on the materialistic principles he had been taught: "Who still speaks to us of free-will? As the stone which falls to the ground obeys the laws of weight, man obeys the laws which are proper to him. . . . Responsibility is the same for all, that is to say, *none.*" And again: "Physicians must not be accomplices of the magistrates and judges, who punish men for acts for which they are not responsible"—pp. 32, 33. Here we have a sample of the teaching of the School of Medicine of Paris, not only the first medical school of France, but among the first schools of Europe. And this sample is, unfortunately, not a solitary one. The Medical Faculty of the University of Paris gave medals in 1866 for two dissertations, in one of which we find a denial of the act of creation and of God the Creator, and a rejection of every metaphysical idea, *as useless and dangerous;* while human thought is set down as produced *by heat!* In the other we read the following propositions: "Matter is eternal." "The action of a *First Cause* is useless and irrational—*it is chimerical!*" Again: "It is absolutely impossible to explain the existence of a creative power"; and "an immaterial being is not necessary for the production of life." And, "to attribute the phenomena of life to an immaterial soul, is to substitute a chimerical being for the hypothesis of machinists." "Materialists have done good service to physiology by eliminating metaphysical entities from this study. The idea of the soul, as an immaterial power, is a mere abstraction; in fact, nothing of the kind exists."

Unhappily these principles, subversive of all morality, are not advanced by the aspirants only to academical distinctions; most certainly the students would not advance these theories had they not learned them from their masters. Hence we find one of the Professors of the University of France, in Bordeaux, asserting, that "even among civilized nations moral ideas are so relative, contradictory, and dependent on exterior and individual relations, that it is impossible, and will always be impossible, to find an absolute definition of goodness."—p. 38, *note.* And the "Medical Review" published the discourse pronounced by one of the physicians of the Faculty of Paris, M. Verneuil, over the grave of a member of their learned body, Dr. Foucher, in which we find the following:

> "'We are reproached with believing with the sages of old, that Fate is blind, and as such presides over our lot. And why should we not believe it?. . . Humbling and sad as is this admission, still we must make it: imperceptible elements of the great social organization appearing upon this earth as living beings, fragments of matter agitated by a spirit, we are born, we live, and we die, unconscious of our destiny, playing our part without any precise notion of the end, and in the midst of the darkness which covers

[4] Vive le Materialisme.

our origin and our end, having only one consolation—the love of our fellow-man.

"'This simple philosophy alone,' M. Verneuil continues, 'assuages our grief and ends by drying our tears. By the side of the half-open tomb we ask, whether he whom it contains served the good cause without deceit. . . . If, by his intelligence or his kindness of heart, he labored in the great work, we say he has paid his part of the common debt, and whether he returns to his original nothing or not, whether he is destroyed or merely changes his form, whether he hears our words or not, we thank him in the name of the past and of the future.'"

Another distinguished Professor published, in 1866, *Lectures on the Physiology of the Nervous System*, in which we find the following passage:

"We admit,' he says, '*without any restriction*, that intellectual phenomena in animals are of the same order as in man. . . .' 'As for *free-will*, we comprehend a certain kind of free-will in the more intelligent animals; and, on the other hand, we may add, that perhaps man is not so free as he would fain persuade himself he is.' And '*as to feeling the distinction between good and evil*, it is a grave question, *which we must first study in man himself!*'"

Let it not be supposed that these principles are merely announced as abstractions; conclusions are drawn from them which must fill every thinking mind with horror. Eighty students of the Normal School, the great training institution of teachers for the North of France, applauded such conclusions in a public letter. Several of the infidel Professors of the Faculty of Medicine received ovations from crowded class-rooms; millions of immoral and irreligious books were scattered throughout the country. Thus Freemasonry, under the pretext of combating ignorance, wages a deceitful and implacable war against religion. "We too," says the organ of Freemasons,[5] "we too expect our Messiah, the true Messiah, of the mind and reason—universal education!"

"It is scarcely necessary for us to remind you, dearly beloved brethren, that the seeds of irreligion and anarchy thus sown broadcast over the fair face of France, have already produced a too abundant harvest of evils, perhaps the most disastrous recorded on the page of history. All Europe has been horrified by the atrocities perpetrated within the last few months in the name of liberty in that city, which was looked on as the centre of the civilization of the world. National monuments have been destroyed, peaceable citizens robbed and murdered, the venerable Archbishop, many of the clergy, and leading members of the civil and military authorities, massacred in cold blood. In other cities of France, too, we have seen anarchy and irreligion proclaimed—miscreants in arms against the property, and liberty, and lives of their fellow-citizens, often of the helpless and unprotected; and all this at a moment when the country was invaded, and a part of it occupied,

[5] Le Monde Maconnique, June, 1866.

by its enemies. The storm had been sown, and in very truth unfortunate France has reaped the whirlwind.

"SPREAD OF INFIDELITY THROUGH BAD EDUCATION NOT CONFINED TO FRANCE.

"And unhappily, dearly beloved brethren, the spread of infidel principles by means of bad education is not confined to France. A few years ago a congress of students was held in Liège, in Belgium, where infidel and anti-social principles in their worst form were proclaimed amidst the plaudits of the assembly. In England irreligion and socialism are publicly taught. Even in our own country it is a matter of notoriety, that a Chair in one of the Queen's Colleges has been occupied since their foundation by a gentleman, who, in a published work, extolled the first French revolution, and, in another place of the same book, compared our Saviour, whose name be praised forever, to Luther and to Mahomet! Again: In Trinity College one of the Fellows denies the fundamental truth of Christianity respecting the eternity of the punishment of sin; and others call in question the inspiration of the Holy Scriptures, or of portions of them, and impugn many truths which constitute the foundation of all revealed religion. In the same University, too, the doctrines of Positivism, a late form of infidel philosophy, have a large number of followers. The nature of that philosophy may be gathered from the following passages in the 'Catechism of Positivism, or Summary Exposition of the Universal Religion,' translated from the French of Auguste Comte. The preface begins thus:

> "'In the name of the past and of the future, the servants of humanity—both its philosophical and practical servants—come forward to claim, as their due, the general direction of this world. Their object is to constitute at length a real Providence in all departments—moral, intellectual, and material. Consequently they exclude, once for all, from political supremacy, all the different servants of God—Catholic, Protestant, or Deist—as being at once behind-hand and a cause of disturbance.'

"The work consists of 'Thirteen Systematic Conversations between a Woman and a Priest of Humanity,' and the doctrines contained in it are epitomized in the following blasphemous lines:

> *"'In a word, Humanity definitely occupies the place of God, but she does not forget the services which the idea of God provisionally rendered.'*

"TESTIMONY OF REV. PROFESSOR LIDDON.

"Again, during the last two sessions of Parliament, a Select Committee of the House of Lords sat to inquire into the condition of the English Universities. The Marquis of Salisbury was the chairman. The evidence taken before that committee reveals the appalling fact that infidelity, or doubt as to the first principles of the Christian religion, nay, of belief in God, is wide-spread in the Universities of England, and especially among the most intellectual of the students; and that this sad result is due in a great measure to the teaching and examinations. In the first report for the session 1871, pp. 67, 69, and 70, in the evidence of the Rev. Professor Liddon, D.D., Canon of St. Paul's, London, and Professor of Exegesis in the University of Oxford, we find the following passages:

> "*Quest.* 695. *Chairman.*—'Very strong evidence has been given to us upon the influence of the Final School' (the examination for degrees with honors) 'upon Oxford thought, as tending to produce at least momentary disbelief.'
>
> "*Witness.*—'I have no doubt whatever it is one of the main causes of our present embarrassments.'
>
> "696.—'That, I suppose, is a comparatively new phenomenon?'
>
> "'Yes; it dates from the last great modification in the system pursued in the Honors School of *literæ humaniores*. It is mainly the one-sided system, as I should venture to call it, of modern philosophical writers.'
>
> "697.—'Is there any special defect in the management which produces this state of things, or is it essential to the nature of the school?'
>
> "'I fear it is to a great extent essential to the nature of the school, as its subjects are at present distributed.'

"Again, in answer to Question 706, the same witness says:

> "'I ought to have stated to the noble Chairman just now that cases have come within my own experience of men who have come up from school as Christians, and have been earnest Christians up to the time of beginning to read philosophy for the Final School, but who, during the year and a half or two years employed in this study, have surrendered first their Christianity, and next their belief in God, and have left the University not believing in a Supreme Being.'"

Now what kind of a being is the infidel, or the man without religion? To have no religion is a crime, and to boast of having none is the height of folly. He that has no religion must necessarily lose the esteem and confidence of his friends. What confidence, I ask, can be placed in a man who has no religion, and, consequently, no knowledge of his duties? What confidence can you place in a man who never feels himself bound by any obligation of conscience, who has no higher motive to direct him than his self-love, his own interests? The pagan Roman, though enlightened only by reason, had yet virtue enough to say: "I live not for *myself*, but for the Republic"; but the infidel's motto is: "I live only for myself; I care for no one but myself." Oh, what a monster would such a man be in society were he really to think as he speaks, and to act as he thinks!

A man who has no religion, must first prove that he is honest before we can believe him to be so. It is said of kings and rulers, they must prove that they have a heart, and it may also be said of the man who has no religion, that *he must prove* that he has a *conscience.* And I fear he would not find it so easy a task.

A man without religion is a man without reason, a man without principle, a man sunk in the grossest ignorance of what religion is. He blasphemes what he does not understand. He rails at the doctrines of Christianity, without really knowing what these doctrines are. He sneers at the doctrines and practices of religion, because he cannot refute them. He speaks with the utmost gravity of the fine arts, the fashions, and even matters the most trivial, and he turns into ridicule the most sacred subjects. In the midst of his own circle of fops and silly women, he utters his shallow conceits with all the pompous assurance of a pedant.

The man without religion is a dishonest plagiarist, who copies from Christian writers all the objections made against the Church by the infidels of former and modern times; but he takes good care to omit all the excellent answers and complete refutations which are contained in these very same writings. His object is not to seek the truth, but to propagate falsehood.

The man without religion is a slave of the most degrading superstition. Instead of worshipping the true, free, living God, who governs all things by His Providence, he bows before the horrid phantom of blind chance or inexorable destiny. He is a man who obstinately refuses to believe the most solidly-established facts in favor of religion, and yet, with blind credulity, greedily swallows the most absurd falsehoods uttered *against religion*. He is a man whose reason has fled, and whose passions speak, object and decide in the name of reason.

The man without religion often pretends to be an infidel merely in order to appear fashionable. He is usually conceited, obstinate, puffed up with pride, a great talker, always shallow and fickle, skipping from one subject to another without even thoroughly examining a single one. At one moment he is a Deist, at another a Materialist, then he is a Sceptic, and again an Atheist; always changing his views, but always a slave of his passions, always an enemy of Christ.

The man without religion is a slave of the most shameful passions. He tries to prove to the world that man is a brute, in order that he might have the gratification of leading the life of a brute. I ask you, what virtue can that man have who believes that whatever he desires is lawful, who designates the most shameful crimes by the refined name of innocent pleasures? What virtue can that man have who knows no other law than his passions; who believes that God regards with equal eye truth and falsehood, vice and virtue? He may indeed practise some natural virtues, but these virtues are in general only *exterior*. They are practised merely out of human respect; they do not come from the heart. Now the seat of true virtue is in the heart, and not in the exterior. He that acts merely to please man and not to please God, has no real virtue.

The man without religion often praises all religions; he is a true knave. He says: "If I were to choose my religion, I would become a Catholic, for it is the most reasonable of all religions." But in his heart he despises all religion. He is a man who scrapes together all the wicked and absurd calumnies he can find against the Church. He falsely accuses her of teaching monstrous doctrines which she has always abhorred and condemned, and he displays his ingenuity by combating those monstrous doctrines which he himself has invented, or copied from authors as dishonest as himself. The infidel is a monster without faith, without law, without religion, without God.

There are many who call themselves "free-thinkers," many who reject all revealed religion, merely out of silly puerile vanity. They affect singularity in order to attract notice, in order to make people believe that they are strong-minded, that they are independent. Poor deluded slaves of human respect! They affect singularity in order to attract notice, and they forget that there is another class of people in the world also noted for singularity. In fact they are so singular that they have to be shut up for safe keeping in a mad-house.

What is the difference between an infidel and a madman? The only difference is, that the madness of the infidel is wilful, while the madness of the poor lunatic is entirely involuntary. The one arouses our compassion, while the other excites our contempt and just indignation.

Finally, the man without religion says: "There is no God." He says so *"in his heart"*, says Holy Writ; he says not so in his head, because he knows better. Let him be in imminent danger of death, or of a considerable loss of fortune, and you will see how quick, on such occasions, he lays aside the mask of infidelity; he makes his profession of faith in an Almighty God; he cries out: "Lord save me, I am perishing! Lord have mercy on me!" and the like.

There is still another proof to show that the infidel does not believe what he says: why is it that he makes his impious doctrines the subject of conversation on every occasion? It is, of course, first to communicate his devilish principles to others, and make them as bad as he himself is; but this is not the only reason. The good Catholic seldom speaks of his religion; he feels assured, by the grace of God, that his religion is the only true one, and that he will be saved if he lives up to his religion. This, however, is not the case with the infidel. He is constantly tormented in his soul. "There is no peace, no happiness for the impious," says Holy Scripture.—(Isa. xlviii. 22.) He tries to quiet the fears of his soul, the remorse of his conscience. So he communicates to others, on every occasion, his perverse principles, hoping that he may meet with some of his fellow-men who may approve of his impious views, and that thus he may find some relief for his interior torments. He resembles a timid night-traveller. A timid man, who is obliged to travel during a dark night, begins to sing and to cry in order to keep away too great fear. The infidel is a sort of night-traveller; he certainly travels in the horrible darkness of his impiety. His interior conviction tells him that there is a God, who will certainly punish him in the most frightful manner. This fills him with great fear, and makes him extremely unhappy every moment of his life. He cannot bear the sight of a Catholic church, of a Catholic procession, of an image of our Lord, of a picture of a saint, of a prayer-book, of a good Catholic, of a priest; in a word, he cannot bear anything that reminds him of God, of religion, of his guilt, and of his impiety. So he cries, on every occasion, against faith in God, in all that God has revealed and proposes to us for our belief by the Holy Church. What is the object of his impious cries? It is to deafen, to keep down in some measure, the clamors of his bad conscience. Our hand will involuntarily touch that part of the body where we feel pain. So, in like manner, the tongue of the infidel touches, on all occasions, involuntarily as it were, upon all those truths of our holy religion which inspire him with fear of the judgments of Almighty God. He feels but too keenly that he cannot do away with God and His sacred religion, by denying His existence.

I have given you the true portrait—the true likeness—of the man without religion. Were you given to see a devil and the soul of an infidel at the same time, you would find the sight of the devil more bearable than that of the infidel. For St. James the Apostle tells us, that "the devil believes and trembles."—(Chap. ii. 19.) Now the Public School system was invented and introduced into this country to turn the rising generations into men of the above description.

Spread of Infidelity through Bad Education in America; or, The Object of the Public School System.

Mr. O. A. Brownson, in his book "The Convert," Chaps. VII. and VIII., gives us the following information on the origin of the Public Schools in this country:

> "Frances Wright was born in Scotland, and inherited a considerable property. She had been highly educated, and was a woman of rare original powers, and extensive and varied information. She was brought up in the utilitarian principles of Jeremy Bentham. She visited this country in 1824. Returning to England in 1825, she wrote a book in a strain of almost unbounded eulogy of the American people and their institutions. She saw only one stain upon the American character, one thing in the condition of the American people to censure or to deplore—that was negro-slavery.
>
> "When, in the next year, Mr. Owen came, with his friends, to commence his experiment of creating a new moral world at New Harmony, Frances Wright came with him, not as a full believer in his crotchets, but to try an experiment, devised with Jefferson, Lafayette, and others, for the emancipation of the negro-slave.
>
> "Fanny Wright, however, failed in her negro experiment. She soon discovered that the American people were not, as yet, prepared to engage in earnest for the abolition of slavery. On more mature reflection she came to the conclusion that slavery must be abolished only as the result of a general emancipation, and a radical reform of the American people themselves.
>
> "The first step to be taken for this purpose was to rouse the American mind to a sense of its rights and dignity, to emancipate it from superstition, from its subjection to the clergy, and its fear of unseen powers, to withdraw it from the contemplation of the stars or an imaginary heaven after death, and fix it on the great and glorious work of promoting *man's earthly well-being*.
>
> "The second step was, by political action, to get adopted, at

the earliest practical moment, a system of State schools, in which all the children from two years old and upward should be fed, clothed, in a word, maintained, instructed, and educated at the public expense.

"In furtherance of the first object, Fanny prepared a course of Lectures on *Knowledge,* which she delivered in the principal cities of the Union. She thought that she possessed advantages in the fact that she was a woman; for there would, for that reason, be a greater curiosity to hear her, and she would be permitted to speak with greater boldness and directness against the clergy and superstition than would be one of the other sex.

"The great measure, however, on which Fanny and her friends relied for ultimate success, was the system of public schools. These schools were intended to deprive, as well as to relieve, parents of all care and responsibility of their children after a year or two years of age. It was assumed that parents were, in general, incompetent to train up their children, provide proper establishments, teachers and governors for them, till they should reach the age of majority.

"The *aim* was, on the one hand, to relieve marriage of its burdens, and to remove the principal reasons for making it *indissoluble;* and, on the other hand, to provide for bringing up all children, in a rational manner, to be reasonable men and women, that is, *free from superstition, free from all belief in God and immortality,* free from all regard for the invisible, and make them look *upon this life* as *their only life,* this earth as their only home, and *the promotion of their earthly interests and enjoyments as their only end.* The three great enemies to earthly happiness were held to be religion, marriage, or family and private property. Once get rid of these three institutions, and we may hope soon to realize our earthly paradise. For religion is to be substituted science, that is, science of the world, of the five senses only; for private property, a community of goods; and for private families, a community of wives.

"Fanny Wright and her school saw clearly that their principles could not be carried into practice in the present state of society. So they proposed them to be adopted only by a future generation, trained and prepared in a system of schools founded and sustained by the Public. They placed their dependence on education in a system of *Public Schools,* managed after a plan of William Phiquepal, a Frenchman, and subsequently the husband of Fanny Wright.

"In order to get their system of schools adopted, they proposed to organize the whole Union, secretly, very much on the plan of the Carbonari of Europe. The members of this secret society were to avail themselves of all the means in their power, each in his own locality, to form public opinion in favor of education by the State at the public expense, and to get such men elected to the Legislatures as would be likely to favor their purposes. This secret organization commenced in the State of New York, and was to extend over the whole Union. Mr. O. A. Brownson was one of the agents for organizing the State of New York. He, however, became tired of the work, and abandoned it after a few months."

"The attention of so-called philanthropic men in all parts of the country, was directed to the subject. In 1817, and the following years, commenced what has been improperly termed a revival of education. To form public opinion in favor of Public Schools, the following means were employed: Public School societies and organizations were established in New York, Philadelphia, Boston, Portland, Lancaster, Pittsburgh, Worcester, Hartford, Lowell, Providence, Cincinnati, etc.; Thomas H. Gallaudet, James G. Carter, and Walter R. Johnson, made great efforts through the press; there were established the 'American Journal of Education,' in January, 1826, and the 'American Annals of Education.' Conventions were held throughout New England from 1826 to 1830, in behalf of Public Schools; lectures were delivered in every precinct in the States, on the subject of education; there were also established local school periodicals, as well as others of a more general character, to contribute towards forming public opinion in favor of Public Schools, in every corner of the country. All these means, and the zealous and unwearied efforts of Horace Mann, Henry Barnard, and others, have contributed towards the success in establishing the Public Schools in our country." —*American Encyclopædia.*

This is a brief history of the Public Schools. It tells, in clear terms, all that they are, and all that they are to bring about, namely: a generation without belief in God and immortality, free from all regard for the invisible—a generation that looks upon this life as their only life, this earth as their only home, and the promotion of their earthly interests and enjoyments as their only end—a generation that looks upon religion, marriage, or family and private property as the greatest enemies to worldly happiness—a generation that substitutes science of this world for religion, a community of goods for private property, a community of wives for private family; in other words, a generation that substitutes the devil for God, hell for heaven, sin and vice for virtue and holiness of life.

We may, then, confidently assert that the defenders and upholders of *Public Schools without religion* seek in America, as well as in Europe, to turn the people into refined Pagans. They recently betrayed themselves. They wish, as Dr. Wehrenphennig and Dr. Wirgow openly said, for an equalization of religious contradictories, a religion and an education which stands above creeds, and knows nothing about dogmas; in other words, they wish for a religion of which a certain poet says: "My religion is to have no religion." The object, then, of these godless, irreligious *Public Schools* is to spread among the people the worst of religions, the *no religion,* the religion which pleases most hardened adulterers and criminals—the religion of irrational animals. How far this diabolical scheme has succeeded is well known, for there are at present from twenty to twenty-five millions of people in the United States who profess no distinct religious belief. Everywhere the same effects have been observed. Licentiousness, cruelty, and vice—"Positivism," or the substitution of the harlotry of the passions for the calm and elevating influences of reason and religion. How can it be otherwise?

CHAPTER IV.

EXPOSÉ OF THE PUBLIC SCHOOL SYSTEM.

It is a fundamental principle of Christianity, admitted even by Protestants, that man cannot reach his destiny without a knowledge of the religion which Jesus Christ taught, and which He sealed with His precious Blood. Now this fundamental principle is virtually ignored in our present school system, which proposes to educate without religion. The whole course of instruction is imparted without any reference to religion, without any of those occasional observations that are so necessary in our days, and especially in this country, in order to explain the seeming inconsistencies between scientific facts and the doctrines of faith. Instruction, to be useful, must show that the discoveries of science are, as is really the case, evidences of religion. It must show the harmony that exists between history and philosophy and the truths of faith. Secular knowledge should be the handmaid of religion; but no religion, no knowledge of God, is permitted to be taught in these schools.

Let a stranger, say an educated Pagan, enter one of our public schools; will he discover sign, symbol or token of any kind to indicate that either the teacher or children are Christians? Or suppose this Pagan, or a Turk, or Atheist sends children there to be educated, they can do so with perfect safety to their Pagan, Mohammedan, or infidel superstitions or opinions. They will not, through the whole course of instruction, hear a prayer, a lecture, or a single advice, lesson, or precept of the Church; they will, as far as the State plan of teaching extends, remain ignorant of the "holy name of God," or the Blessed Trinity, or the Lord's Prayer, or the Ten Commandments, or the Gospels, or the death and sufferings of our Lord, or the resurrection of the body, or a future state of reward and punishment. *No prayer* is offered up or even permitted to be taught to those little ones whom our Lord loves so tenderly. The teacher is not even permitted by law to explain what is meant by the term "our Saviour," "our Redeemer"!

Should a child ask, in a reading-lesson, what "our Lord and Saviour" meant, the teacher must tell him: "Hush! if you want to know that you must ask somebody out of school! We don't teach anything about religion here! We have no Lord, or God, or Saviour here!"

In reference to this manner of educating the youth of America, the Protestant Bishop of Tennessee said some time ago:

> "The secular system took no notice of God or of Christ, or of the Church of the Living God, or, except in the most incidental way, of God's Holy Word. The intellect was stimulated to the

> highest degree, but the heart and the affections were left uncultivated. It was a system which trained for the business of life, not for the duties of life. As there were differences of opinion about Christianity, it was not allowed to be spoken of, and a knowledge of it was not one of the qualifications for a teacher. A man might be a Mohammedan or a Hindoo if he were only a proficient in geography, arithmetic, or the exact sciences. The teachers in the normal schools might be infidels provided they did not openly inculcate their scepticism; and, in point of fact, in the schools which were designed to train teachers only, a vast majority were not Christians."

The school-books must be made unchristian lest they give offence to the countless sects of Protestantism. Voltaire, Paine, or Renan may be read in the Public Schools, but nothing of God.

If our Public Schools differ in any degree from the ancient heathen, it is to our greater shame and confusion, and to their advantage. They taught piety to *"their gods;"* we ignore the *true God altogether,* and bring the false gods of the heathens down to earth to be made the slaves and instruments of our sensual gratifications. Thus the mind of the child is, and remains, a religious void; at least, there is but a religious mist in his intellect. The child even unlearns, in the society of the school, whatever principles of religion he may have learned from his parents.

The present common school system of education necessarily begets contempt of religion. Men trained under such a system learn to look upon religion as a dress which is to be worn only on Sunday, and to be laid aside during the rest of the week; they look upon religion as something which may do very well in the church, or in the meeting-house, but which is entirely out of place in business, in society, and in the daily transactions of life. The child has logic enough to think that he is taught whatever is necessary for his future career, and that religion must not be necessary, otherwise it would be taught in school.

And what will the child learn, in this Pagan system of education, to press down his rising passions? What precept of positive virtue does he learn? What principle of self-restraint? What does he learn in such a school to make him obedient, honest, chaste, a good citizen, a good Christian? The common school system proceeds on the principle of suffering the passions of youth to take any development which fallen nature may bring about, and then trusting to a riper age for a change for the better, just as if it were possible "to gather grapes of briars, or figs of thorns."

In these Public Schools the whole education of children is directed to the cultivation of their heads or intellectual faculties alone. The heart, with all its moral and mysterious emotions, is entirely neglected. Every mental power and acquirement is intended and directed to promote their prosperity, success, and happiness in this life; at least this is what is sought and promised as the reward of study and application. They are constantly presented with the bright side of the world. Scientific knowledge, they are taught, will do away with the old drudgery of labor, and bring the acquirement of wealth and honor within the reach of all, no matter how poor or humble the condition of their fathers or mothers. They have all, no doubt, read the Declaration of Independence, and learned that all men are created free and equal. They have shared the equal bounty of the State in the way of education, and have, in the language of the day, "an equal right on the world for a living."

I ask if this is not a pretty fair and not overdrawn statement of the case? You will bear in mind that all this time the free-and-easy social intercourse of the sexes is going on; that while their studies and exercises are strictly confined to dry, secular knowledge, or such other pursuits as might excite their vanity, pride, or imagination, not one line or lesson, caution or command, as stated before, is used or administered to curb or control the natural, I might say inevitable, cry of the youthful passions clamoring for their gratification.

CHAPTER V.

EVIL CONSEQUENCES OF THE PUBLIC SCHOOL SYSTEM ON THE MALE PORTION OF SOCIETY.

Let us now suppose the young men educated under the present Public School system fairly launched into the world, and, for the first time, thrown on their own resources. They are all well, indeed *over-educated.* The greater part of their families are necessarily in poor or moderate circumstances. Will their learned and accomplished sons take the humble and laborious trades or occupations of their fathers? I fear not. We should not expect more from human nature than there is in it. All these fine young public school graduates cannot get nice situations as clerks, professors, editors, teachers, etc., etc., and the professions are all full to overflowing.

You must remember that, as I have said, not one of the boys have ever been taught the first principle, prayer, or moral duty. They are, as far as the Public School-training went, perfectly ignorant of the Divine law as rule of our life; they are, in fact, but educated apes or animals. How can this young man reconcile "poverty and wealth," "labor and ease," "sickness and health," "adversity and prosperity," "rich and poor," "obedience and authority," "liberty and law," etc., etc. All these are enigmas to him, or, if he affects to understand them at all, he thinks they arise from bad management or bad government, and can and ought to be remedied by repression or sumptuary legislation. He will be a tyrant or slave, a glutton or miser, a fanatic or libertine, a sneak-thief or highway robber, as circumstances may influence him. Think you that the common "fall back" on principle of self-interest—well or ill understood—will ever restrain such a one from doing any act of impulse or indulgence, provided he thinks it can be safely done? He will look on life as a game of address or force, in which the best man is he who carries off the prize.

He will look upon power as belonging of right to the strongest; the weak, or those who differ from him in opinion, he will treat with contempt and cruelty, and will think they have no rights he is bound to respect. In power, such a man will be arbitrary and cruel; out of power, he will be faithless, hypocritical and subservient. Trust him with authority, he will abuse it; trust him with money, he will steal it; trust him with your confidence, and he will betray it. Such a man—Pagan and unprincipled as he is—may nevertheless affect, when it suits his purpose, great religious zeal and purity. He will talk of "*Philanthropy*" and the "*Humanities,*" have great compassion, perhaps, for "a dray-horse," and give the cold shoulder to the houseless pauper or orphan.

The heart of such a man is cold, insincere, destitute of every tender chord for a tender vibration, of every particle of right or just feeling or principle that can be touched; on the contrary, it is roused to rage, revenge and falsehood if interfered with. How is such a heart to be touched or moved, or placed under such influences as could move it? Indeed, it would require a miracle! Nay, even a miracle would fail to make a salutary impression upon such a heart. A French infidel declared that, should he be told that the most remarkable miracle was occurring close by his house, he would not take a step out of his way to see it. Pride never surrenders; it prefers rather to take an illogical position than to bow even to the authority of reason. Furious, beside itself, and absurd, it revolts against evidence. To all reasoning, to undeniable evidence, the infidel—the man without religion—opposes his own will: "Such is my determination." It is sweet to him to be stronger, single-handed, than common sense, stronger than miracles, than even the God who manifests Himself by them.

Such a man is always in favor of *strong government*, provided he can get to run it. He will talk loudly of loyalty and the *"life of the nation."* He worships the *State*, because, to his gross animal understanding, it represents *power*, and makes money his God, because it gives him this power. Such a man may be called civilized, but he is only an *accomplished barbarian*. His head and hands are instructed, his heart, and low passions and appetites, unbridled and untamed. Such a man can never be made to understand the beautiful and benign principles of our republican form of government. Like all brutes, he relies on force, and tries and judges every issue by success. What he calls *"the final arbitrament of arms"* is to such a one a righteous decision, provided always it be in his favor. He may affect the demagogue, and talk loudly about the power of the people, but you will observe that this refers to them *en masse*, in the whole or concrete. He cannot understand the individual man as entitled to any consideration or rights (unless he happened to be made rich) independently of the State. Indeed, he looks upon poor men as made for the State, and it can be only on this ground that he claims the children as its property—"children of the State"!! He insists on educating them by the *State*, and for the State, and not for the comfort and support of their fathers and mothers, nor that they should thereby fulfil the immortal destiny for which they were created. He holds the life, the dignity, the comfort or happiness of the family or individual as nought in the balance against *"the life, the power, the wealth and glory of the nation." "Perish the People*—live the State"; this is his motto, and such have ever been the principles and motto of all Pagans from the beginning.

CHAPTER VI.

EVIL CONSEQUENCES OF THE PUBLIC SCHOOL SYSTEM ON THE FEMALE PORTION OF SOCIETY.

What I have said in the preceding chapter is but a faint picture of the bad effects of what is called *polite education*, as given in the Public Schools, on the male portion of society. It is with some reluctance that I am now going to trace the same evil influence in its still more injurious consequences on the female portion. It is very difficult to treat this part of the subject with the necessary freedom, not only on account of its intrinsic delicacy, but also because of that false (and indeed to themselves injurious) idea that there is nothing wanting to the absolute perfection of our women.

Let it not be said, that in calling public attention to these evil consequences on the female portion of the community, we are overstepping the boundaries of propriety or decency. There is a license for the poet; a license for the stage; a license for the bar; a license for the writer of fiction; a license for the press, and why should there not be a license for a Christian writer? It is high time for *true* modesty to take the place of that *false modesty* which has driven virtue, like an exile, out of the land, and peopled it largely with Fourrierites, Owenites, and other socialists and free-lovers.

Now, whatever success a "godless system of education" may have on boys, I think all must admit that it must prove not only a failure, but a positive injury, to girls. It is not that moral and religious education is not equally required by both, in a spiritual sense, but that women, in an especial manner, have certain duties assigned them, in the Order of Providence, of so high and holy a character, that it requires, in some sense, a special education to fit them for the faithful discharge of these duties.

Let us remember that the Public School-girls of to-day will be the mothers of to-morrow. Mothers are called by God to take particular care of the bodily and spiritual life of their children. This care is a heavy, a very heavy burden indeed, and mothers cannot carry this burden without a tender love for their children. Now God has made the love of mothers for their children a necessary love. It is for this reason that there is no command in the Divine Law for parents to love their children, whilst, on the contrary, children are commanded to love their parents. Love towards one's own offspring is a love so deeply planted in the heart by Nature herself, that the wild beasts never fail to love their young. It is said that even tigers, hearing the cry of their whelps when they are taken by the hunters, will plunge into the sea to swim after the vessels where they are confined.

A mother's love is proverbial. Indeed, there is no love so pure and so thoroughly disinterested as the love of a good mother for her child. Her love knows no change; brothers and sisters have forgotten each other; fathers have proved unforgiving to their children; husbands have been false to their wives, and wives to their husbands, and children too often forget their parents; but you rarely hear of a mother forgetting even her ungrateful, disobedient children, whose actions have lacerated her heart, and caused dark shadows to glide before her eyes, and enter her very soul. Still there are moments when her faithful heart yearns towards them; there are moments when the reminiscences of the happy *past* obliterate the *present* sorrow, and the poor wounded spirit is cheered for a while, because there is still one of the fibres of the root of hope left in her forlorn breast, and a languid smile will flit over her wan and prematurely faded face. Yes, she forgives, though there is no River Lethe for her to drink from in this life; showing that her love is the most pure in this world, and the nearest approach to the love that God has so graciously bestowed upon her.

Some years ago a vessel sailed from the coast of Ireland. It was filled with passengers who were coming to this country to better their future. The vessel set sail with a favorable wind. The sky was clear, and the sun shone gayly upon the sparkling sea. But suddenly the heavens grew dark. A fierce storm arose. The winds howled madly around the vessel. The ship was hurried on—on, till it was dashed against the rocks. The wild, surging waves dashed over it. The vessel split in twain. Part remained hanging amid the rocks, and the rest sank, with those on board, beneath the waves, far down into the depth of the sea. The storm continued to rage for several days. At last, when the wind had died away, some hardy fishermen, who lived on the coast, took a skiff and rowed out to the wreck. They entered the part of the vessel that remained hanging amid the rocks. They broke open the cabin door. They heard distinctly the feeble wail of a child. They rushed in. They found a little babe lying upon the breast of its dead mother. The child was eagerly sucking the blood which oozed from a large wound in its mother's breast. The mother had died of cold and hunger; but, even amid her fearful sufferings, she did not forget her child. She took a sharp knife, and, with the wonderful love of a mother's heart, she made a deep gash in her breast, in order that her child might preserve its life by drinking her own heart's blood!

And when the darling child of the Christian mother is on the point of death, ah! how tender is not her prayer to the Author of Life that He spare the child.

"Oh, God of mercy," she prays, "spare my child! Heaven is already full of light and gladness. Do not then take to heaven the light and joy of my heart. Thou art ever happy, O my God! do not then deprive me of my only happiness. God of compassion, O leave me the sweet babe whom Thou hast given me! my love, and all my happiness, is centred in him. Since he has come to me, the earth, and sea, and sky, the whole world around has grown doubly beautiful. The air seems filled with light, and song, and sweetness. Ah, do not take my child away, for when his tender body lies beneath the sod, my heart and life shall lie there with it, and this whole world shall grow dark and dreary as one vast gloomy graveyard. O God!

remember I am yet so young. I am not used to tears. Deal gently with my poor weak heart! I have never yet known what it is to lose a friend, a relative, or beloved one. O God! shall, then, the first that teaches me the dread meaning of grave and shroud be my own, my first-born child? O Jesus, I conjure Thee, by Thy wounded Heart—wounded for love of me—do not crush my tender heart, for Thou hast made it tender. Thou hast made me a mother; oh, spare my darling child!"

Ah! who can measure the depth of the wonderful love of a mother's heart! But this natural love of a mother for her offspring, in order to be persevering and untiring, must be cultivated—must be ennobled and supernaturalized by religious education; otherwise this love will decrease, and be lost in the end, and with the loss of this love the Christian woman has lost her divine calling. Now as no religious education is imparted to the girls in the Public Schools, can we wonder to see thousands and thousands of them who have lost their divine calling—can we wonder that we hear of a countless number of unnatural crimes, committed under the veil of marriage, that are becoming so common at the present day? Dr. Storer, of Massachusetts, declares that increase of children in Massachusetts is limited almost wholly to the foreign population. Mr. Warren Johnson, State Superintendent of Common Schools in Maine, reports to the Legislature a decrease of 16,683, between the ages of four and twenty-one years, from the census of 1858. Total decrease from maximum of 1860 is nearly 20,000. Mr. Johnson asks: "Are the modern fashionable criminalities of infanticide creeping into our State community?" Dr. H. R. Storer, of Massachusetts, in 1859, declared that forced abortions in America were of frequent occurrence, and that this frequency was increasing so, that from 1 in 1,633 of the population in 1805, it had risen to 1 in 340 in 1849; and Dr. Kyle, of Xenia, Ohio, asserted that abortions occurred most frequently among those who are known as the better class; among church members, and those generally who pretend to be the most polite, virtuous, moral and religious. And, without mincing matters at all, this eminent physician boldly declares that "a venal press, a demoralized clergy, and the prevalence of medical charlatanism, are the principal causes of the fearful increase of this abominable crime." The paucity of children in the families of wealthy and well-to-do Americans has been publicly noticed and commented upon time and again; but the true cause thereof, if known, was carefully concealed. And can we wonder that the crime has descended from the highest to the lowest, and now pervades all classes of society? Statistics have been frequently published to show that in certain States of the Union, and in certain districts of those States, the births did not, and do not, equal the deaths; and were it not for the foreign population among us many of those districts, and not a few of those States, would be depopulated in a few years. Massachusetts and New York lead the van in this criminal record. Dr. T. A. Reamy, of Zanesville, Ohio, in 1867, wrote, that after a careful survey of the field he was ready to say that "to-day no sin approaches with such stealth and dangerous power the altars of the Church as fœticide; and, unless it can be stayed, not only will it work its legitimate moral depravity and social ruin, but (he believed) God will visit dreadful judgment upon us no less severe, perhaps, than He did upon the Cities of the Plain."

In 1865, Dr. Morse Stewart, of Detroit, Michigan, declared that few of either sex entered the marital relation without full information as to the ways and means of destroying the legitimate results of matrimony. And among married persons so extensive has this practice become, that people of high repute not only commit this crime, but do not even blush to speak boastingly among their intimates of the deed, and the means of accomplishing it.

Dr. Nathan Allen, of Lowell, Mass., at a meeting of the Social Science Association, Boston, entitled "Wanted—More Mothers," remarked "that the increase of population for twenty-five years has been mainly in cities and towns, and it will be found to be largely made up of foreign element; and in the smaller villages, chiefly American, the stock has hardly increased at all.

"We find there are absolutely more deaths than births among the strictly American children; so that, aside from immigration, and births of children of foreign parentage, the population of Massachusetts is really decreasing.

"Another fact developed by report is, that whereas, in 1765, nearly one-half of the population of Massachusetts was under fifteen years of age, it is believed that, at the *present* time, *not* more than *one-fifth* of the purely American population is under that age. In an equal number of American and foreign families, the births will be nearly three times as many in the latter as in the former. In some of the old towns, the records of a hundred years do not show a single instance of a married couple without children. The New York census of 1865 shows that, out of nine hundred and ninety-three thousand two hundred and thirty-six married women, one hundred and thirty-seven thousand seven hundred and forty-five had no children, and three hundred and thirty-three thousand only had one or two.

"In the small town of Billerica, there are ninety families with ten or more children; five of these had fourteen, and one twenty-one: the total in the ninety families is ten hundred and ninety-three. The birth-rates show that American families *do not* increase at *all*, and the inspection of the registration in other States shows that the same remark applies to all."

Many parts of Vermont are undergoing a gradual depopulation. Sandgate had a population of 1,187 in 1810, and 805 in 1860.

The town of Rupert had a population of 1,848 in 1800, which had diminished to 1,103 in 1860.

The town of Arlington was settled in the year 1762. In the year 1800 all the arable and pasturage land was occupied, and the inhabitants numbered 1,569. In 1830 the number had decreased to 1,207, and in 1860 to 1,146.

Mrs. A. B. Boone says, in her book "The Increase of Crime," "I have frequently heard women say 'I don't mind having one or two children, but no more for me.' When I first heard these expressions I thought it merely a joke, but eventually I found out they *meant* what they said, and I was amazed. And when these women do condescend to have one or two children, what sort of a lifelong inheritance are they giving their offspring? ill-health even unto death. Frequently I come in contact with women of thirty, and even twenty-five, so debilitated that they are far more fit for hospitals than to fill the sacred office of either wife or mother.

"I am sorry to add that the crime of *child-murder* is carried on to the greatest extent among the wealthy. In Cambridgeport, a medical lady informed me that she was continually applied to for this purpose, and always refused in the most decided manner; but, to her knowledge, one woman performed, on an average, from a hundred to a hundred and fifty cases in a week. And yet churches abound in this place.

"The Rev. Dr. Todd has written two most truthful lectures, one entitled 'Fashionable Murders,' and the other 'A Cloud with a Dark Lining.' His revelations with regard to the determination that the Americans evince not to have children, is fearfully true, more especially among the women.

"Speaking of having children, reminds me of a circumstance that happened some fifteen years ago. I had a letter of introduction to a lady who wished to engage my children to read at a party she was about to give. She received me with an air of melancholy politeness, at the same time informing me that the gathering was postponed, as dear little Fanny was 'real sick.' I saw a wine-glass and teaspoon on the table by the side of the sofa, which had a small blanket on it bound with sky-blue ribbon, covering up something that I supposed to be a sick child. I approached, and gently drew aside the blanket. I jumped back—it was a poodle-dog, whose black eyes winked at me as if about to cry: a sort of appeal for sympathy shone in its glowing orbs. I was almost convulsed with laughter, it was so unexpected. When able to speak, I said, 'Pardon me, madam, for laughing; but I thought it was a baby.' She replied indignantly, 'Oh, dear, no! I never had a baby; nor I don't want one either!' And it would be a blessing, I say, if such women as these *never* became mothers. When I was a young girl, and heard people say they hated children, and saw them fondling dogs, and feeding kittens with a spoon because the *old cat* was too weak to attend to so many, and knew, at the same time, that poor *human mothers* were compelled (just as *slaves once* were) to separate from their husbands and children when *poverty* demanded that they should go into the '*Union*,' or, rather, *Dis*union—I say, when I pondered on these things, thoughts would flit through my mind, whether, when death severed the body from the *souls* of these people, that their spirits were not instantly infused into cats and dogs, and that they came back in those shapes as a penance for their *brutality* to mankind, and their *loving-kindness* to *brutes*. However, we never went to the party. The woman remarked to a friend that she thought me devoid of all feeling, to laugh at a little, sick, *innocent* dog!

"Three doors from the rooms I lived in is the stylish house of Dr. and Mrs. Grindle, where there are hundreds of 'fashionable murders' committed yearly. And twice the papers have teemed with accounts of the unhappy mothers dying, and on the last occasion the child was not to be found, although born alive—and nothing done to either the doctor or his lady!"

A gentleman of one of the smaller towns of Connecticut writes to the *Independent* as follows: "I have just read, with great interest, your editorial on the 'Murder of Helplessness.' The paper will go into hundreds of families where the crime is practised, to bear witness against it; for, thank God, it is fashionable to take the *Independent*. For more than a year it has been on my mind to write to you upon this question. You will have the thanks of every well-wisher of the human race. But you make a great mistake when you speak of the crime of fœticide as being confined to the large cities. It prevails all over the country. I dare not tell you what I know—and the information has been given me unsolicited—in reference to this horrid practice in the land. I do not believe there is a village in the New England States but this crime is practised more or less. There are men who make it their business, with medicine and instruments, to carry on this slaughter. And even M.D.'s (physicians) in good and regular standing in the church have practised it. Men are making here, in this highly moral State, $3,000 and $4,000 a year in the small towns alone, at this business. Their patients are from the highly religious and fashionable to the low and vicious. Their scale of charges is according to the cupidity and size of purse of the victims. Delicate females go, in the dead of night, dressed in masculine attire, to avoid detection, to obtain the means to hide their shame. The cause of the evil lies in 'lust, which is as near to the murder as fire to smoke.' The demoralization of the people at large, in the practice of licentiousness, furnishes a topic of the greatest anxiety to the philanthropist. When American women lose their shame, the race is lost—church-membership is no bar. The continence of man and the chastity of woman is the only hope."

Trustworthy physicians assure us there are not less than sixty ghouls (gules) in New York City, who grow rich by killing infants. We have seen the number stated at six times sixty. Those who have passed through Fifth Avenue, New York, must have noticed a magnificent dwelling, or rather palace, in the neighborhood of the Central Park. It was built by a certain doctress who has acquired her wealth by the murder of helpless innocents.

The unhappy victims of these ghouls are not generally of the low and debased sort. Most of these illegitimate mothers are of the educated classes, many of them, shocking to say, under the age of fifteen; many of them delicate, sensitive females, who make use of these unhallowed means to hide their shame from the eyes of their friends and relatives.

The number of marriages (outside the Catholic Church) has largely decreased within the past few years. The crime of infanticide is largely increasing. A certain species of it is practised in the first families, and the drugs and implements for committing such murders are publicly sold everywhere. Physicians advertise publicly, offering their services to enable people, as they say, "to enjoy the pleasures of marriage without the burden." At least 25,000 fœticides are annually committed. How to preserve their looks, and how to avoid having children, seem to be the chief aim of many women nowadays. In the upper classes of society, in some of our large cities, a lady who is the mother of more than two children is looked upon as unfashionable.

The author of the book "Satan in Society" writes, on page 130-131, as follows: "A medical writer of some note published, in 1861, a pamphlet, in which he declared himself the hero of three hundred abortions." He admits, in a work of his, that he only found abortion necessary to save the life of the mother in four instances, thus publicly confessing that in an immense number of cases he has performed the operation on other grounds; and yet, in the face of all this self-accusation, several attempts at his expulsion from his county medical society have been defeated, and he is accounted "a brother in good standing" of several learned bodies, and holds an enviable position in a fashionable church and fashionable society. This rascal walks unhung; for this the "Medical Code" is primarily responsible, and after that the "ministers of the Gospel," the "worshippers" in the churches, the dwellers in "south fronts."

I have said above that the love of children has always been deemed a sign of superior intelligence—of noble manhood. Affection for its offspring is a quality possessed alike by all animals, with scarcely an exception; and few indeed of the millions of the animal creation seek to destroy their own offspring after birth, or to so neglect them as to leave them liable to destruction by other bodies or forces. It was left for human intelligences to encompass the death of their children, both before birth and after, and it was left to the anti-Christian civilization of this nineteenth century also to discover and adopt the most revolting and barbarous means to accomplish this end. The crime of fœticide, or infanticide, is not of recent growth. Like every other crime, it has had a venerable existence, but its beastly development among us has been mainly the work of a few years. Thirteen years ago its prevalence attracted the attention of medical jurists in all parts of our country, and essays, tracts, and bound volumes were issued against it. But the crime grew apace, and its deadly and dastardly fruits appear before us to-day, sickening to the moral conscience and religious sentiments of the nation.

And in view of the alarming increase of this crime of child-murder, the prediction of Dr. M. B. Wright to the Medical Society of Ohio, in 1860, will soon be fulfilled, namely: "The time is not far distant when children will be sacrificed among us with as little hesitation as among the Hindoos, unless we stop it here and now."

The frightful increase of immorality, of unnatural crimes, in these latter years, and especially in those very States where the common school system of education is fully carried out, as in New England, proves, beyond doubt, that there is something essentially wrong in this system. Some years ago the public were startled by the shocking developments of depravity in one of the female Public Schools of Boston; so shocking, indeed, as almost to stagger belief. The Boston *Times* published the whole occurrence at the time, but after creating great excitement for a few weeks, the matter was quietly hushed up, for fear of injuring the character of the common schools.

Only a few years ago other startling transactions came to light in New York, involving the character of some of the leading school commissioners, and some of the principal female teachers in the common schools. These scandals became so notorious, that they could be no longer blinked at or smothered, and several of the leading papers came out openly, to lash vice in high places. The Chicago papers assert openly that the Public Schools there are *assignation houses*, for boys and girls above a certain age.

"It is but six or seven years ago that Mr. Wilbur H. Storey, who owns the *Chicago Times*—the paper, at that time, of largest circulation in Chicago—published in his paper, and sustained the assertion, that the Public School system in Chicago had become so corrupt, that any school-boy attending, who had reached fourteen years of age, was whistled at by his companions as a *spooney*, if he had not a *liaison* with some one or more of the Public School-girls!

"The Daily *Sentinel*, of Indianapolis, quoted Mr. Storey's articles, and said, with great regret, that it was only too true of Indianapolis also, judging by the wanton manners of troops of the girls attending Public Schools in Indianapolis."

And there are but too many cities to which the same order of remark applies. Far be it from me to say that *all* the children of the Public Schools of any of these cities are corrupted. It is marvellous how some are protected from even the *knowledge* of vice, in these hot-beds of pollution. But the *system* of schools without the control of positive religious teaching and discipline, tends only to one vile end. We are assured, as to the City of New York, that smart girls, even of most immature years, show their discontent at their neglected fate, from hearing girls only a few years older tell what "*nice*" acquaintances they have made on the streets, or in the cars, going or coming, and what delicious lunches they have taken with these "gentlemen" at restaurants of most unquestionably bad repute. These things I have learned from a friend who heard them from members of the City Police, and from others that could not avoid the unhappy knowledge of the facts indicated.

The moral character of the Public Schools in many of our cities has sunk so low, that even courtesans have disguised themselves as school-girls, in order the more surely to ply their foul avocation.

Does any one wonder, then, that we hear and read of "Trunk Horrors"? Does any one wonder that we have divorces, despair, infanticides, fœticides, suicides, bagnios, etc., and that other class, I fear not less numerous, but certainly more dangerous, "*the assignation houses*"? These you cannot "police," or "localize." They, like a subtle poison, circulate through all the veins and arteries of that society called in fashionable phrase "genteel," penetrating the vital tissues of the social body, and corrupting, too often, the very fountains of life.

CHAPTER VII.

WHAT IS IT TO BE A MOTHER?

Let us again bear in mind that the Public School-girls of to-day will be the mothers of to-morrow. Mothers are destined, by God, to bring up children for heaven. This is their grand mission. What a happiness, what an honor for a mother to give angels to heaven! Would to God she only knew the real dignity and importance of her mission, and comprehended the qualifications in the moral and religious order that best prepare her for the duties of her sublime calling! What mission can be more sublime, more sacred, what mission can be more meritorious before God than that of giving to the young child the primary lessons of religion?

There is indeed nothing more honorable, nothing more meritorious, nothing which conducts to higher perfection, than to instruct children in their religious duties. This instruction of children is a royal, apostolic, angelic, and divine function. *Royal,* because the office of a king is to protect his people from danger. *Apostolic,* because our Lord commissioned apostles to instruct the nations, and, as St. Jerome says, thus made them the saviours of men. *Angelic,* because the angelical spirits in heaven enlighten, purify, and perfect each other according to their spheres, and their earthly mission is to labor without ceasing for the salvation of man. St. Peter Chrysologus calls those who instruct others in the way of salvation, "the substitutes of angels." Indeed this mission of mothers is divine; they are called to carry on the very work of God Himself. Everything that Almighty God has done from the creation of the world, and which He will continue to do to the end, has been, and will be, for the salvation of mankind. For this He sent His Son from heaven, who enlightened the world by His doctrine, and who still continues to instruct His people by His chosen disciples. Those mothers, then, who direct their children in the paths to heaven, who allure them from vice, who form them to virtue, may fitly be termed apostles, angels, and saviours. Oh! what glory awaits those mothers who perform the office of angels, and even of God Himself, in laboring for the salvation of the souls of their children. If this employment is honorable for mothers, it is also not less meritorious for them. What is the religious instruction of children, but conferring on a class of our race, the weakest and most helpless, with inconceivable labor and fatigue, the greatest of all blessings? For while the physical development of the child advances with age, it is not so with the mental; for religious instruction only can develop the noble faculties of the soul. The soul of a child, so to speak, would continue to live enshrouded in Pagan darkness, if the mother did not impart and infuse the light of truth. All the gold in the world is but dross in comparison with true religious knowledge.

Our Saviour says: "Whosoever shall give to drink to one of these little ones, even a cup of cold water, shall not lose his reward."—(Matt. x. 42.) May we not infer that those mothers who bestow upon children the treasures of divine knowledge will receive an exceedingly great reward? If God denounces so severely those who scandalize little children: "But he that shall scandalize one of these little ones, it were better for him that a mill-stone were hanged about his neck, and he were drowned in the depth of the sea" (Matt. xviii. 6), what recompense will mothers not receive who instruct and sanctify them?

Mothers who give their efforts and means to this object, choose the surest way to appease the anger of God, and to insure their own salvation. They choose the best means of attaining a high degree of perfection. Almighty God gives to each one the graces proper to his vocation. Mothers, therefore, who are devoted to the religious instruction of their children, must rest assured that God will give them extraordinary graces to arrive at perfection. "Whoever," says our Lord, "shall receive one such little child in My name, receiveth Me."—(Matt. xviii. 5.) Whosoever, then, believes that our Saviour will not allow Himself to be surpassed in liberality, must also believe that He will bestow His choicest blessings on those mothers who instruct their children in the knowledge of God and the love of virtue.

What obligations have not the "angels" of children "who always see the face of the Father who is in heaven" (Matt. xviii. 10), to pray for these mothers—their dear colleagues and charitable substitutes, who perform their office and hold their place on earth. The children will pray for their mothers, and God can refuse nothing to the prayers of children, and their supplications will ascend with the prayers of the angels.

Do you desire, O Christian mother, to be saved? Do you wish to acquire great treasures in heaven, and to attain great perfection in this life?—Employ yourself diligently in the religious instruction of your children. Do you wish to gain the love of our Lord, and to deserve His protection?—Teach your children to fear and love God; you cannot do anything more pleasing to His Divine Heart.

It is related in the Gospel that mothers brought to Him little children, that He might touch them. And the disciples rebuked them that brought them. And when Jesus saw it, He was much displeased, and said to them: "Suffer little children to come to me, and forbid them not: for of such is the kingdom of God; and embracing them, and laying His hands on them, He blessed them." If Jesus was displeased with those who prevented little children from coming to Him, what love and tenderness will He not have for those mothers by whose means they come to Him?

Oh! how consoled will they not be in their last hour, when they shall see the souls of those whom they prepared for heaven, accompanied by their good angels, surrounding their bed of death, forming, as it were, a guard to protect them from the snares and assaults of the enemy!

This is a happiness which those mothers may confidently expect who labor assiduously to give their children a good religious education. Ah! would to God, I say once more, that mothers would understand their sublime mission on earth!

But it is just here that the difficulty lies: how can a mother give the child these early lessons of piety and devotion, if she has never learned them herself? How can she train it to raise its young heart to that Heavenly Father, and ask Him for His continued mercy and blessings, of whose name or law she has never been informed or instructed in the Public Schools? How can she impart to her child that knowledge which she herself has never learned in the Public Schools, and which she has always been taught to look upon as unnecessary? Can she teach the child to love God and keep His commandments, to hate sin, and avoid it for the love of God?—To love, honor, and obey its parents, not from natural motives alone, but because, in so doing, it would love, honor, and obey God in the person of its father and mother, and have thus not only a great reward, and length of days here below, but also the joys of heaven above? This lesson the poor mother was never taught in the Public Schools. How can she teach her sweet child that it has an immortal soul, that God sees even the inmost thoughts of the soul, that it is this soul that sins by consenting to the evil inclinations of the heart; that when the child is tempted to pride, gluttony, anger, disobedience, theft, lies, or any manner of uncleanness, even in thought as well as deed, that it must call on God and its good guardian angel to come to its assistance, and keep its soul from consenting, and its body from doing, any of those things that might offend its good God? All this the poor mother has not been taught in the Public Schools. The State claims the right to educate her, and it did not regard this kind of knowledge necessary, else it would have provided it.

Let us again bear in mind that the Public School-girls of to-day will be the women of to-morrow.

The most majestic kingdom for woman to reign in is home. A woman nowhere looks more lovely, more truly great, more fascinating, and more really beautiful and useful, than when in her own house, surrounded by her children, giving them what instruction she is capable of, or devising some plan of intellectual entertainment. Depend on it that this is the grandest position in this world for a woman, and this home-audience is nearer and sweeter to the affectionate heart of a mother whose brain is properly developed, than all the applause and flatteries that the outer world can bestow. It is not in the court-room, the pulpit, and rostrum, but it is among the household congregation that woman's influence can achieve so much, and reign paramount. This, however, is not easily understood and practised by women who have been educated without religion. And it is for this reason that such women cannot make faithful wives and tender mothers.

Young ladies whose education has been devoid of moral and religious instruction, whose imagination, always over-ardent and vivacious, has been still more stimulated by a class of exercises, public examinations, and studies better calculated to give them an unreal than a sober view of life, are not prepared to fulfil their divine mission on earth. An illustration of this truth is the fact that quite recently over six hundred personal applications—mostly made by girls of from fifteen to twenty—were made in one day at the Grand Opera House in New York to fill places in the ballet and Oriental marches of the spectacle of Lalla Rookh. Assuredly this fact is evidence that the women in New York, like so many women in all quarters of the land, are unwilling to do the work which properly belongs to them to do, and prefer any shift, even the degrading one mentioned above, to honest household labor. There are thousands of ladies to whom the following description, written by a lady herself, may well be applied:

"How is it that there is not more nature in the present age, and less sophistication in society, and that mothers do not teach their daughters to fit themselves for wives and mothers? For they all seem to be setting traps to get husbands. Why, the young ladies of the present day are quite ashamed should they be ignorant of the name of the last new opera and its composer, but would feel quite indignant if they were asked whether they knew how to make good soup, or broil a beefsteak, or mend stockings.

"Above all, you can notice in the young ladies of the present day a madness beyond description for dress, for balls, theatres, watering-places, and all kinds of worldly amusements; you can see in them the greatest desire to appear ladies. They go and spend the whole day at the perfumer's, where they purchase their complexion; at the goldsmith's and the milliner's, where they get their figures. A few days ago, the father of one of these ladies had to pay a bill of forty-nine hundred dollars at the milliner's, for his daughter. The chief mental agony of the masses of the young women of the present day seems to be, who shall have the largest possible waterfall, the smallest bonnet, and make themselves the greatest fright. They do nothing from morning till night but read novels, and look at their white hands, or the passers-by in the street. They all seem to be senseless creatures, for their capacious brain soars no higher than dress, fashion, pleasure, comfort of life. Were it not for their vain daughters, hundreds of parents at this moment would have a happier countenance, and not that careworn, wretched look that we so frequently see when honest people get in debt, incurred by living beyond their *means*. Were it not for the extravagancy of young women, young men would not be afraid to marry, consequently would not be led into the temptations that they are in the single state, for marriage is one sure step towards morality, and consequently tends to the decrease of crime.

"Very many young ladies act as catch-traps, with their painted faces and affected sweetness, to lure young men into the swamps of iniquity.

"I frequently read comments about servants not knowing and performing their proper duties; in fact, of their incompetency to fill the office they apply for: *and it is true.*

"In Boston, a short time ago, one hundred and eighty unfortunate girls were arrested in *one night*; and I doubt not that the greater portion of them could have *once* been respectable servants, but considered the office and *name too low*! Men think it no disgrace to become carpenters and masons, and it is certainly as respectable to clean a house, and keep it in order, as it is to build it. And what kind of a name have these girls now? What future have these women to look forward to? Generally the world's cold, nipping scorn, combined with ill-health and destitution. A girl would much rather work in a factory, or a 'saloon,' because she can be called 'Miss,' dress finer, and imagine she will be thought a *lady*! Poor girl! It is this delusion, this false pride, that crowds the streets nightly with pretty young girls, some of whom count only twelve short summers. With Hamlet, I exclaim, 'Oh, horrible! most horrible!' I lived in a house in which there was a girl, Annie C., not seventeen, and she attended in a restaurant. I once said to her, 'Why do you not take the situation of a seamstress, or a nurse in a gentleman's family?' She turned upon me in the most insolent way, saying, 'Me be a servant! That will do very well for Irish, or Dutch, or English girls, but I am an *American*, and feel myself as *good as anybody*.'

"However, this girl afterwards went as a ballet-girl at one of the lowest places in Boston; and the last account I heard of her was, she was travelling with an Ethiopian troop *alone*. Poor young creature! what will be her end? The truth is, that after a girl is fifteen years old, in this country, she considers herself a person of *sound judgment*, and the parents look up to these sprites with a sort of deferential fear. These girls are simply living pictures walking about the earth, deriding everything they are incapable of understanding. And who could be charmed with such women? with such 'Grecian Bends,' Grecian noses? The genuine well-bred woman will shine out from beneath the plainest garb; and shoddy vulgarity, even should it be incased in rubies and diamonds, will only be rendered the more obvious and conspicuous to those who at a glance can discover the difference—to those who cannot be deceived, even by the radiant sparkling of these richest of gems."

This sort of women wish to have the "women's rights." They would like, if they knew how, to turn the world upside down, and inside out. This great desire among a certain class of women, to have the world think that they possess masculine power, generally proceeds from persons who wish to create a sensation, and fail to do so in the station they belong to. When a woman wishes to go out of her natural element, she shows that her intellect is shallow, and she is desirous of being thought greater than her sex generally; while, in reality, she discovers to us her own littleness. These people seem to wish to be what it is impossible for them ever to become—"men."

"When God created man in his own image, He said, 'It is not good that man should live alone: I will make him a helpmeet.' Now, had God meant to create merely a companion capable of following the same pursuits, and capable of the same herculean labors that evidently is meant to be man's destiny, why, He would have made *another man*. But no! When God caused a deep sleep to fall upon Adam, he took out one of his ribs, and made a *woman*—a being in EVERY WAY THE COMPLEMENT OF MAN. And, after they ate of the tree of knowledge, God said to the woman, 'Thy desire shall be to thy husband, and he shall RULE *over thee*.' And unto Adam he said, 'Because thou hast *hearkened* unto the voice of thy wife, and hast eaten of the tree which I commanded thee, saying, *Thou shalt* not eat of it, cursed is the ground for thy sake; in sorrow shalt thou eat of it all the days of thy life;' thus plainly demonstrating to us, that MAN was meant to *rule*. Bear in mind that God was *angry* because Adam HEARKENED unto the voice of his WIFE; and Adam called his wife Eve because she was the mother of all living. So it is clear to be seen, that woman was meant to attend to the duties of a mother in caring for her offspring, and man was intended to labor as the provider for her whom he chose as a helpmeet, as well as for the entire household. Woman has natural nourishment sent to her for the babe long before she is able to leave her couch. Does not all this prove to every thinking person that woman's sphere and calling are *widely different*?"

The good and perfection of women consist in remaining contentedly in the place which God has assigned them, and in performing well the duties of their divine calling. If the hand wishes to be in the place of the eye, and the eye wishes to be where the hand is, they become burdensome, and disturb the good order and harmony of the body. Now it is the same with the members of the social body. If women are in the place, or engaged in the occupation which God has chosen for them, they enjoy a profound peace; they rest under His protection; they are nourished by His grace; they are enriched by His blessings, and work out their eternal happiness with but little pain.

This truth, however, is considered by many women as one of trifling importance; they seem not to care as to whether they live up to their divine calling or not. The Holy Ghost, however, admonishes every one thus: "Let every man abide in the vocation to which he was called" (1 Cor. vii. 20); for, "Blessed is the man that shall continue in wisdom—and that considereth her ways in his heart."—(Eccles. xiv. 22, 23.) Blessed that woman who well considers her divine calling, penetrates into, and admires its greatness, and endeavors, with all her strength and heart, to comply with all its duties. One of the most usual temptations which the arch-enemy of mankind makes use of to shake women's happiness, in the present day, is to excite in them disgust and dissatisfaction for their divine calling. Hence it is that we so often hear them complain of their state of life; they fancy that, by changing their condition of life, they shall fare better: yes, provided they changed themselves. Would to God they were sworn enemies of these useless, dangerous, and bad desires! God wills to speak to them amidst the thorns, and out of the midst of the bush (Exod. iii. 2), and they will Him to speak to them in *"the whistling of a gentle air."*—(III Kings, xix. 12.) They ought, then, to remain on board the ship in which they are, in order to cross from this life to the other; and they ought to remain there willingly, and with affection. Let them not think of anything else; let them not wish for that which they are not, but let them earnestly desire to be the very best of what they are. Let them endeavor to do their best to perfect themselves where they are, and bear courageously all the crosses, light or heavy, that they may encounter. Let them *believe that this is the leading principle, and yet the one least understood in the Christian life*. Every one follows his own taste; very few place their happiness in fulfilling their duty according to the pleasure of our Lord. What is the use of building castles in Spain, when we are obliged to live in America? "As a bird that wandereth from her nest, so is a man that leaveth his place" (Prov. xxvii. 8), his occupation, or station of life. Let every woman remain firm in her calling, if she wishes to insure her tranquillity of mind, her peace of heart, her temporal and eternal happiness.

To become unfaithful to their vocation is for women to suffer as many pangs as a limb which, through some accident, has been wrenched out of place. They are continually tormented by evil spirits, who have power over a soul that is out of its proper sphere. They are no longer under the protection of God, since they have withdrawn from His guidance, and voluntarily abandoned His watchful Providence. They fall often into grievous sins, because they are not sustained by the grace which belongs to the state in which God desires them to be. A woman, therefore, can never show her superior intellectual powers better than by cheerfully accepting the calling for which the Creator evidently intended her; that is, for *woman, wife, and mother*.

CHAPTER VIII.

EVIL CONSEQUENCES OF THE PUBLIC SCHOOL SYSTEM CONTINUED.

Few questions affect so directly the welfare and interests of the people as the question of education; and assuredly, in this country, there is none of more moment as regards the well-being and permanence of our national institutions. These, our institutions, our prosperity and civilization, depend for their permanence and perpetuity, not so much on the culture of the arts, sciences, literature, or philosophy, as on the general diffusion of the salutary and vivifying principles of religion. History tells us in its every page, that the decline and downfall of nations have ever been caused by irreligion and immorality.

Indeed, it is not the State that has made men free, nor can it, on its own professed origin, keep *itself* or *them* free. It has no mission to reform men or manners; its boasted material civilization is no civilization at all. For steam, railroads, telegraphs, printing, and in fact all the arts and natural sciences, have never civilized or converted one man, not even a naked savage, and never will. They are the results of civilization, and even then the least part. Nor are they adequate to maintain or preserve the State. What is called *material civilization* is nothing else than *polished barbarism,*—a kind of monster, with the intelligence of a man, and the cruelty and instincts of a beast. It may flatter the vanity of modern nations to think they are superior to the ancients in scientific and industrial developments, but if they rely on this alone, they are greatly mistaken. I admit the superiority of the moderns, but not on this account. In the first place, many arts and products of head and hands have been lost, but even those that remain are the envy and despair of modern competitors. Besides, every age must be judged by comparison with its contemporaries. Yet they have fallen; and antiquarian travellers search in vain for the ruins of the proudest and greatest cities of the past. The nation and people—the most gallant and accomplished of all antiquity—who engraved their names on the imperishable fields of Platæa and Marathon, who conquered at Salamis, or died at Thermopylæ—that carried eloquence, heroism, and art to a pitch never since attained—the age which boasted of Pericles and Praxitelles, of Plato and Aristides—perished from excess of its material civilization, deprived, as it was, of the vital element of true religion. Without this no nation can live, nor exhibit in its actions true grandeur, or nobility of character. There is among such a cruelty, a perfidy, and a beastly lust, which sooner or later bring on their decay and ruin.

Look at ancient Rome, the once proud mistress of the world. In her palmiest days, amidst her thousands of marble palaces and triumphal arches, amidst her innumerable temples and altars, there was *not one to Mercy*. Nor was there, amidst all this barbaric display, a single *hospital* for the poor of any age or condition. The Roman eagle was carried at the head of victorious legions to the *"Hither Inde,"* and far beyond the depths of *"Hercynian forests."* Conquered kings marched at the head of subjugated nations to swell her triumphs; the wealth and strength of the then known world lay at her feet.

Here was exhibited on a scale—the grandest the world ever saw or will see—the triumphs of *"material civilization."* Yet all this crumbled and fell before the rude hatchets of the long-haired *"barbarian hordes,"* coming they knew not from whence, and going they knew not whither, only able to give the single answer, that they were *"the scourge of God."* Where, then, was the power to save? It was not in their material civilization, nor in their impotent and terrified legions. What all these could not do was accomplished by an unarmed man—Pope Leo the Great, speaking in the name of that mighty God, unknown alike to Attila and to Roman wisdom. That God still reigns, and Him it is the State would exclude from the Public Schools! thereby denying alike the lessons of history and its Christian duty. These United States, or no existing nation (relatively to the age), has never attained the point of artistic, æsthetic, social or material perfection of the Greco-Roman States; yet they fell, as I have just said, to slavery and ruin, not so much from the blows of the barbarians, as from the dissolving influence of a *material civilization*, resulting inevitably in public and private impotence and demoralization.

Only keep up the present godless system of State education, and depend on it, as sure as effect follows cause, every species of villany and defilement will flood the land. It is certain that all education which is not based on religion is heathenish, and must prove destructive in the end. It will destroy the very people whom it was expected to save. It will consume them as a fire.

Nor can it be otherwise; for what brought on the "Cities of the Plain" the material fires of heaven? Or what were the sins and crimes of the Gentile nations that called forth the terrible chastisements predicted by the prophets? Why, the self-same pride, worldly-mindedness, ambition, sensuality, and *disregard of God and His laws* which is at this hour taught in the Public Schools. This, I am aware, is a grave charge, but it is made with all deliberation and sense of responsibility. Indeed, the ancients were in many respects more excusable than we are. They had but the Old Law, always incomplete and obscure, whilst we live under the fulfilment of the new law, with all its aids and graces. Now, if God did not spare the "Cities of the Plain," if He destroyed the ancient nations in punishment for their wicked lives and disregard of Himself and His law, what reason have our modern heathens and infidels to escape God's vengeance—they who in every respect are more guilty in His sight? Let the measure of the evil consequences of the Public School system become full, and rest assured the wrath of God will not fail to come down upon the American people. The late American war was a great punishment for the whole country. Thousands of men were launched into eternity unprepared to appear before their Eternal Judge. Yet this punishment is only a forerunner of a far more terrible one. The Lord is patient, and slow in punishing a whole nation, which He may spare for many years for the sake of His just. Yet for all that He will not fail to punish private families, fathers, and mothers, and children, if they have no regard for Him and His law—if they are practical infidels, and give themselves up to their beastly passions. Let me give you some instances, taken from the little book "Fate of Infidelity," by a Converted Infidel.

"You all have, undoubtedly, heard of Blind Palmer, a professed infidel. After he had tried to lecture against Christ he lost his sight, and died suddenly in Philadelphia, in the forty-second year of his age. You will also have heard of the so-called Orange County Infidel Society. They held, among other tenets, that it was right to indulge in lasciviousness, and that it was right to regulate their conduct as their propensities and appetites should dictate; and as these principles were carried into practical operation by some families belonging to the association, in one instance a son held criminal intercourse with his mother, and publicly justified his conduct. The step-father, and husband to the mother who thus debased herself, boldly avowed that, in his opinion, it was morally right to hold such intercourse. The members of this impious society were visited by God in a remarkable manner. They all died, within five years, in some strange or unnatural manner. One of these was seized with a sudden and violent illness, and in his agony exclaimed: 'My bowels are on fire—die I must,' and his spirit passed away.

"Dr. H., another of the party, was found dead in his bed the next morning.

"D. D., a printer, fell in a fit and died immediately, and three others were drowned within a few days.

"B. A., a lawyer, came to his death by starvation, and C. C., also educated for the bar, and a man of superior intellectual endowments, died of want, hunger, and filth.

"Another one, who had studied to be a preacher, suddenly disappeared, but at length his remains were found fast in the ice, where he evidently had been for a long time, as the fowls of the air, and the inhabitants of the deep, had consumed the most of his flesh.

"Joshua Miller, notorious as a teacher of infidelity, was found upon a stolen horse, and was shot by Col. J. Woodhull; N. Miller, his brother, who was discovered one Sunday morning seated upon a log playing cards, was also shot.

"Benjamin Kelly was shot off his horse by a boy, the son of one Clark, who had been murdered by Kelly; his body remained upon the ground until his flesh had been consumed by birds.

"I. Smith committed suicide by stabbing himself, while he was in prison for crime.

"W. Smith was shot by B. Thorpe and others, for robbery.

"S. T. betrayed his own confidential friend for a few dollars; his friend was hung, and he was afterwards shot by D. Lancaster.

"I. V. was shot by a company of militia. I. D., in a drunken fit, was frozen to death.

"I. B., and I. Smith, and J. Vervellen, B. R., and one other individual, were hung for heinous crimes they had committed. N. B., W. T., and W. H., were drowned. C. C. hung himself. A. S. was struck with an axe, and bled to death.

"F. S. fell from his horse and was killed. W. Clark drank himself to death; he was eaten by the hogs before his bones were found, which were recognized by his clothing. J. A., sen., died in the woods, his rum-jug by his side; he was not found until a dog brought home one of his legs, which was identified by his stocking; his bones had been picked by animals.

"S. C. hung himself, and another destroyed himself by taking laudanum. D. D. was hired for ten dollars to shoot a man, for which offence he died upon the gallows.

"The most of those who survived were either sent to the State Prison, or were publicly whipped for crimes committed against the peace and dignity of the State."

This is a brief history of the Orange County "Liberals," as they called themselves. To the infidel and evil-doer, it presents matter worthy of serious reflection, while the believer will recognize in each event the special judgment of God, which is too clearly indicated to be doubted by any honest mind. I ask, will the Lord fail to visit with similar judgments all those who are guilty of the same crimes? Will the Lord fail to visit with similar judgments all those who, by keeping up and defending a godless system of education, prepare the young for infidelity, and all kinds of crimes and iniquities? If the Lord punished so severely the King Antiochus for carrying away the sacred vessels from the temple of Jerusalem; if He sent so many plagues upon the Egyptians, and drowned, at last, the King Pharaoh and his whole army in the Red Sea, for refusing to let the people of God offer sacrifices where and in the manner the Lord desired it, what will be the punishments for those who, by a godless system of education, abolish religion? If God slew twenty-four thousand men of the Israelites for having fallen into fornication (Numb. xxv.), with what punishments will He visit those who add, to the sin of fornication and adultery, even the crime of child-murder! Numberless child-murders are committed daily in the land. Assuredly the voice of these innocent victims will cry to heaven for vengeance, and the Lord will not deafen His ear to their voice. If the American people will not soon put an end to the godless system of education, if they permit any longer the rising generation to be raised to infidelity, the wrath of the Lord, enkindled against them ever since the introduction of the godless system of education, will fall upon them. In former times, when the Lord threatened the people with His chastisements, they entered into themselves, and did penance, because they had faith, and the Lord was appeased. But our modern heathens laugh at the very idea of doing penance. So the wrath of the Lord will surely overtake them when they least expect it.

CHAPTER IX.

THE STATE.—ITS USURPATION OF THE INDIVIDUAL RIGHTS.—ITS INCOMPETENCY TO EDUCATE.

It is certain and undeniable that two orders of things actually exist in this world, the natural order and the supernatural—nature and grace. These two orders have the same ultimate end, though, in themselves, they are distinct. Nature is, and must be, always subordinate to grace; the natural must be always subservient to the supernatural. This is God's immutable decree. Hence religion must always hold the first place in everything. A system of education that places the natural and the supernatural on the same level is absurd, and must be condemned; but a system of education that ignores the supernatural altogether, is, if possible, even more wicked and detestable. Yet this wicked, detestable, irreligious system, diabolical in its origin, and subversive of all political, social, and religious order, is imposed by the State upon all Christian denominations, whether they approve of it or not. Now the State has no right whatever to force such a godless system upon its subjects.

For the right understanding of this most important point, I attach great importance to a clear understanding of what is commonly called the State.

What is the State?

People in general have a vague and confused conception of this matter. You will hear the people talk of the "sovereignty of the State," "the life of the State," "the power of the State," "the absolute authority of the State," "the paramount allegiance due to the State," etc., etc. Not only the Public at large, but even those who assume to lead and direct public opinion, are constantly blundering on this subject.

There is nothing so *fertile* as an idea; it will, like every other germ or seed, bring forth in time according to its kind. If it be a good one, it will bring forth good fruit; if it be a false or bad one, it will spread its evil fruits over society. Be it one or the other, it is never barren; sooner or later, the idea or maxim takes form and substance in an *Institution*; then it operates, in a material manner, for good or evil.

To illustrate: a false conception of the nature and authority, of the legitimate functions, rights and duties of what is called the "State," has led, and will, if not corrected, ever lead to the most deplorable political, social, and religious disorder and oppression. As diverging lines in mathematics can never approximate, but must continue to widen as they are extended, so a false departure from a political "standpoint" can never be rectified unless by a return to correct first principles. This is what is meant by the democratic maxim, "that a frequent return to first principles is necessary to secure the ends of public liberty."

Indeed, this error, this diverging point in constitutional interpretation, has been the real cause—the "causa causarum"—of the late war; and not the "negro," or "cotton," or the "spirit of domination," or "difference of race," or what not, might serve as the "*proximate cause*," but the real cause lay far back of them. I am willing to admit that political events do not always proceed on a strictly logical order, but nevertheless there is a sequence, indeed an inevitable chain of cause and effect in the progress of public affairs, such as we see in individual conduct, but only on a broader scale.

Now what is the *civil power*, or *State*; what its origin, its authority, its legitimate functions, its rights and duties? Here I must, of necessity, be very brief. The State originated from the natural desire which men experience to obtain certain goods, such as peace, security of life and property, of personal rights and privileges, etc., etc. These are goods which neither individuals, nor families, nor private corporations can procure for themselves satisfactorily. People therefore unite to establish a State, in order to attain, through the State, what they cannot do by their own private exertions. The State, then, is made by the people and for the people. In our form of government it is a mere corporate agency. Its duty is to see that justice is administered, and personal rights and property protected. It holds the sword of justice not for *itself*, but for *others*; it is the *servant*, and not the *master*. The people were not made for the State, or given to the State, but the State is posterior to the people; it was, as I said before, established by the people and for the people. In them, under God, resides the sovereignty and ultimate permanent authority. The right of the State is to discharge the duties assigned it within the sphere of its delegated authority—that is all.

That sphere of action of the State in this country is clearly defined in the written Constitution. The State, then, must scrupulously abstain from violating any of the rights it was organized to protect.

There never has been, and never will be, but two forms of government—one seeking to restrain, the other to enlarge, the liberties of the people. To the former belong the centralized and despotic governments of the past and present; to the latter, the limited and representative ones.

Russia, without doubt, is the highest type of that despotism so common among Pagan nations. The Czar is the successor of the Gentile Cæsar; he unites in himself the civil and spiritual power; the inevitable result is social oppression, denial of the rights of conscience, of the family, and of the political society. Our government has already made gigantic steps in the same direction. Many of the political minds of this country have been drawn within the circle of *monarchial* ideas. They are unconsciously, as it were, adopting their forms of thought, and applying their forms of expression to our government, and claiming for it the prerogatives and supremacy appertaining to the feudal institutions of Asia and Europe. Our simple democratic form of government seems to be getting ashamed of its plebeian origin, and ambitious to ape the language and pretensions of its former masters. This decadence was made apparent not long ago, in the discussions "for the removal of the United States Capitol." In a two-hours' discussion, the word "Republic," or "Federal Government," or "United States," was not once mentioned!! It was "*Nation,*" "Empire," etc., etc., *usque ad nauseam,* from beginning to end. To a reflecting mind, this language has an ominous significance. It smacks strongly of monarchy.

But some one will perhaps say, "Sir, what has all this dissertation to do with your subject? You commence by disclaiming against the *Public School System,* and here you are giving a grave lecture on the nation relapsing into imperialism or monarchy."

It has a great deal to do; it is an attempt to trace effects to their causes. This government of ours, both in its Federal and State capacity, is growing ambitious to play the *King.* It is setting itself up as master. It is using the language of all tyrants: "*Sic volo, sic jubeo,*" etc., etc. It claims, after the example of Prussia or Russia, or some other despotism, *to direct the education of the children* of the people. It even claims them as belonging to itself. It is the great feudal master. It takes upon itself the old duty of providing instruction for the sons and daughters of its dependents. It takes upon itself the discharge of duties imposed on parents by Divine Law, just as if fathers and mothers had lost their natural instincts as well as sense of duty; just as if the State had all the intelligence, virtue, and forethought of the public in her keeping. It dispenses parents from a duty from which God will never dispense them. It has usurped the office of teacher; it will, if not checked, set itself up as preacher. It makes Sunday laws, temperance laws; it places marriage on the footing of simple contracts, facilitates divorce; it is constantly, in all these things and many others, repeating the "mot" ascribed to a King of France: "*L'état c'est moi.*" In fine, it makes, as it has been aptly, but not very reverently, said, God a little man, and itself and the State a little god, not in love and charity, indeed, but in power and authority.

Here is where the danger comes from, and it is against this that the people must provide. The people must see to it that the State, or those who are charged with its authority, keep within their proper place. The people can never be too vigilant or jealous of their constituted authority, never permit themselves to be the victims of misplaced confidence. The State is not seldom the usurper—the rebel that should be watched. The allegiance is not to it, but from it to the people—its master. "Eternal vigilance is the price of liberty."

The people have been greatly deceived and wronged by the State on the establishment of the Public School system. The better to understand this, let us see again, in a few words, what are the *principles* on which the establishment of public schools is based. How did men arrive at the idea that the State should be a school-master? If we consult history, we shall find that this idea rests upon most objectionable grounds. In Europe—in Protestant countries—the education of youth was held to belong to the church. But as the Protestant prince was also the chief bishop of his church, he had the care of schools, as well as the administration of other religious matters. According to this principle of the *State-church,* all the schools were *State-schools*. At the present day, Protestant princes and princesses are not looked upon as chief bishops, but the consequence of this objectionable system does still remain, and has gained a foothold even in this free country.

The French Revolution, among other things, diffused communistic and socialistic theories. Nay, communism and socialism seemed to have, for a moment, the fullest sway in those revolutionary proceedings. It is from such socialistic revolutionists that came the idea, or rather principle, which was made a law, that the State should educate the children of its subjects. Accordingly the school-system was arranged, which Napoleon I. highly welcomed and retained, as he saw in it a welcome instrument of his despotism. In fact, nothing pleases State-absolutism or despotism so much as the complete control of education through the system of State-schools. As the result of impartial history, then, we see that the foundation of the State-school system is nothing else than the objectionable Protestant State-church, and especially revolutionary socialism.

But most absurd did the State-school system appear after it had been transplanted into free America. Here this "State system of education" was at first applied to the poor, and other unprovided-for "waifs of society." But not long after, the State claimed to have a paramount interest in the children of all classes; it made no distinction, it knew not the rich from the poor, but opened its scholastic treasures alike, and it was thought to be all right.

What an absurdity! The State, as I have remarked, must scrupulously abstain from violating any of those rights which it was organized to protect. It must not paralyze or take away the industry of the individual, family, or private institutions by substituting for it its own industry. The State should rather protect and promote the industry of its subjects, as well as other rights and liberties. Let me speak more plainly: the State, for instance, should protect trade, but it should not be itself a tradesman; the State should encourage agriculture, but it should not be itself a farmer; the State should sustain honest handicraft, but it should not work at shoe-making or tailoring, and bread-baking. So, in the same manner, the State should promote and protect education, but it should not be itself a school-master, and give instruction.

What a cry would be raised if the State erected State workshops, and thereby ruined all other similar trades! Now the State does the same thing, as far as possible, in regard to education. What an absurdity! In our free country, State education has no more foundation in good sense than the old sumptuary laws, that regulated the length of a boot or the dimensions of a skirt.

If the State claims the right to educate our children, why does it not just as well claim the right to nurse, feed, clothe, doctor, and lodge them? Indeed these necessities are more indispensable, and must be supplied to a considerable extent before education can be given at all. Why should the State throw all these burdens on the parents, and assume that of instruction? It cannot claim to know more of grammar than of the art of nursing and cooking. It is even said that the tailor and barber have more to do in fashioning the man than the school-master.

Again, how absurd is it not for the State to undertake to teach all alike, without regard to their circumstances or prospects in life, the same business. This scholastic equality soon ends, if it ever had a reality. They cannot all expect to be Newtons, Humboldts, or La Places. They cannot be all, nay, not one in ten thousand, "professors," or "editors," or what not. We cannot, if we would, escape the sentence imposed on our forefather in the garden: "Thou shalt eat thy bread in the sweat of thy face." As well might the State claim that all the children from seven to seventeen years of age should sit at the same table, provided at public expense, and be served with the same food and the same number of dishes. If the State (in order to prepare the rising generation to make citizens, which must be its reason, if any) thinks it necessary to prescribe a State education, it is equally important that their food, and even their clothing, should be of the approved State quality and pattern!!! All know that this was the old Lacædemonian plan, and how it ended history tells;—in ferocity, avarice, dishonesty and disruption. All admit the folly and wickedness of forcing a people into uniformity in matter of religion. Now it is just as unreasonable, just as absurd, just as wicked to force the people into uniformity in the matter of education. One species of tyranny as well as the other disregards the just claims of conscience, tramples on the most vital rights of individuals, and usurps the most sacred right of the family.

The State may, indeed, require that the children should be educated, in order that they may one day become worthy members of society, and fit subjects for the State; but claim, and give, and control their education, the State cannot. There is in all this matter a feature not always clearly represented. It is this: any provision made by the "State" for education, must refer *to the poor and otherwise unprovided,* and be justified on the grounds of the State standing to these classes *in loco parentis*; beyond this, though the State, as to "charitable uses," may be defined *parens patria,* yet, as to the people at large, *it has nothing to do with their education whatever*. If this simple though undeniable fact were properly understood, it would save a world of trouble and confusion.

I am speaking of a "*Christian State,*" and the State in America is Christian. The very graves, if necessary, would open and give up their dead to bear testimony to its Christian origin. Its civilization is Christian, and is the product of the principles of the "*New Law*" as taught and promulgated by the Church. The distinguishing feature of this civilization is, that it has asserted the dignity of freedom of the *individual man,* while the ancient, or Gentile, civilization, *sunk* the *individual man* in the composite society called the State. In that case it was but reasonable that the *State* should, *as owner,* take upon itself the burden of providing, not only for his government, but also for the education of his offspring. These, too, belonged to it, on the maxim of Roman or Pagan law, that *partus sequitur ventrem,* or the offspring follows the parent. This is the origin of the Pagan doctrine, "*the children of the State*"—a miserable relic of barbarism. It is important to keep this fact in mind, when we deny the *supremacy of the State* in the matter of education.

Our children, then, are not the *children of the State*. The State has no children, and never had, nor will. The State does not own them, nor their fathers nor mothers, nor anybody else in this country, thank God! We have not got that far yet on the road to civil slavery, and I hope we never shall. We are not Pagans, nor Mahometans, nor Russians. We have not sold out, and don't intend to! We are free, for with a great price our forefathers have bought this freedom; and better still, we are made, through the mercy of our Divine Author, Christians, and heirs to a heavenly kingdom. Our children, too, are free; they belong by the order of nature to their parents, and by the order of grace to our Lord Jesus Christ. They are children of God and heirs to His heavenly kingdom. It is not on the State, but on parents, that God imposed the duty to educate their children, a duty from which no State can dispense, nor can fathers and mothers relieve themselves of this duty by the vicarious assumption of the State. They have to give a severe account of their children on the Day of Judgment, and they cannot allow any power to disturb them in insisting upon their rights and making free use of them. The State has no more authority or control rightfully over our children, than over a man's wife. The right to educate our children is a right of conscience, and a right of the family. Now these rights do not belong to the temporal order at all; and outside of this the State has no claim, no right, no authority. When the State has children, it will be time enough to teach them. How long will it take our enlightened age to learn this simple but important truth?

Nothing shows better the absurdity of the State in claiming the right of education, than its incompetency for the task. The State is forbidden any interference with religion.

I have shown that the whole system is infidel in principle. The State says we want no religion taught in the Public Schools, because, as we cannot teach you religion without inculcating some form or other professed by some sect or other, and as we do not wish to give offence, we will teach you none. Let the child believe anything or nothing, so as it is not some form of "sectarianism." I worship in the "Pantheon;" all are alike to me, of course. In all this the State is perfectly consistent, and cannot do otherwise. It has undertaken a part *it is not competent to perform.* The State, as State, professes no form of belief. Its gods, its worships, its altars, its victims, its rewards, its punishments, its heaven, its hell—are here. It teaches no religion, because it don't profess any. It was not born, it will not die, it has no soul, it was not created, it will not be judged in the world to come, like men.

But let me not be misunderstood as concluding that states, nations, or kingdoms are not moral persons, and are not responsible for their acts and conduct to Almighty God. They have no right to do wrong more than an individual. "States" have their lives, their mission, their destiny; they have their sphere here below. They represent the temporal, or the things which belong to Cæsar.

The State, then, is a moral person, and *a fortiori,* a religious person, *for there can be no morality without religion.* But though religion, in a general sense, be recognized by the State, it has no authority to control or direct it. It must respect the conscience of an individual. This is his birthright, and cannot be voted away, whether to support Public Schools or Public Churches.

If there be amongst us any number, great or small, who deny the common faith, it is the duty of the State to tolerate them. A greater power—God—does this. But the State itself cannot profess or *play infidel,* or, under pretence of avoiding sectarian partiality, strike at the root of all Christianity. I admit the State is of the "temporal order," and cannot discriminate between the various modes of belief; but not for that can it place itself *outside* of them. It is *distinguishable*, but not *separable*, from the spiritual order. It is simply a means to a greater end. It is a mischievous error to say that the State has nothing to do with religion, and may act outside of its obligations. If by this it is meant that the State cannot establish or maintain any special form of religion, or interfere with its profession, or even denial by others, I admit the proposition; but if, on the other hand, it is meant that it regards Christianity and infidelity, God or no God, truth and error, either as equal or unimportant, then I utterly deny and condemn it. To bear with and tolerate error is its duty; to foster or provide for its support or propagation, or place it on the same footing with revealed truth, is another and very different thing.

The constitutions of the State guarantee to every citizen the right to worship God according to the dictates of his own conscience; but this is not guaranteeing to every one the liberty of not worshipping God at all, to deny His existence, His revelation, or to worship a false god. The freedom guaranteed is the freedom of religion, not the freedom of infidelity. The American Constitution grants to the infidel the right of protection in his civil and political equality, but it grants him no right to protection and support in his infidelity; for infidelity is not a religion, but the denial of all religion. The American State is Christian, and under the Christian law, and is based upon Christian principles. It is bound to protect and enforce Christian morals and its laws, whether assailed by Mormonism, Spiritism, Freelovism, Pantheism, or Atheism. But the State does the contrary. For, I ask, is not the State indirectly prohibiting the profession of Christianity by establishing a system of education which prohibits all religious instruction? The State forbids the teacher to speak a word on the subject of religion.

The State says that "it is an admitted axiom that our form of government, more than all others, depends on the *virtue and intelligence of the people*. The State proposes to furnish this *virtue* and *intelligence* through the *Public Schools*." That is, the safety of the State depends on the virtue and intelligence of the people, and the latter is derived from the virtue and intelligence of the "State." But where does the virtue and intelligence of the State come from? The only answer on this theory is, from the people. So the "State" enlightens and purifies the people, and the people enlighten and purify the "State." The people support the State, the State supports the Public Schools, and they support the State. If this is not what logicians call a "vicious circle," it looks very much like it. It puts me in mind of the Brahmin's theory of the support of the earth. The Hindoo says, "The world rests on the back of an elephant—the elephant rests on the back of a turtle." But what does the turtle rest on? So it is with our "*Public School Brahmins*." They will tell you, with all the coolness of Hindoo hypocrisy and pretension, that the "State depends on the schools—the schools on the State or people," but they do not say what the turtle stands on. This is the dilemma that all who rest society on the State, or on an atheistical basis, get into. They would cut the world loose from its assigned order of dependence on Divine Law, and "set it a-going on its own hook." But the trouble is, they have no support for this turtle; they have an earth without axis. The Public

School savans would have a self-supporting, a self-adjusting, and a self-created State, balanced on nothing, resting on nothing, responsible to nothing, and believing in nothing but in its own perfection and immortality. They pretend, "through godless schools," to give virtue without morality, morality without religion, and religion without God; thereby sinking below the level of the poor Indian, whose untutored mind sees God in the clouds, and hears Him in the wind.

The nameless abominations of the Communists, Fourrierists, and other such vile and degraded fraternities; the cold-blooded murders and frightful suicides that fill so many domestic hearths with grief and shame; the scarcely-concealed corruption of public and professional men; the adroit peculation and wilful embezzlement of the public money; those monopolizing speculations and voluntary insolvencies so ruinous to the community at large; and, above all, those shocking atrocities so common in our country of unbelief—the legal dissolution of the matrimonial tie, and the wanton tampering with life in its very bud; all these are humiliating facts sufficient to convince any impartial mind that there can be no social virtue, no morality, no true and lasting greatness, without religion.

"Religion," says Lord Derby, "is not a thing apart from education, but is interwoven with its whole system; it is a principle which controls and regulates the whole mind and happiness of the people." And, "Popular education," says Guizot, "to be truly good and socially useful, must be fundamentally religious."

The essential element of education—its pith and marrow, so to speak—is the religious element. By excluding it from the school-room the State has committed a crying injustice to the rising generation, and one of the worst—if not the very worst—of crimes against society. It is not one portion of the "triple man," but the whole—the physical, intellectual, and moral being—the body, the mind, the head, as stated in a previous chapter—that must be cultivated and "brought up." Neglect any one part of man's nature, and you at once disturb the equilibrium of the whole, and produce disorder; educate the body at the expense of the mind and soul, and you will have only animated clay; educate the intelligence at the expense of the moral and religious feelings, and you but fearfully increase a man's power to effect evil. You store the arsenal of his mind with weapons to sap alike the altar and the throne, to carry on a war of extermination against every holy principle, against the welfare and the very existence of society.

Science, without religion, is more destructive than the sword in the hands of unprincipled men; it will prove more of a demon than a god. It is these upholders of the present Public School system that arrest the progress of true happiness in our country, and prepare terrible catastrophes, which may deluge the land with blood.

Who were the leaders in the work of destruction and wholesale butchery in the Reign of Terror? The nurslings of lyceums in which the chaotic principles of the "philosophers" were proclaimed as *oracles of truth*.

Who are those turbulent revolutionists who now long to erect the guillotine by the Tuilleries? And who are those secret conspirators and their myrmidon partisans who have sworn to unify Italy or lay it in ruins? Men who were taught to scout the idea of a God and rail at religion, to consider Christianity as a thing of the past; men who revel in wild chimeras by night, and seek to realize their mad dreams by day.

Let us, then, dear American fellow-citizens, rest assured that intellectual discipline, without the coöperation of any religious element, will not, and cannot, produce the greatness of a nation, nor can it maintain its life and splendor and prevent its decay; let us, on the contrary, be persuaded that the only safety for a commonwealth, the only source of greatness and prosperity for a nation, as well as of tranquillity and happiness for the individual, is the true religion of Jesus Christ; it is this religion alone that is the safeguard of morality, and morality is the best security of law, as well as the surest pledge of freedom.

CHAPTER X.

THE STATE A ROBBER.—VIOLATION OF OUR CONSTITUTION AND COMMON LAW.

We have seen, so far, that the irreligious, godless system of the Public Schools tends directly to turn the youth of both sexes into the worst kind of infidels; to make them disregard good principles, and hold iniquity in veneration; to do away, not only with all revealed religion, but even with the law of nature; to make them practise fraud, theft, and robbery almost as a common trade; to make them regardless of their parents and of all divinely constituted authority; we have seen that this godless system of education is the most powerful means to create confusion, not only in religion, but also in government and in the family circle; to increase the number of apostates, and make of these apostates members of such secret societies as aim at the overthrow of governments and all good order, and Christian religion itself.

Truly, this godless system of education, if carried out to its logical consequences, will disrupt society, destroy the right of the Christian family entirely, bring back on the world the barbarism, tyranny and brutality of Pagan antiquity, and make slaves and victims of its children and their posterity forever!

Who does not feel most indignant at the State for having introduced such a godless system of education? And for the support of this system of education—of this *prolific mother of children of anti-Christ*—we are enormously tithed and taxed! Horrible!

I have shown that the State in America is Christian; that it cannot profess or play infidel. What right, then, has a Christian State to compel Christians to support infidel schools? Is not this compulsory support most violative of constitutional and religious rights? According to the Constitution of the State, "no human authority can control or interfere with the rights of conscience." Now, the direction and control of the education of our children is clearly not only a duty, but a "right of conscience." This right, of course, belongs to all denominations, whether few or many. By what authority, then, does the State impose *an established system* of education at our expense against this constitutionally guaranteed right of conscience? I would like to know wherein this differs from an established church, such as has been lately removed, after having been imposed for centuries by State supremacy on the Irish people, without their consent.

It is, in fact, much worse; for though the Episcopal Church was not in accordance with the religious belief of a majority, yet it was, nevertheless, a Christian Church of a sect of high orthodox pretensions. But these "*Public Schools*," for whose support we and all other Christian denominations are taxed, are, by their own confession, utterly *irreligious*. The early Christians refused to burn even a little gum-rosin (incense) before the Pagan idols, and preferred rather to go to the lions; but we Christians, in this late day, and in what is boastingly called "Free America," are forced to pay taxes to support what is worse than heathen idols—schools from which the name of God is excluded, and, to our shame, we submit.

Referring to the wrong done to Catholics who cannot, in conscience, send their children to these schools, Judge Taft, of Ohio, said not long ago:

"This is too large a circumstance to be covered by the Latin phrase, 'De minimis non curat lex.' These Catholics (paying their proportion of the taxes) are constrained, every year, on conscientious grounds, to yield to others their right to one-third of the school-money, a sum averaging, at the present time, about $200,000 every year. That is to say, these people are *punished* every year, for believing as they do, to the extent of $200,000; and to that extent those of us who send our children to these excellent common schools *become beneficiaries of the Catholic money*. What a shame for Protestants to have their children educated for money robbed from Catholics! Mercantile life is supposed to cultivate, in some, a relish for hard bargains. But if it were a business matter, and not a matter of religious concern, could business men be found willing to exact such a pecuniary advantage as this? I think it would shock the secular conscience!"

The State, in creating *free schools*, is like the Turkish Bashaw's mode of making pork cheap. He first compelled the Jews to buy it at a rate fixed by himself; but the Jews had no use for it, so it was left for every one to pick up at will. Indeed, what is a school worth when a man will pay a premium to be exempt from sending his children to it? The State, boasting of its splendid Public Schools, is also like that poor fellow who wore a gold watch and boasted of it. "Where did you get it?" he was asked. "I got it as a present," he answered. Then he related how one day he met with a rich man: "I knocked him down," he said, "put my foot on his throat, and said: 'Give me your watch, or I kill you.' So he gave it to me." "Pay your taxes for the erection and support of our Public Schools," says the lord State to the poor and to the rich, "or I sell your property." What a shame! The Catholics ask no favor, but they insist on their rights. In this country, whose discoverer was a Catholic—in this country, where the principle of religious toleration was first established by a Catholic nobleman, the famous and chivalric Calvert, Earl of Baltimore—in this country, whose people are largely indebted for their freedom to the armed coöperation and generous aid of Catholic France—in this country, whose constitutional freedom has been struck down by the malevolent Puritanism *which in one breath declares that Catholics are opposed to education, and in the next insists that they shall be deprived of the means necessary for its maintenance*—in this country, I say, we Catholics are entitled to equal rights, and to a fair share, to a just apportionment of the annual amount raised by taxation for the support of our charitable and educational institutions. We ask only what is fair, what is just, what is right; and we base our demand upon principle, and not upon the ground of favors granted or received.

If the State taxes us, as a religious and Christian people, for the education of our children, it must give us a Christian education. If it cannot, or will not do that, it must cease to tax us, and leave the education of our children to ourselves. If the Christian gives to Cæsar what belongs to Cæsar, he has a right to demand of Cæsar that he allow him to give to God what belongs to God.

Again, the Constitution says, "That no person shall be compelled to erect, support, or attend any place of public worship, nor support any minister of the gospel, or teacher of religion," etc.; and it says, "That no private property ought to be taken or applied to public use without just compensation." Now let us apply these constitutional principles to State-schools, and see if our compulsory support of them is not violative of our constitution as well as common law. Why is it "that no person shall be compelled to erect, support, or attend any place of public worship, nor support any minister of religion"? Simply because he "don't want to"; and he don't want to, "because it is against his conscience"; and "no human authority," says the Constitution, "can control or interfere with the rights of conscience"; that is all the reason, and no other. The State believes that all places of worship, and ministers of the gospel, are good; but, knowing that there is a difference of opinion among the people on that subject, wisely leaves such matters to their choice, and will not take private property for public use without compensation. Why, then, is private property taken for Public Schools without compensation? We cannot use them in conscience, and we have seen there is no lawful power or authority to "control or interfere with conscience." I ask, then, if I am not right in stating that our compulsory support of an odious and infidel system of Public Schools, against our conscience and against our consent, is not far worse than the support of any form of church establishment?

Moreover, according to the Constitution, "No preference can ever be given by law to any church, sect, or mode of worship." This section is often quoted as the authority and reason for excluding religious teachings from the Public Schools; but, strange enough, it is flagrantly violated by the present system, giving a *preference by law* to the *unbelievers*, and thereby discriminating against the believers of all sects and denominations. For, after all, there can be but two churches, or, if you please, sects, in the eye of the State—the believers and unbelievers. To the former belong the various Christian denominations, and to the latter those who deny and *protest* against all religious faith and belief. Those certainly are the last, and for that reason, if for no other, are the *best or worst* (as people may choose to view them) sect. It is, then, this last product, this "*caput mortuum*" of all sects and believers of every shade and kind, that is favored by the no-belief system of education.

"Though the State may not give any preference to any church or sect," it is not, on that account, authorized to ignore and reject all; but, on the contrary, is obliged in justice to assist all or none, as, by this course alone, it avoids giving preference to any. This is what the law contemplates, and the only course that comports with reason and justice. If it suits the *last sect*—the *unbelievers or no-believers*—to exclude morals or religion from schools, all right; let them keep on as at present. But if it suits the various other churches or sects to modify the system to suit their conscientious views and beliefs, to apply their own proportion of the school tax for that purpose, it is their undeniable and lawful right.

There is one view in which the public will agree in regard to the Public Schools: it is that they cost too much money. For the management of the godless Public Schools there is a costly array of "Commissioners," and "Inspectors," and "Trustees," and "Superintendents," and "Secretaries of Boards," and "Central Officers," all in league with "Contractors," to make "a good thing"—so-called—out of the plan. We have, now, contractors for buildings and repairs, contractors for furniture, contractors for books, contractors for furnaces, contractors for fuel, contractors even for pianos, and all making money out of it. The "Boards" that give the contracts do not make any money by way of commissions, do they? Ah! you know full well that hundreds of thousands of dollars are annually spent or squandered in running these Public Schools, and which are recommended, in a particular manner, for their *economy*!

But aside, for a moment, from these *Public Schools*, so numerous, so costly, so grand and imposing in their exterior, managed by a little army of high-paid professors, teachers, superintendents and assistants, costing the people of every city and State hundreds of thousands of dollars annually, there is another army, yea, a volunteer army, not commissioned or paid by the State, but by a greater power—God—who, for His love, and that uncomparable reward which only God bestows, devote themselves to teaching, instructing, training and educating the poor, the needy, the orphan, the houseless, the homeless, the forlorn, the despised, as well as the more favored of the earth. These make no grandiloquent printed reports in costly binding; they have no official stenographers or reporters to noise their proceedings in "morning papers"; they have no "Polytechnic Halls," fitted up with pretentious libraries, and all the surroundings of upholstery, and heating and cooling apparatus; but winter and summer, early and late, they keep the even tenor of their way with an "*eye single*" to their humble and laborious duties.

In nearly all the cities of America, in those busy and worldly centres of traffic and trade, of luxury and wealth, with their average of good and evil, virtue and crime, this "*volunteer army*" distributes itself noiselessly, quietly, and as it were obscurely, not heralded nor preceded by the emblems of pomp or worldly power, but nevertheless making its conquests and asserting its quiet influence in lanes and alleys, gathering up the little children, taking them to its camps, and instructing and educating them in the service of God and society.

You may have seen, in some of those cities, that long line of little boys or girls, two by two, extending to the length of a block or more; you may have observed how regularly they are assorted, the tallest in first, and ranging down to the little ones, whose busy feet are trying to keep up with the column. You may also have noted the order and silence (so unusual among children), and your attention was arrested, and perhaps you know not how all this order in this beautiful panorama was brought about. Well, with these boys you may have observed two men, one at the head, the other at the foot of this long line. If you saw this for the first time you may have wondered, and I suppose been even amused, at the figure and costume of those men;—the broad-brimmed hat, the long, strange-fashioned robe, the white collar, the collected air and mien, all bespeak the *Christian Brother*. These men, nevertheless, are "profoundly learned in all the sciences of the schools." They have abandoned home, family, friends, and have devoted themselves, merely for a scant support, to the education of the young.

If, on the other hand, the long line are girls, you may have observed two ladies; one at the head, the other at the foot. You will at a glance conclude they are not of the world. Their costume is of the homeliest cut and quality, but scrupulously clean; there is a something about their very presence that impresses you with reverence and respect, and you must be a very hardened sinner indeed if you did not feel the better of having even their shadow fall upon you. These silent, collected, but impressive women are "*Nuns*" of one order or another. They, too, have left all to serve God in the persons of these little children. They have made sacrifices greater than the world can appreciate or understand, and which only the Divine Master can reward. Their whole life is a silent but an eloquent sermon, their whole conduct the gospel in action. You will remember they are women like others of their sex, and mayhap have been flattered and petted, and once filled with the natural vanity and expectations of their sex; but all these they have put *behind* them, and henceforth and forever their walk, and life, and conversation is with God, and in the service of His little ones. Now it will be easily seen that the personal influence of such men and women over the life and manners of children, must be immensely beneficial. It is granted that the influence of father and mother is potential for good or evil. So it is with teachers. Children are shrewd observers, and are apt to take some one as a prototype and exemplar. This one they copy as near as may be. These "Christian Brothers," and "Nuns, or Sisters," are good models; they teach the children to pray in the best of all ways—by praying themselves first; they try to impress on these tender souls sentiments of love, obedience, and respect to their fathers and mothers, and, above all, their duties to our dear Lord. They accompany them to His altar on Sundays and holy days, beginning and ending all their daily lessons with a little prayer or devotion. For the rest, they give them, in their schools, a plain, practical education.

Every day (we are told) there are instances of men slipping from the high rounds to the lowest one in the ladder of wealth. Business men find themselves engulphed in the sea of financial embarrassment, from which they emerge with nothing but their personal resources to depend upon for a living. Clerks, salesmen, and others find themselves thrown out of employment, with no prospect of speedily obtaining places which they are competent to fill, and with no other means of gaining a livelihood. How many men are there in every city to-day, some of whom have families dependent on them for support, who bewail the mistake they made in not learning useful trades in their younger days? There are hundreds of them. There are men in every city who have seen better days, men of education and business ability, who envy the mechanic, who has a sure support for himself and family in his handicraft. Parents make a great mistake when they impose upon the brain of their boy the task of supporting him, without preparing his hands for emergencies.

No matter how favorable a boy's circumstances may be, he should enter the battle of life as every prudent general enters the battle of armies: with a reliable reserve to fall back upon in case of disaster. Every man is liable to be reduced to the lowest pecuniary point at some stage of his life, and it is hardly necessary to refer to the large proportion of men who reach that point. No man is poor who is the master of a trade. It is a kind of capital that defies the storm of financial reverse, and that clings to a man when all else has been swept away. It consoles him, in the hour of adversity, with the assurance that, let whatever may befall him, he need have no fear for the support of himself and his family.

Unfortunately a silly notion—the offspring of a sham aristocracy—has, of late years, led many parents to regard a trade as something disreputable, with which their children should not be tainted. Labor disreputable! What would the world be without it? It is the very power that moves the world. A Power higher than the throne of the aristocracy has ennobled labor, and he who would disparage it must set himself above the Divine principle, "In the sweat of thy face shalt thou eat bread!" A trade is a "friend in need"; it is independence and wealth—a rich legacy which the poorest father may give to his son, and which the richest should regard as more valuable than gold.

Now what kind of education is necessary for a tradesman to carry on business successfully? Only a plain, practical education; that is to say, that kind and amount of knowledge of daily ordinary use and appreciation. It is reading, writing, arithmetic, English grammar, and geography, and possibly a knowledge of the German language, sufficient to speak it.

If we look around we will see that all the important and every-day duties of life are carried on by the use of industry, common sense, reading, writing, and arithmetic.

And it might almost be said that the failures are to be ascribed, in part, if not to over-education, at least to the common misdirection of acquirements, accompanied with the vague ambition and desires which they invariably excite, but rarely serve to satisfy. Why, I could find, for instance, in the history, management, and success of every newspaper editor, a living proof of my proposition. Not that I leave it to be inferred that there is not, in these newspapers, the evidences of every kind of acquirements and ability; but that the founders within my knowledge, and those who have made it the *power* and *success* that it is, have worked with these ordinary instruments. But why give one instance when there are so many on every side—so much so that the success of what is called the learned class is so rare, that it must be put among the exceptions.

As to those who are able, and desire further information, they can have it to any extent at the colleges, convents, academies and higher schools.

Many of our "dissenting brethren," of the various denominations, are equally diligent, according to the measure of grace and light given them, to bring their children up in Christian morals and education. They have their own schools, and support them, or they send their children to Catholic institutions, and will not have them tempted or corrupted by the evil influences, moral, social, and intellectual, that emanate and surround those *"whited sepulchres"*—the godless schools—as the miasm emanates and surrounds the pestilent marsh. In all these schools the children are carefully trained in Christian practices, prayers, and religious duties, as well as taught a good, plain, practical course of studies. In fact, they are truly *educated;* while in the Public Schools they are simply instructed, as you might irrational animals, according to their instinct. The Jews also teach and bring up their children in the religion of their fathers, at their own expense; so that more than one-half are, fortunately for themselves, and fortunately for society, the good order and well-being of the State, educated outside of immoral and dangerous pest-houses. It is on this element of our population that the future of the State depends; for if we are to have a sound public conscience and a controlling conservative influence in public or private affairs, we must, under God and His Church, obtain it from a true Christian education.

At these parish schools, supported by voluntary aid, the expenses of pupils per year is under seven dollars; at the Public Schools, it is, I am informed, about thirty-two dollars; so that it costs about four times as much to give the poor, miserable, shallow, infidel instruction in the Public Schools, as it does to give a good Christian education in the denominational ones; or, in plainer language, to educate 20,000 children in denominational schools saves to tax-payers not less than the *small sum*! of $500,000.

"If thy right hand scandalize thee, cut it off and cast it from thee; for it is expedient for thee that one of thy members should perish, rather than thy whole body be cast into hell."—(Matt. v. 30.) By the present Public School system, the State scandalizes the family, because it usurps the rights and duties that belong alone to parents; it scandalizes the tax-payer, because it takes money from him which it has no right to take; it scandalizes society, because, instead of teaching virtue, it teaches vice; it scandalizes the young men and the young women, because, instead of inspiring them with love for Christianity and their religious duties, it inspires them rather with contempt for religion, and turns them into actual unbelievers, and thus destroys the very life of society and the basis of every government; it scandalizes all nations, because there is not, and there has never been, any nation inculcating education without religion.

By its present system of education, the State has weakened, and will finally break up and destroy, the Christian family. The social unit is the family, not the individual; and the greatest danger to American society is, that we are rapidly becoming a nation of isolated individuals, without family ties or affections. The family has already been much weakened, and is fast disappearing. We have broken away from the old homestead, have lost the restraining and purifying associations that gathered round it, and live away from home in hotels and boarding-houses. A large and influential class of women not only neglect, but disdain, the retired and simple domestic virtues, and scorn to be tied down to the modest but essential duties—the drudgery, they call it—of wives and mothers. We are daily losing the faith, the virtues, the habits, and the manners, without which the family cannot be sustained. This, coupled with the separate pecuniary interests of husband and wife secured, make the family, to a fearful extent, the mere shadow of what it was and of what it should be. What remains of the family is only held together by the graces and virtue of women. But even this last hope is fast breaking down, by the great facility of obtaining a divorce *a vinculo matrimonii*—a facility by which the laws of most of the States of the Union grant to lust the widest margin of license, and legalize concubinage and adultery. Now when the family goes, the nation goes too, or ceases to be worth preserving. God made the family the type and basis of society; "male and female made he them."

By its present system of education, the State makes war on God and His Christ, and says, with Lucifer, "Non servio"; and this is the daring rebel against God and His law, that would claim the innocent children of the Christian family as its own; teach them its false maxims, promising them, as Satan, its master, did the Saviour, riches, and honors, and power, if they will but fall down and worship it. How incomprehensibly strange it is, that good men and women who profess Christianity, and acknowledge the obligations of its commandments, should give ear to this tempter, instead of saying, "Get behind me, Satan," and, "Thou art a liar and a cheat from the beginning." The State, in this subject of education, represents the world; and religion, as well as experience, teaches us its folly, its wickedness, its treachery and its ambition. "The State promises bread and gives a stone." It promises wealth, and honor, and gives taxes, slavery, and degradation. It is blind, and it attempts to lead; it is ignorant, and it offers to teach and direct the young. It will not receive the law, and it claims the right to give it. It arrogates the *"higher law,"* and *"would be as God."* There is the danger; and it is against this the fight must be made, if we would not surrender our civil and religious freedom, our temporal and eternal happiness.

Surely it is time for all good Christians of America to cry out to our rulers, "And now, O ye rulers, understand; receive instruction, you that judge the earth."—(Ps. ii. x.) Do not force any longer upon a Christian nation an educational system which produces such results; do not train any longer our children without religion—to infidelity, and consequently to revolution. Do not teach the youth of America any longer to reject God and His religion; they will not be long faithful to you if you make them unfaithful to the faith of their fathers. You, and all the classes in society who delight in seeing the influence of religion weakened or destroyed, never seem to realize, until it is too late, that you are sure to be the especial victims of your own success. The man who scorns to love God and His law, how shall he continue to love his neighbor? The man who has said "there is no God," is he not on the point of also saying "lust is lawful," "property is robbery"? If you raise instruments to deny God and to do away with all religious principles, God will use these very instruments to do away with you also.

Your Pagan system of education will ultimately overturn all order in the land. Among ancient Pagan nations, where the poor were comparatively ignorant—where they did not know their rights—it was easy to hold them in bondage; but now things have changed. Discontent in the lower order of society can no longer be smothered. Education has become general; and, unfortunately, the very element, without which education is often a curse, is omitted. Religious education has been separated from secular instruction. Without religion, the poor are unable to control their passions, or to bear their hard lot. They see wealth around them, and, unless taught by religion, they see no reason why that wealth should not be divided amongst them. Why should they starve, while their neighbors roll in splendor and luxury? If the poor were ignorant, they would not, perhaps, notice all the sad privations of their state; they would not, perhaps, feel them so keenly. But they are partially educated, and "a little learning is a dangerous thing."

They know their power, and, not having the soothing influence of religion to restrain them, they use their power. They have done so in France and elsewhere, and if they do not always succeed in producing revolution, and anarchy, it is only the bayonet that prevents them. Such is the abyss that yawns beneath the feet of our country, and into which the advocates of *education without religion*—perhaps some of them unconsciously—seek to precipitate us, by continuing to force upon this Christian nation an anti-Christian, an anti-American system of education.

Surely the grievance is not simply an affair of taxes, or so much money unjustly levied and collected. This we might bear, as we have to do in other cases of injustice, for righteousness' sake. But we have a duty to God, ourselves, and our children. We recognize the office and obligations of the State as *temporal ruler*, but we do not acknowledge in it an absolute and *unconditional* authority. We do not admit the doctrine of *passive obedience*. We will not and cannot surrender the education of our children to its dictation and control, for that is a trust placed in our hands by a higher power, and for which we will have to answer, at the last day, on our salvation. I ask—am I right in all that I have said upon the State and its godless system of education? If I am, then I think I have a right to ask for a verdict of "Guilty." If there are still some who cannot see that I am right, then let them, without delay, be operated upon for *amaurosis*. But then, in God's name, is it not high time to inquire what should be done to correct the system, and stop the torrent of its evil influences? This is a great question; it demands a speedy and satisfactory solution. The interests it involves are commensurate with time and eternity.

CHAPTER XI.

REMEDY FOR THE DIABOLICAL SPIRIT AND THE CRIMES IN OUR COUNTRY.

Men look around, and ask, Where is the remedy for the so wide-spread corruption of all classes of society? This is a most important question. It is not difficult for a Christian to answer it. A skilful physician, who wishes to cure his patient, endeavors first to remove the cause of the disease. So, in like manner, if we wish to stem the torrent of the evils that flood the land, we must stop the source from which they flow.

Now the leading men and the most prominent journals of New York and New England, confess that the greater part of the wide-spread immorality in our day and country is to be traced to the separation of religion from the instruction in our Public Schools.

Governor Brown, addressing the Seventh National Teachers' Convention in St. Louis, in August last, said: "It is a very customary declaration to pronounce that education is the great safeguard of republics against the decay of virtue and the reign of immorality. Yet the facts can scarcely bear out the proposition. The highest civilizations, both ancient and modern, have sometimes been the most flagitious. Nowadays, certainly, your prime rascals have been educated rascals."

And indeed if we go to Auburn, Sing Sing, and other prisons, and examine some of the criminals confined there, we will find that there is truth in the Governor's words.

Do the managers of the Erie Railway lack any kind of intelligence that could be communicated in a common school? Are not those pests, the Washington and Albany lobbies, rather *too* knowing? Had not those blood-suckers, the shoddy-ites and army contractors, an average common school education? Do not the "gold rings" and the "whiskey rings" know how to read and write? Were not Catiline of old, and Aaron Burr and Benedict Arnold of more recent times, men of intelligence? Were not the parties to the recent tragedy, two of whom Mr. Beecher united in unholy wedlock, passable enough in point of merely intellectual cultivation? Mephistopheles was a person of surprising accomplishments, and the ablest debates in literature are those which Milton puts in the mouths of the grand synod of devils in Pandemonium. Byron was a prodigy of intelligence; but, whether Mrs. Stowe's revolting accusation be true or not, he was certainly a profligate.

No one, certainly, gifted with ordinary power of observation, will ascribe crime solely to ignorance, nor will such a one fail to see that a large class of the most audacious and dangerous offenders of both sexes are educated, nay, over-educated, according to the Public School standard.

The Boston Daily *Herald*, of October 20th, published the following as an editorial article:

"Year after year the Chief of Police publishes his statistics of prostitution in this city, but how few of the citizens bestow more than a passing thought upon the misery that they represent! Although these figures are large enough to make every lover of humanity hang his head with feelings of sorrow and shame at the picture, we are assured that they represent but a little, as it were, of the actual licentiousness that prevails among all classes of society. Within a few months, a gentleman[6] whose scientific attainments have made his name a household word in all lands, has personally investigated the subject, and the result has filled him with dismay; when he sees the depths of degradation to which men and women have fallen, he has almost lost faith in the boasted civilization of the nineteenth century. In the course of his inquiries he has visited both the well-known 'houses of pleasure' and the 'private establishments' scattered all over the city. He states that he has a list of both, with the street and number, the number of inmates, and many other facts that would perfectly astonish the people if made public. He freely conversed with the inmates, and the life-histories that were revealed were sad indeed. To his utter surprise, a large proportion of the 'soiled doves' *traced their fall to influences that met them in the Public Schools*; and although Boston is justly proud of its schools, it would seem, from his story, that they need a thorough purification. In too many of them the most obscene and soul-polluting books and pictures circulate among both sexes. The very secrecy with which it is done throws an almost irresistible charm about it; and to such an extent has the evil gone, that we fear a large proportion of both boys and girls possess some of the articles, which they kindly (?) lend to each other. The natural result follows, and frequently the most debasing and revolting practises are indulged in. And the evil is not confined alone to Boston. Other cities suffer in the same way. It is but a few years since the second city in the Commonwealth was stirred almost to its foundations by the discovery of an association of boys and girls who were wont to indulge their passions in one of the school-houses of the city; and not long ago another somewhat similar affair was discovered by the authorities, but hushed up for fear of depopulating the schools."

"That the devil is in the *Public Schools*, raging and rampant there among the *pupils* as well as among the *teachers*, no one can well doubt who has sent a little child into them, as guiltless of evil or unclean thoughts as a newly fallen snowflake, and had him come home, in a short time, contaminated almost beyond belief by the vileness and filth which he has seen, and heard, and learned *there*." —(Hathe Tyng Griswold, in *Old and New*, for March; or *Boston Pilot*, April 6, 1872.)

A celebrated physician of this country says in his book, "Satan in Society," as follows:

"The evils and dangers of the present system of educating and bringing up

[6] Prof. Aggassiz.

the boys and girls of our country, are too obvious to require minute description. Irreligion and infidelity are progressing *pari passu* with the advance guards of immorality and crime, and all are *fostered,* if *not engendered,* by the *materialistic system of school instruction,* and the consequent wretched training at home and on the play-ground. The entire absence of all religious instruction from the school-room is fast bearing fruit in a generation of infidels, and we are becoming worse even than the Pagans of old, who had at least their positive sciences of philosophy, and their religion, such as it was, to oppose which was a criminal offence. To those who would dispute this somewhat horrible assertion, the author would point to the published statistics of church attendance, from which it appears that of the entire population but a very small proportion are habitual church-goers. Deducting from these, again, those who attend church simply as a matter of fashion, or from other than religious motives, and there remains a minimum almost too small to be considered, abundantly sustaining our charge. The disintegration of the prevalent forms of religious belief, the rapid multiplication of sects, the increase in the ranks of intellectual sceptics, the fashionable detractions from, and perversions of, the Holy Scriptures, acting with the influences already mentioned, may well cause alarm.

"But we have not only the removal of the salutary restraints of religious influence from our popular system of education; we have the promiscuous intermingling of the sexes in our Public Schools, which, however much we may theorize to the contrary, is, to say the least, subversive of that modest reserve and shyness which in all ages have proved the true ægis of virtue. We are bound to accept human nature as it is, and not as we would wish it to be, and both Christian and Pagan philosophy agree in detecting therein certain very dangerous elements. Among the most dangerous and inevitable is the sexual instinct, which, implanted by the Creator for the wisest purposes, is, perhaps, the most potent of all evils when not properly restrained, retarded, and directed. This mysterious instinct develops earlier in proportion as the eye and the imagination are soonest furnished the materials upon which it thrives; and, long before the age of puberty, it is strong, and well-nigh ungovernable, in those who have been allowed these unfortunate occasions. The boy of the present generation has more practical knowledge of this instinct at the age of fifteen, than, under proper training, he should be entitled to at the time of his marriage; and the boy of eleven or twelve boastfully announces to his companions the evidences of his approaching virility. Nourished by languishing glances during the hours passed in the school-room, fanned by more intimate association on the journey to and from school, fed by stolen interviews and openly-arranged festivities—picnics, excursions, parties and the like—stimulated by the prurient gossip of the newspaper, the flash novels, sentimental weeklies, and magazines, the gallant of twelve years is the libertine of fourteen. That this picture is not overdrawn, every experienced physician will bear witness.

"And as for the Public School-girls, they return from their *'polishing schools'*—these demoiselles—cursed with a superficial smattering of everything but what they ought to have learned—physical and moral wrecks, whom we physicians are expected to *wind up* in the morning for the husband-hunting excitements of the evening. And these creatures are intended for wives! But *wives* only, for it is fast going out of fashion to intend them for *mothers*—an 'accident' of the kind being regarded as'*foolish*'!

"We assert, then, that the present system of education, by its faults of omission and commission, is directly responsible, not, it is true, for the bare existence, but for the enormous prevalence of vices and crimes which we deplore; and we call upon the civil authorities to so modify the obnoxious arrangements of our schools, and upon parents and guardians to so instruct and govern their charges, that the evils may be suppressed, if not extinguished."

The attempt to prepare man for his duties in social life with morals and religion left out, is not only a failure, but a crime. Yes, it is not only a failure, but a crime of such magnitude, that society has already begun to suffer its consequences in a demoralization and *general libertinage* of the most shameful kind. This education without religion and morals is the poisoned fountain from which flows, and will flow, if not purified by adding the essential elements now omitted, the impure streams of all kinds of vice. If God is despised, governments will be trampled on; if God's law is hated, the laws of men will be violated; man will see only his own interest, his neighbor's property will only whet his appetite; his neighbor's life will be only a secondary consideration; he would, according to his creed, be a fool not to shed blood when his interest requires it; his fellow-men become imbued with his principles—anarchy succeeds subordination—vice takes the place of virtue—what was sacred is profaned—what was honorable becomes disgraceful—might becomes right—treatises are waste paper—honor is an empty name—the most sacred obligations dwindle down into mere optional practices—youth despises age—wisdom is folly—subjection to authority is laughed at as a foolish dream—the moral code itself soon becomes little more than the bugbear of the weak-minded—crowns are trampled under foot—thrones are overturned—nations steeped in blood, and republics swept from the face of the earth.

Yes, continue a little longer to educate the greater part of the community according to the present system of the Public Schools, and rest assured we shall soon have a hell upon earth—society will be stabbed to the heart by the ruffian assassin called *godless Public School education*—it will reel, stagger, and sink a bleeding victim to the ground, expiring, like the suicide, by the wound itself has inflicted. I truly believe that if Satan was presented with a blank sheet of paper, and bade to write on it the most fatal gift to man, he would simply write one word—"godless schools." He might then turn his attention from this planet; "godless Public Schools" would do the rest.

Now what is to be done to stop the poisoned source from which the diabolical spirit and the crimes of our country flow? A certain class come forward and say, "Let the Bible be read in our Public Schools. The Bible is the grand source of religion and morality. The Bible alone, without note or comment, is the grand source of life and civilization."

Very well, let the Bible be admitted, but with the Bible you must send the key—the interpreter. And then, which of all the Bibles, and whom among the numerous sects, shall be sent?

To read the Bible, without note or comment, to young children, is to abandon them to dangerous speculation, or to leave them dry and barren of all Christian knowledge. In mixed schools there is no other resource, because it is impossible to make any comment upon any doctrinal teaching of Christ and His Apostles, without trenching upon the conscientious opinions of some one or other of the listeners. "The Father and I are One." "The Father is greater than I." Here at once we have the Unitarian and the Trinitarian at a dead-lock! "This is My Body." "It is the spirit which quickeneth, the flesh profiteth nothing." Here we have the primitive Lutheran, who believed in the real presence (consubstantially), and his Calvinistic coadjutor in reform, squarely at issue! "Unless you be born again of water and the Holy Ghost," etc. Here we have the Baptist and the Quaker very seriously divided in opinion. Nevertheless, widely as they differ the one from the other, there is a fundamental assimilation between all the Protestant sects which may render it possible for them to unite in one educational organization; and yet we find many of the most enlightened and earnest among the Protestant clergy of America now zealously advocating the denominational system, such as we find it in the European countries. They believe that education should be distinctly based upon doctrinal religion, and they are liberal enough to insist that, by natural right as well as by the constitutional guarantees of our free country, no doctrine adverse to the faith of a parent may lawfully be forced or surreptitiously imposed upon his child. It is well known, however, that between the Catholic faith and all Protestant creeds, there is a gulf which cannot be bridged over. It would, therefore, be simply impossible to adopt any religious teaching whatever in mixed schools, without at once interfering with Catholic conscience. No such teaching is attempted, as a general rule, we believe, in the Public Schools of the United States, and hence we have only a vague announcement of moral precepts, the utter futility and barrenness of which must be evident to every one. Catholics, agreeing with very many enlightened and zealous Protestants, believe that secular education, administered without religion, is not only vain, but exceedingly pernicious; that it is fast undermining the Christian faith of this nation; that it is rapidly filling the land with rationalism; that it is destroying the authority of the Holy Scriptures; that it is educating men who prefix "Reverend" and affix "D.D." to their names, the more effectually to preach covert infidelity and immorality to Christian congregations; that, instead of the saving morality of the Gospel of Christ, which rests upon revealed mysteries and supernatural gifts, it is offering us that same old array of the natural virtues or qualities which helped, for a while, like rotten pillars, to prop up the heathen nations of old. It must, then, be evident to every man of common sense that the reading of the Bible alone, though it be the Word of God, will *not* counterbalance the results of Pagan education. Indeed the reading of the Bible alone is by no means an adequate remedy to stem the torrent of the evils in our country. What impurities have not been committed under the sanction of those words of the Lord, "Increase and multiply"! A host of sectarians, following in the wake of the Anabaptists of Munster, in Germany, have, on the authority of those words, dared to legitimate polygamy. On such misapplication of a text from the Gospel, Luther, Bucerus, and Melanchthon have permitted Philip, the Landgrave of Hesse, to have two wives.

In the name of the Bible, of the Word of God, Luther at first incited the German peasantry to revolt against their rulers, and then, frightened at his own work, he persuaded the princes to massacre the peasants. John of Leyden found, in his studies of the Bible, that he should marry eleven women at once. Herman felt himself clearly designated, in the Bible, as the Envoy of the Lord. Nicholas learned from it that there was no necessity of anything connected with faith, and that we must live in sin in order that grace may abound. Sympson pretends to find in the Scriptures an ordination that men should walk in the streets stark naked, to teach the rich a lesson that they must divest themselves of everything. Richard Hill justified, with the Bible in hand, adultery and manslaughter as deeds never failing to work out some good purpose, especially when joined to incest, in which case more saints are added to the earth and more blessed to the heavens. Even on the avowal of honest Protestants, no crime or abomination has ever failed to find its pretended justification in some scriptural text.

What, then, must we think of the reading of the Bible, when its reading, without note or comment, leads to such consequences? Indeed what has been said on the evil consequences of the Public School system on society proves sufficiently that the reading of the Bible is no adequate means at all to stem the torrent of crimes in our country. Nowhere has the Bible been read more frequently, during school-hours, than in the Public Schools of the New England States, and yet nowhere have the results of these schools proved more fatal than in these very States. The reading of the Bible alone, therefore, though it be the Word of God, will *not* counterbalance the results of Pagan education.

There are others who maintain "that religious instruction should be left to parents."

Now it is not only idle, but cruel, to say that the place and provision for such Christian instruction and formation is under the roof of the parents' home; that the best school is the family. This is indeed true of the early formation by affection, influence, example, by which fathers and mothers fashion the first outlines of character, and mature them while the education of their children is advancing. None have reminded parents of this more faithfully than the Pastors of the Church. But to say that fathers and mothers are to educate their children, and that their home is to be the school of Christian instruction, catechetical teaching, formation of conscience, preparation for sacraments, and the like, is either the shallow talk of men who know nothing of Christian education, or care nothing for it, or a heartless mockery of our poor. The rich, the refined, the educated, whose time is their own, do not educate their own children. They systematically send them to schools and colleges, or pay for tutors or governesses under their own roof. They wisely shrink from a work for which, if they have the time, they seldom have the acquirements or the gift, or the method of the perseverance or the patience. And if this be, as it is, universally true of those who are the most competent, and the most provided with all the means and opportunities for the work, now is it not hardness of heart, or want of common sense, to say that the children of the poor are to learn reading, and writing, and summing, indeed, at school, but that their Christian teaching and formation must be provided at home? The workingmen of these countries are at labor from twilight to twilight. Their wives have the burden of the whole family; the poor mother is alone both the head and the servant of the whole house. When is she to teach, and train, and shape, and fashion the characters, hearts, consciences, intellects of the children? Is it to be done in the midst of a day's work, or in the weariness after the day's work is done? And are they competent to do what the mother of the rich cannot do? Broken with cares, wearied by work, suffering from poverty, often fainting from sickness because worn out with all these burdens, how shall the father or mother of a family, huddled into a single room, do what the rich and the educated, in their spacious houses, and with abundant leisure, never dream of attempting?

Moreover, as I have shown in a preceding chapter, it must be admitted that a mother not educated in religious and moral principles cannot inform the mind and heart of the young child; this fully disposes of the argument that domestic teaching alone will supply what is acknowledged to be wanting in the "Public Schools." It is to be hoped that we shall hear no more of this heartless talk.

"Well, then," some will say, "let our children receive, *in Sunday-schools,* that amount of religious culture and instruction which the State says shall not be given in the school, and which is believed to be so essential in the education of the young."

Now it is in vain to open our Sunday-schools and expect to cure, on one day of the week, or rather a few hours of that day (when this even depends, in a great part, on the weather), the work not only of the other six, but the fruits of years of an ill-directed and godless State education. The Sunday-schools are nothing but so many *"Poor-man's soothing plasters"* on Christian consciences. The want of religious training for six days in the week, added to the positive knowledge of error on all religious subjects which youths may acquire during that time, will more than counterbalance the best-directed efforts of parents and the clergy to give any definite knowledge on the truths of revelation. The question whether or not religious education is compatible with Public School education, has been tried in all English-speaking countries, and in parts of Germany, with this result: that, a class, the Public School children are without any adequate religious knowledge or training. The clergy may have Sunday-schools, as they have, in all their churches; but what can children learn, in a few hours, of a subject which took three years from the Saviour of man to teach even to the apostles? And then the apostles, after three years of instruction from the lips of Christ, did not understand the Christian religion; they were slow to understand, and, after His resurrection, Christ upbraided them with incredulity and hardness of heart. Even the children of the Public Schools, as far as experience goes, lose all taste for the study of religion, which is developed among the children of Christian schools without any effort. Sunday-schools, at best, may train children to be Christians *one day* in the week, and Pagans six days. School-days over, the usual result will be *Pagans* all the seven days of the week.

If it is in vain to say, "Let the Bible be read in our Public Schools," or "let our children receive religious instruction from their parents, or in Sunday-schools, in order to arrest the fast-spreading crimes of the land," it is still more in vain to say, "Let the Legislature be called upon."

It cannot be denied that the higher culture of America has, from the time of the introduction of the present Public School system, ceased to be Christian. What is the natural harvest of this sowing? It is that we have already a generation of men, thousands of whom are not fit to be the heads and fathers of families. But this is not all; we have also ever so many guides of public opinion, ever so many ministers of public affairs, and ever so many lawgivers of the United States, who are infidels and profligates; who see *only themselves* in all they do, who desire only to fret out their little hour on the political stage *with a sharp eye to their own interests,* without the smallest desire to secure the Republic against future disasters—who cannot, or *will* not, see the disastrous storms the ship of the Republic will soon have to encounter. What good, then, could be expected from calling upon the Legislature? It would only show its impotency, or, what is more, its own corruption. The executive is unable, suspected, or often found in the *"ring,"* or, to use a common expression, "Justice stinks." The judiciary, by its very nature, always timid, and too often time-serving, can do nothing. Well, then, the press: what shall be said of it? Only this: that it would be unreasonable to expect it to possess the supernatural powers of healing such a multitude of foul lepers, or to be able at any time to lift itself far above the level of the general average of the age and country.

What, then, must be done to save society from the perils that menace it—to stem the tide that bids fair to sweep away, eventually, even civilization itself? We must proceed on a true principle. When we proceed on a true principle, the more logically and completely we carry it out the better; but when we start with a false principle, the more logical we are, and the farther we push it, the worse. Our consistency increases, instead of diminishing, the evils we would cure. The reformers started wrong. They would reform the Church by placing her under human control. Their successors have in each generation found they did not go far enough, and have, each in its turn, struggled to push it farther and farther, till they find themselves without any church life, without faith, without religion, and beginning to doubt if there be even a God. So, in the question of education, the upholders of the Public School system have pushed the false principle "that all individual, domestic, social, and political evils are due to ignorance, and can only be prevented by high intellectual culture," till they have nearly taught away all religious belief and morality, have well-nigh abolished the family which is the social unit, and find that the evils they pretended to prevent, and the wrongs they sought to redress, are fast increasing.

We must, then, proceed on a true principle in trying to remedy the profligacy that disgraces so many of our crowded centres, and the demoralization that is fast gangrening even our rural districts.

One thousand eight hundred and forty-odd years ago, you might have observed a poor, meanly-clad wanderer, wending his steps on the Appian way to the Capitol of the world,—the wealthy, magnificent, and ungodly city of Rome. He has passed its gates, and threads his way unobserved through its populous streets. On every side he beholds gorgeous palaces raised at the expense of downtrodden nationalities; stately temples dedicated to as many false gods as nations were congregated in Rome; public baths and amphitheatres devoted to pleasure and to cruelty; statues, monuments, and triumphal arches raised to the memory of blood-thirsty tyrants. He passes warriors and senators, beggars and cripples, effeminate and dissolute women, gladiators and slaves, merchants and statesmen, orators and philosophers;—all classes, all ranks, all conditions of men of every language and color under the sun. Everywhere he sees a maddening race for pleasure; everywhere the impress of luxury, everywhere the full growth of crime, side by side with indescribable suffering, diabolical cruelty and barbarity. And this poor, meanly-clad wanderer was St. Peter. Oh! how the noble heart of the fisherman of Galilee must have bled, when he observed the empire of Satan so supreme—when he witnessed the shocking licentiousness of the temple and the homestead; when he saw the fearful degradation of woman groaning under the load of her own infamy; when he saw the heart-rending inhumanity which slew the innocent babes and threw them into the Tiber; when he saw how prisoners of war, slaves, and soldiers were trained for bloody fights, and entered the arena of the amphitheatre, and strove whole days to strangle one another, for the special entertainment of the Roman people. When Peter came to Rome, that city was the condensation of all the idolatry, all the oppression, all the injustice, all the immoralities of the world; for the world was centred in Rome.

Here, then, were evils to be remedied similar to those of our day and country. Pagan philosophers, poets and orators, had tried their best to cure these evils and to elevate mankind, but they had tried in vain. What they were unable to bring about, St. Peter accomplished by preaching to the Roman people Christianity—the religion of Jesus Christ—which imparts to the mind infallibly the light of truth, and lays down for the will authoritatively the unchangeable principles of supernatural morality, true prosperity, true happiness, and peace on earth and for eternity. Indeed, it is a well-known fact that the Capitoline temple, and with it the many shrines of idolatry, the golden house of Nero, and with it Roman excess and Roman cruelty, the throne of the Cæsars, and with it Roman oppression and Roman injustice, gave way and disappeared in proportion as the light of Christianity was infused into that foul mass, into that rotten society, centred in Rome. It was this Christian religion that changed a sinful people into saints, and so many holy inhabitants of heaven. And what the blessings of the religion of Christ brought about in Rome, they bring about wherever they are diffused. Hence all true lovers of the country tell us that there is but one remedy for the cure of the diabolical spirit and the crimes of our country—it is to teach our children the truth and blessings of the Christian religion. It is the Christian religion that infallibly and authoritatively teaches the duties of civil authorities towards their subjects, of husbands towards their wives, of parents towards their children, of masters towards their servants, of pastors towards their flocks, of the faithful towards their pastors, of servants towards their masters, of wives towards their husbands, of children towards their parents, of subjects towards their lawfully constituted civil authorities, of all men towards God, their Supreme Master, and just Rewarder of good and evil. Moreover, it is the Christian religion alone that affords men the means to obtain God's grace, which enlightens the mind to see the beauty of virtue, inflames the heart with love for it, and inclines the will to practise it with perseverance. If we then wish to be sure of having a virtuous and virile people, we must Christianize our youth, especially during their school hours; we must bring up our children in a religious atmosphere. I have already remarked that religion may be compared to leaven. As leaven must be diffused throughout the entire mass in order to produce its effects, so the Christian religion must be thoroughly diffused throughout the child's entire education, in order to be solid and effective.

Not a moment of the hours of school should be left without religious influence. It is the constant breathing of the air that preserves our bodily life, and it is the constant dwelling in a religious atmosphere that preserves the life of the youthful soul. Religion is not a study, or an exercise that may be restricted to a certain place, or a certain hour. It is a faith and a law which ought to be felt everywhere, and which in this manner alone can exercise all its beneficent influence upon our minds and lives. It will never do to suffer the child to devote six days in the week to worldly science, and to depend on Sunday for a religious training. This would be like reserving the salt which should season our food during the week, and taking it all in a dose on Sunday. By such a system we may make expert shop-boys, first-rate accountants, shrewd and thriving "earth-worms"; but it would be presumption to think of thus making good citizens, still less virtuous Christians.

Let us be assured that our young men know their duties to God, to their neighbors, and to themselves, and they will then, but not till then, be true Christians. In being true Christians they will be dutiful sons, faithful husbands, affectionate fathers, gentle masters, honest servants, law-loving and law-abiding citizens, true statesmen, good soldiers, and valiant defenders of the country, chaste and sober companions, the joy of God and of society.

But, above all, let us be assured that our daughters are educated as women, not as men. Women are not needed as men; they are needed as women: to do, not what men can do as well as they, but what men cannot do. Woman was created to be a wife and a mother; that is her destiny. To that destiny all her instincts point, and for it nature has specially qualified her. Her proper sphere is home, and her proper function is the care of the household, to manage a family, to take care of children, and attend to their early training. For this she is endowed with patience, endurance, passive courage, quick sensibilities, a sympathetic nature, and great executive and administrative ability. She was born to be a queen in her own household, and make home cheerful, bright, and happy. There it is that she is really great, noble, almost divine.

Now the general complaint is that the greater part of our Public School-girls are not fit to be good wives, mothers and housekeepers. As wives, they forget what they owe to their husbands, are capricious and vain, often light and frivolous, extravagant and foolish, bent on having their own way, though ruinous to the family, and generally contriving, by coaxings, blandishments, or poutings, to get it. They hold obedience in horror, and seek only to govern their husbands and all around them.

As mothers, they not only neglect, but disdain, the retired and simple domestic virtues, and scorn to be tied down to the modest but essential duties—the drudgery, they call it—of mothers; they manage to be relieved of household cares, especially of child-bearing, and of the duty of bringing up children. They repress their maternal instincts, and the horrible crime of infanticide before birth now becomes so fearfully prevalent, that the American nation is actually threatened with extinction. If they condescend to have one or two children, they set them an ill example; for if children see that their mother, as a wife, forgets to honor and obey her husband, and always wants to have her own way with him, they soon lose all respect for her, and insist on having their own way with her, and usually succeed.

As housekeepers they devote their time to pleasure or amusement, wasting their life in luxurious ease, in reading sentimental or sensational novels, or in following the caprices of fashion; thus they let the household go to ruin, and the honest earnings of the husband becomes speedily insufficient for the family expenses, and he is sorely tempted to provide for them by rash speculation or by fraud, which, though it may be carried on for a while without detection, is sure to end in disgrace and ruin at last.

There is indeed nothing which more grieves the wise and good, or makes them tremble for the future of the country, than the way in which our daughters are educated in the Public Schools. When they become wives and mothers, they have none of the habits or character necessary to govern their household and to train their children properly. Hence arise that growing neglect or laxity of family discipline; that insubordination, that lawlessness, and precocious depravity of Young America; that almost total lack of filial reverence and obedience with the children of this generation. Exceptions there happily are; but the number of children that grow up without any proper training or discipline at home is fearfully large, and their evil example corrupts not a few of those who are well brought up. The country is no better than the town. As a rule, children are no longer subjected to a steady and firm, but mild and judicious, discipline, or trained to habits of filial love, respect and obedience. These habits are acquired only in a school of obedience, made pleasant and cheerful by a mother's playful smile and a mother's love. The care and management of children during their early years belong specially to the mother. The education of children may be said to commence from the moment they open their eyes and ears to the sights and sounds of the world about them; and of these sights and sounds the words and example of the mother are the most impressive and the most enduring. Of all lessons, those learned at the knees of a good mother sink the deepest into the mind and heart, and last the longest. Many of the noblest and best men that ever lived, and adorned and benefited the world, have declared that, under God, they owed everything that was good and useful in their lives to the love of virtue, and truthfulness, and piety, and the fear of God instilled into their hearts by the lips of a pious mother. It is her special function to plant and develop in their young and impressible minds the seeds of virtue, love, reverence, and obedience, and to train her daughters, by precept and example, not to catch husbands that will give them splendid establishments, but to be, in due time, modest and affectionate wives, tender and judicious mothers, and prudent and careful housekeepers. This the father cannot do; and his interference, except by wise counsel, and to honor and sustain the mother, will generally be worse than nothing. The task devolves specially on the mother; for it demands the sympathy with children which is peculiar to the female heart, the strong maternal instinct implanted by nature, and directed by a judicious education, that blending of love and authority, sentiment and reason, sweetness and power, so characteristic of the noble and true-hearted woman, and which so admirably fit her to be loved and honored, only less than adored, in her own household. But though the duties and responsibilities of mothers in this matter are the heaviest and most important for themselves, and for the society of all others, yet there are none which are more neglected.

Now wives and mothers, by neglecting their domestic duties and the proper family discipline, fail to offer the necessary resistance to growing lawlessness and crime, aggravated, if not generated, by the false notions of freedom and equality so widely entertained. It is only by home discipline, and the early habits of reverence and obedience to which our children are trained, that the license the government tolerates, and the courts hardly dare attempt to restrain, can be counteracted, and the community made a law-loving and a law-abiding community.

Why is it that the very bases of society have been sapped, and the conditions of good government despised, or denounced under the name of despotism? Why is it that social and political life is poisoned in its source, and the blood of the nation corrupted? It is because wives and mothers have failed in their domestic duties, and the discipline of their families. And they have failed in this, because the State did not, and could not, bring them up to it.

The evils we have to cure cannot be reached by the reading of the Bible, by Sunday-school training, nor by any possible political or legislative action. Men or women cannot be legislated into virtue. That the remedy, to a great extent, must be supplied by woman's action and influence, we not only concede, but claim. But it is only as woman, as wife, as mother, that she must do the work: as woman, to soften asperities, and to refine what else were coarse and brutal; as wife, to sustain with her affection the resolutions and just aspirations of her husband, and render home bright and cheerful—"the sweetest place on earth"; as mother, to direct and inspire the noble and righteous aspirations of her sons—to train and form her children to early habits of piety, filial love and reverence, of obedience to God's law, and respect for authority.

There are, in our day, comparatively few mothers who are qualified to do this. But what they can and should do is to see that they have a better and more thorough system of education for their sons, but especially for their daughters—a system of education that specially adapts them to the destiny of their sex, and prepares them to find their happiness in their homes, and the satisfaction of their highest ambition in discharging its manifold duties, so much higher, nobler, and more essential to the virtue and well-being of the community, the nation, the society, and to the life and progress of the human race, than any which devolve on king or emperor, magistrate or legislator. We would not have their generous instincts repressed, their quick sensibilities blunted, or their warm, sympathetic nature chilled, nor even the lighter graces and accomplishments neglected; but we would have them all directed and harmonized by solid intellectual instruction, and moral and religious culture. We would have them, whether rich or poor, trained to find the centre of their affections in their home; their chief ambition in making it cheerful, bright, radiant and happy. Whether destined to grace a magnificent palace, or to adorn the humble cottage of poverty, this should be the ideal aimed at in their education. They should be trained to love home, and to find their pleasure in sharing its cares and performing its duties, however arduous or painful.

There are, as I have said, comparatively few mothers qualified to give their daughters such an education, especially in our own country; for comparatively few have received such an education themselves, or are able fully to appreciate its importance. They can find little help in the fashionable boarding-schools for finishing young ladies; and, in general, these schools only aggravate the evils to be cured. The best and the only respectable schools for daughters that we have in the country are the conventual schools taught by women consecrated to God, and specially devoted to the work of education. These schools, indeed, are not always all that might be wished. The religious cannot, certainly, supply the place of the mother in giving their pupils that practical home-training so necessary, and which can be given only by mothers who have themselves been properly educated; but they go as far as is possible in remedying the defects of the present generation of mothers, and in counteracting their follies and vain ambitions. With all the faults that can be alleged against any of them, the conventual schools, even as they are, it must be conceded, are infinitely the best schools for daughters in the land, and, upon the whole, worthy of the high praise and liberal patronage their devotedness and disinterestedness secure them. We have seldom found their graduates weak and sickly sentimentalists. They develop in their pupils a cheerful and healthy tone, and a high sense of duty; give them solid moral, religious instruction; cultivate successfully their moral and religious affections; refine their manners, purify their tastes, and send them out feeling that life is serious, life is earnest, and resolved always to act under a deep sense of their personal responsibilities; meet whatever may be their lot with brave hearts, and without murmuring and repining.

The editor of the *New York Herald* prefaces an account of a Catholic academy with the following remarks:

"However divided public opinion may be as to secular and religious schools—no matter what differences in opinion may exist in the community as to the policy of aiding or discouraging purely sectarian systems of education—there can be but little opposition from any quarter to the verdict of experience given by many thousand families, that these devoted women—the Sisters of the Catholic Church—are the best teachers of young girls, the safest instructors in this age of loose, worldly, and rampant New Englandism. Those matters of education which make the lady, in their hands, subordinate to the great object of making every girl committed to their care a true woman, are imbued with those principles which have made our mothers our pride and boast. Those of us who cavil at Catholic pretensions, sneer at their assumption, and ridicule their observances, must acknowledge that the Sisters are far ahead and above any organization of the sort of which Protestantism can boast. The self-sacrifice, the devotion, the single-mindedness, the calm trust in a Power unseen, the humility of manner and rare unselfishness which characterize the Sisters, has no parallel in any organization of the reformed faith. The war placed the claims of the Sisters of Charity fairly before the country; but these Sisters of the different branches have, in peace, 'victories no less renowned than in war.' Educating the poor children, directing the untutored mind of the youthful alien savage in our midst, or holding the beacon of intellectual advancement bright and burning before the female youth of the country, and beckoning them to advance, they are ever doing a good and noble work."

We do not disguise the fact that our hopes for the future, in great measure, rest on these conventual schools; if they are multiplied, and the number of their graduates increase, and enter upon the serious duties of life, the ideal of female education will become higher and broader; a nobler class of wives and mothers will exert a healthy and purifying influence; religion will become a real power in the Republic; the moral tone of the community, and the standard of private and public morality, will be elevated; and thus may gradually be acquired the virtues that will enable us, as a people, to escape the dangers that now threaten us, and to save the Republic as well as our own souls.

Sectarians, indeed, declaim against these schools, and denounce them as a subtle device of Satan to make their daughters "Romanists"; but Satan probably dislikes "Romanism" even more than sectarians do, and is much more in earnest to suppress or ruin our conventual schools, in which he is not held in much honor, than he is to sustain and encourage them. At any rate, our countrymen who have such a horror of the religion it is our glory to profess, that they cannot call it by its true name, would do well, before denouncing these schools, to establish better schools for daughters of their own. These modest, retiring Sisters and Nuns, who have no new theories and schemes of social reform, and upon whom a certain class of women look down with haughty contempt, as weak, spiritless, and narrow-minded, have chosen the better part, and are doing infinitely more to raise woman to her true dignity, and for the political and social, as well as for the moral and religious, progress of the country, than the Woman's Rights party, with all their grand conventions, brilliant speeches, stirring lectures and spirited journals. By way of parenthesis, we dare tell these women who are wasting so much time, energy, philanthropy, and brilliant eloquence in agitating for female suffrage and eligibility, which, if conceded, would only make matters worse, that, if they have the real interest of their sex or of the community at heart, they should turn their attention to the education of daughters for their special functions, not as men, but as women, who are one day to be wives and mothers—woman's true destiny.

Undoubtedly the special destiny of women is to be wives and mothers; but we are told that there are thousands of women who are not and cannot be wives and mothers. In the older and more densely settled States of the Union, there is an excess of females over males, and all cannot get husbands if they would. Yet, we repeat, woman was created to be a wife and a mother, and the woman that is not fails of her special destiny. Under the Christian dispensation honorable provision has been made for that large class of women who, either from preference, or from any other cause, do not marry. Virginity, which was regarded as a reproach, became an honor under the Christian law. Those women who do not wish, or cannot be wives and mothers in the natural order, may be both, in the spiritual order, if they will, and are properly educated for it. They can be wedded to the Holy Spirit, and be the mothers of minds and hearts. The holy virgins and devout widows who consecrated themselves to God, in or out of religious orders, are both, and fulfil in the spiritual order their proper destiny. We hold them in high honor, because they become mothers to the motherless, to the poor, to the forsaken, to the homeless. They instruct the ignorant, nurse the sick, help the helpless, tend the aged, catch the last breath of the dying, pray for the unbelieving and the cold-hearted, and elevate the moral tone of society, and shed a cheering radiance along the pathway of life. They have no need to be idle or useless. In a world of so much sin and sorrow, sickness and suffering, there is always work enough for them to do; it is on the poor and motherless, the destitute and the downtrodden, the sinful and the sorrowful, the aged and infirm, the ignorant and the neglected, that, under proper direction, they can lavish the wealth of their affections, the tenderness of their hearts, and the ardor of their charity, and find true joy and happiness in so doing, ample scope for woman's noblest ambition, and chances enough to acquire merit in the sight of heaven, and true glory, that will shine brighter and brighter forever. They thus are dear to God, dear to the Church, and dear to Christian society. They are to be envied, not pitied. It is only because you have lost faith in Christ, faith in the holy Catholic Church, and have become gross in your minds, of "earth earthy," that you deplore the lot of the women who cannot, in the natural order, find husbands, and call them, contemptuously, "old maids"—a miserable relic of heathenism or Protestantism, neither of which have anything to hold out to old maids. But Jesus Christ has provided for them better than you are able to understand.

The Father of our country, then, was right when he said, in his farewell address to the American nation, that religion and morality are the "props" of society, and the "pillars" of the State. Let us, then, rest assured that the best way to check the torrent of infidelity and immorality, to avert impending evils, to prepare the golden age of our Republic, is to infuse good morals by the most powerful of all means—*Christian Education.*

CHAPTER XII.

THE DENOMINATIONAL SYSTEM ALONE SATISFIES THE WANTS OF ALL, AND CAN SAVE THE REPUBLIC.

We live in a time of great activity and change, and intense worldliness. "Men run to and fro and knowledge is increased." Would that we could feel that there is an increase also in integrity and virtue, and respect for Religion. We all know that it is not so. So far as we can form accurate ideas of the social and religious condition of men at any particular period in the world's history, we may doubt whether the words of the Apostle St. Paul, describing what shall come to pass in what he calls "the last days," ever touched any people so closely as they do those of our times and country. "Men," he says, "shall be lovers of themselves, covetous, haughty, proud, blasphemous, disobedient to parents, ungrateful, wicked, without affection, without peace, slanderers, incontinent, unmerciful, without kindness, traitors, stubborn, puffed up, and lovers of pleasure, more than lovers of God." Well may the Apostle speak of such times as "dangerous times." When the moral atmosphere we breathe is so full of what the Scriptures call "the spirit of this world," we can only hope to escape its corrupting influences by doing all in our power to diffuse Christian principles among the rising generation, by means of truly Christian schools.

The arrangements can be made without disturbing the general system. It is this: "Let the State aid, but not direct, a system of plain English education, confined to all those whose circumstances are limited, or who are left destitute, or orphans. Let all religious denominations, when they desire it, have the privilege of conducting their own schools, subject only to general uniform inspection and examination on the part of the State, and have their proportion of the school-moneys." The wealthy classes will know how to take care of the education of their own children, as they do of their family affairs in other matters.

The advocates of this "Denominational System" yield to none in their endeavors to secure to *all* the children within the State a good, solid, and practical education, according to the religious convictions and circumstances of all. This, they claim, is not, and cannot be furnished on the present plan. They do not, as falsely charged, desire to distract or divide, or introduce sectarianism into the Public Schools; on the contrary, they *wish* to satisfy conscience by yielding *to all others what they claim for themselves*, and cannot help denouncing the present system as practically resulting in a form of sectarianism worse than any yet professed: to wit,

"Indifferentism."

If the "Denominational System" was adopted, it would satisfy and do justice to all, and, at the same time, excite such rivalry and competition among teachers as to advance education, whilst it diminishes its cost in the same ratio. We have seen that it costs about four times as much to give the miserable infidel instruction in the Public Schools, as it does to give a good Christian education in the denominational schools. What possible objection, then, can there be to adopt the denominational, or separate system, when it costs four times less, and imparts, to say the least, as good an education to the greatest number of children? It is no argument to urge that schools would be sectarian. We have sectarian churches, and various shades and differences of belief, already. This would not alter one or the other a particle. The State cannot impose uniformity on churches; why force it on schools? Indeed it is worse, inasmuch as this scholastic conformity or uniformity is against all religions, and in favor of infidelity, or the no-religious sect, if there be such a one. It discriminates against the believers, and is in favor of the unbelievers.

But it is easy to see what the matter is. It is not religion these men fear so much as *competition*. One session's trial of the separate system would so clearly demonstrate to the public the economy and advantages of this plan, that the troop of paid teachers, officers, musicians, and others, who are fattening at the expense of a credulous people, would be exposed, and have to take their "carpet-bags" and tramp. However, I have no cause of quarrel with the employés, male or female, of the Public Schools. They do not elect themselves, nor make their salaries, and they are not to be blamed for taking them. If the clever gentleman who draws (in one State, at least) $2,750 for ten months, four hours' a day work, or the accomplished lady who gets $2,000 for the same time and labor, or the three musicians at $2,000 each, or the humble, but perhaps not less useful, corps of "school-sweepers" (janitors), who are rewarded with $16,886.50, or the officers (three), who pocket $14,457.90 salary, and $20,771.96 office-expenses!! are so handsomely rewarded, it is their good fortune, and not their fault. There is, doubtless, a great deal of human nature in their composition, as well as others.

There is no earthly way of giving satisfaction to all, except by granting the denominational system, thereby leaving to all sects and denominations, as well as to those who do not range themselves under any specific form at all, to apply a fair proportion of the school-money. All those who prefer the present plan would have no change to make, and all those who desire the separate plan would have the right to select their own class-books and teachers; in other words, would have the interior management of their own schools. This is the way church matters are managed to the satisfaction of all. Peoples' views and convictions on education are just as conscientious and distinct as on religion, and they have just as good a right to them. If any man denies this truth, I would like him to give his reasons.

There is one other thing to be taken into consideration here: if, as is claimed, all, from the highest to the lowest, have a right to an education at the hands of the State, and if, as is admitted, all should be instructed in their moral and religious duties, if not by the State, at least by their parents and pastors, who will instruct the poor little orphans, the very class for whose benefit the public provide an education—who, I say, will instruct them in the way they should go? who will answer for these little "waifs of society"? They ask for bread, and the State gives them a stone; it has, with the best intentions in the world, no better to give them. These considerations have compelled most of the European States, as well as our neighbors—the Canadians—to abandon the *godless system*, and establish separate schools, when asked to do so by the members of any denomination.[7]

There *is no exception to this rule, except here!* With all our boasted progress, we are behind all civilized nations in this important particular.

Now by adopting this fair method, the poor orphans and ragged children, who have the first and best claim of all, would be educated. As it is, it is a notorious fact, that as far as Public Schools are concerned, they are left out in the cold. This fact is capable of being demonstrated to any lady or gentleman who will visit the Catholic orphanages and poor schools of any city. If any one doubts this, and does me the honor of putting himself at my disposal, I will show him or her thousands of such poor ragged little ones in one evening. Now is it not drawing largely upon public credulity, as well as on the public purse, to ask for thousands for high schools, and normal schools, etc., to educate the children, in great part, of the rich, or, at best, comparatively well to do, and turn their backs on the poor fatherless orphans and the ragged children of the poor widow or laboring man? Will anybody who has his eyesight doubt or deny this? If so, he can be convinced, any day of the week, by looking at the class and style of boys and girls who go to the upper Public Schools, and observing the boys and girls (several hundreds in number) who go to the poor schools of the Sisters of Mercy, or, in fact, to any other charity convent school.

The Bible, or religious education in schools, will ever come up to vex and torment the public, especially the Catholic portion of the community, until the right of separate schools is granted. It is especially the Catholics that do and must insist upon having separate schools, for it is the Catholics that have always done all in their power to establish and maintain the republican form of government, and it is through the influence of Catholicity alone that our Republic can be maintained, and increased in power and glory.

A body which has lost the principle of its animation becomes dust. Hence it is an axiom that the change or perversion of the principles by which anything was produced, is the destruction of that very thing; if you can change or pervert the principles from which anything springs, you destroy it. For instance, one single foreign element introduced into the blood produces death; one false assumption admitted into science, destroys its certainty; one false principle admitted into mor-

[7] By "An Act to restore to Roman Catholics in Upper Canada certain rights in respect to Separate Schools," passed May 5, 1863, they provided that "the Roman Catholic separate schools shall be entitled to a share in the fund annually granted by the legislature of the province for the support of common schools, and shall be entitled also to a share in all other public grants, investments, and allotments for common school purposes now made or hereafter to be made by the municipal authorities, according to the average number of pupils attending such school, as compared with the whole average number of pupils attending schools in the same city, town, village or township."—Cap. 5, sec. 20.

als, is fatal. Now our American nation is departing from the principles which created their civilization, and upon which their grand Republic is based. Their civilization is becoming every day more and more material, and this material civilization, while more and more material, is becoming less moral; society is becoming less solid, less safe, less stable; individuals are becoming more anarchical, the intellect more licentious, the wills of men more stubborn, and this self-will expresses itself in their actions, so that it is true to say that, by means of godless education, the principles of Christianity upon which the American Republic was founded, and by which it has hitherto been preserved, have been rejected, and are being violated on every side. Our Republic, therefore is no more progressing, but is going back.

About fifteen years ago a number of leading politicians and statesmen of America, of highest name and note, met together to consider the condition of the United States. It was before the war, when there were already many causes of anxiety. It was said that there was a universal and growing license of the individual will, and that law and government were powerless to restrain it; that if the will of the multitude became licentious, it would seriously threaten the public welfare and liberty of the country. The conclusion they came to was, that, *unless there could be found some power which could restrain the individual will*, this danger would at last *seriously menace the United States*.

Now it is easy to say what that power is. It is the power which created the Christian society—it is the power which drew the world out of the darkness of heathenism, abolished slavery, restored woman to her true dignity—it is the power which established and maintained republican governments, and that power is the power of Catholicity. Whensoever this power is weakened or lost, immediately all political society decays. There will be a bright future for America if this power will be maintained and preserved.

The Catholic Church is the grandest Republic that was ever established. But it is a Republic of a supernatural order. It has for its Founder Jesus Christ, the Son of God Himself. He chose St. Peter for its first President. This grand Republic is divided, as it were, into as many States as there are dioceses; each diocese has a Bishop—a true successor of the Apostles—for Governor, and each Bishop has priests to assist him in the spiritual government of the diocese. The Constitution of this Republic was made by Jesus Christ. It cannot be changed or altered at all, either by the President, or by the votes of its citizens. St. Peter and the other Apostles, and their lawful successors, were bound in conscience, by Jesus Christ, to keep His Constitution—His doctrine—and teach others to keep it, under pain of forfeiture of eternal life. The President and the Governors of this Republic—the Pope and the Catholic Bishops—are not at liberty to govern its citizens, the Catholics, as they please; they have to govern them according to the Constitution—the Doctrine of Jesus Christ. Now Almighty God governs men in accordance with the nature with which He has created them, as beings endowed with reason and free-will. God adapts His government to our rational and voluntary faculties, and governs us without violence to either, and by really satisfying both. The rulers of the Catholic Church have to do the same; they must govern men as freemen. Hence the Catholic Church leaves to every people its own nationality, and to every State its own independence; she ameliorates the political and social order, only by infusing into the hearts of the people and their rulers the principles of justice and love, and a sense of accountability to God. The action of the Church in political and social matters is indirect, not direct, and in strict accordance with the free-will of individuals and the autonomy of states. Servile fear does not rank very high among Catholic theologians. The Church, when she can, resorts to coercive measures only to repress disorders in the public body. Hence her rulers are called shepherds, not lords, and shepherds of their Master's flock, not of their own, and are to feed, tend, protect the flock, and take care of its increase for Him, with sole reference to His will, and His honor and glory. The Catholic Church proffers to all every assistance necessary for the attainment of the most heroic sanctity, but she forces no man to accept that assistance. Catholics believe the doctrines of the Church, because they believe the Catholic Church the Church of God—they believe that Jesus Christ commissioned St. Peter and the Apostles, and their lawful successors, to teach all men in His name—to teach them infallibly and authoritatively His divine doctrine—they believe that this Church is the medium through which God manifests His will and dispenses His grace to man, and through which alone we can hope for heaven; they believe that nothing can be more reasonable than to believe God at His word, and that, above all, they must seek the kingdom of God and secure their eternal salvation.

Being governed by the Church, as freemen, in the spirit of a republican government, and enjoying, as they do, the freedom of the children of God, Catholics feel nowhere more at home than under a republican form of government. If a great pope could say in truth that he was nowhere more pope than in America, every Catholic can, and does, also, say in truth, "Nowhere can I be a better Christian than in the United States." Hence it is that Catholics are very generally attached to the republican institutions of the country—no class of our citizens more so—and would defend them at the sacrifice of their lives. Catholics far more readily adjust themselves to our institutions than non-Catholics, and among Catholics it must be observed that *they* succeed best who best understand and best practise their religion. They who are least truly American, and yield most to demagogues, are those who have very little of Catholicity, except the accident of being born of Catholic parents, who had them baptized in infancy.

Practical Catholics are the best Republicans! If we consult history, we find that they were always foremost in establishing and maintaining the republican form of government. Who originated all the free principles which lie at the basis of our own noble Constitution? Who gave us trial by jury, *habeas corpus*, stationary courts, and the principle—for which we fought and conquered in our revolutionary struggle against Protestant England—that taxes are not to be levied without the free consent of those who pay them? All these cardinal elements of free government date back to the good old Catholic times, in the middle ages—some three hundred years before the dawn of the Reformation! Our Catholic forefathers gave them all to us.

Again, we are indebted to Catholics for all the republics which ever existed in Christian times, down to the year 1776: for those of Switzerland, Venice, Genoa,

Andorra, San Marino, and a host of minor free Commonwealths, which sprang up in the "dark ages." Some of these republics still exist, proud monuments and unanswerable evidences of Catholic devotion to freedom. They are acknowledged by Protestants, no less than by Catholics. I subjoin the testimony of an able writer in the New York *Tribune*, believed to be Bayard Taylor. This distinguished traveller—a staunch Protestant—appeals to history, and speaks from personal observation. He writes:

"Truth compels us to add that the oldest republic now existing is that of San Marino, not only Catholic, but wholly surrounded by the especial dominion of the popes, who might have crushed it like an egg-shell at any time these last thousand years—but they didn't. The only republic we ever travelled in besides our own is Switzerland, half of its cantons or states entirely Catholic, yet never, that we have heard of, unfaithful to the cause of freedom. We never heard the Catholics of Hungary accused of backwardness in the late glorious struggle of their country for freedom, though its leaders were Protestants, fighting against a leading Catholic power avowedly in favor of religious as well as civil liberty. And chivalric, unhappy Poland, almost wholly Catholic, has made as gallant struggles for freedom as any other nation; while of the three despotisms that crushed her, but one was Catholic."

Let us bring the subject home to our own times and country. Who, I would ask, first reared in triumph the broad banner of universal freedom on this North American Continent? Who first proclaimed in this new world a truth too wide and expansive to enter into the head of, or to be comprehended by, a narrow-minded bigot—a truth that every man should be free to worship God according to the dictates of his conscience? Who *first* proclaimed, on this broad continent, the glorious principles of universal freedom? Read Bancroft, read Goodrich, read Frost, read every Protestant historian of our country, and you will see there inscribed, on the historic page, a *fact* which reflects immortal honor on our American Catholic ancestry—that Lord Baltimore and his Catholic colonists of Maryland were the *first* to proclaim universal liberty, civil and religious; the *first* to announce, as the basis of their legislation, the great and noble principle that no man's faith and conscience should be a bar to his holding any office, or enjoying any *civil privilege* of the community.

What American can forget the names of Rochambeau, De Grasse, De Kalb, Pulaski, La Fayette, Kosciusko? Without the aid of these noble Catholic heroes, and of the brave troops whom they led on to victory, would we have succeeded at all in our great revolutionary contest? Men of the clearest heads, and of the greatest political forecast, living at that time, thought not; at least they deemed the result exceedingly doubtful.

And during the whole war of the Revolution, who ever heard of a Catholic coward, or of a Catholic traitor? When the Protestant General, Gates, fled from the battle-field of Camden with the Protestant militia of North Carolina and Virginia, who but Catholics stood firm at their posts, and fought and died with the brave old Catholic hero, De Kalb? the veteran who, when others ingloriously fled, seized his good sword, and cried out to the brave old Maryland and Pennsylvania lines,

"Stand firm, for I am too old to fly!" Who ever heard of a Catholic Arnold? And who has not heard of the brave Irish and German soldiers who, at a somewhat later period, mainly composed the invincible army of the impetuous "Mad Anthony" Wayne, and constituted the great bulwark of our defence against the savage invasions which threatened our whole northwestern frontier with devastation and ruin?

All these facts, and many more of a similar kind which might be alleged, cannot have passed away, as yet, from the memory of our American citizens. Americans cannot have forgotten, as yet, that the man who perilled most in signing the Declaration of Independence was a Roman Catholic, and that when Charles Carroll, of Carrolton, put his name to that instrument, Benjamin Franklin observed, "There goes a cool million in support of the cause!"

And when our energies were exhausted, and the stoutest hearts entertained the most gloomy forebodings as to the final issue, Catholic France stepped gallantly forth to the rescue of our infant freedom, almost crushed by an overwhelming English tyranny! Catholic Spain also subsequently lent us her aid against England. Many of our most sagacious statesmen have believed that, but for this timely aid, our Declaration of Independence could scarcely have been made good.

These facts, which are but a few of those which might be adduced, prove conclusively that Catholicity is still what she was in the middle ages—the steadfast friend and support of free institutions.

The great roots of all the evils that press upon society, and make man unhappy, are—

"THE IGNORANCE OF THE MIND, AND THE DEPRAVITY OF THE WILL."

Hence he who wishes to civilize the world, and thus assist in executing the plans of God's providence, must remove these two great roots of evil by imparting to the mind infallibly the light of truth, and by laying down for the will authoritatively the unchangeable principles of morality. It is the Catholic Church that has accomplished in society this twofold task, by means of education.

In the Pagan world, education was an edifice built up on the principles of slavery. The motto was, "Odi profanum vulgus et arceo." Education was the privilege of the aristocracy. The great mass of people was studiously kept in ignorance of the treasures of the mind. This state of things was done away with by the Roman Catholic Church, when she established the monastic institutions of the West. The whole of Europe was soon covered with schools, not only for the wealthy, but for the poorest even of the poor. Yes, education was systematized, and an emulation was created for learning, such as the world had never seen before. Italy, Germany, France, England, and Spain, had their universities; but side by side with these, their colleges, gymnasiums, parish and village schools, as numerous as the churches and monasteries, which the efforts of the Holy See had scattered with lavish hand over the length and breadth of the land.

And where was the source of all this light? I answer, at *Rome*. For when the barbarian hordes poured down upon Europe from the Caspian Mountains, it was the Popes who saved civilization. They collected, in the Vatican, the manuscripts of the ancient authors, gathered from all parts of the earth at enormous expense. The barbarians, who destroyed everything by fire and sword, had already advanced as far as Rome. Attila, who called himself the scourge of God, stood before its walls; there was no emperor, no praetorian guard, no legions present to save the ancient Capital of the world. But there was a Pope—Leo I. And Leo went forth, and by entreaties, and threats of God's displeasure, induced the dreaded king of the Huns to retire. Scarcely had Attila retired, before Genseric, king of the Vandals, made his appearance, invited by Eudoxia, the empress, to the plunder of Rome. Leo met him, and obtained from him the lives and the honor of the Romans, and the sparing of the public monuments which adorned the city in such numbers. Thus Leo the Great saved Europe from barbarism. To the name of Leo, I might add those of Gregory I., Sylvester II., Gregory XIII., Benedict XIV., Julius III., Paul III., Leo X., Clement VIII., John XX., and a host of others, who must be looked upon as the preservers of science and the arts, even amid the very fearful torrent of barbarism that was spreading itself, like an inundation, over the whole of Europe. The principle of the Catholic Church has ever been this: "By the knowledge of Divine things, and the guidance of an infallible teacher, the human mind must gain certainty in regard to the sublimest problems, the great questions of life: by them the origin, the end, the norm and limit of man's activity must be made known, for then alone can he venture fearlessly upon the sphere of human efforts, and human developments, and human science." And, truly, never has science gained the ascendancy outside of the Church that it has always held in the Church. And what I say of science I say also of the arts. I say it of architecture, of sculpture, and of painting. I need only point to the Basilica of Peter, to the museums and libraries of Rome. It is to Rome the youthful artist always turns his steps, in order to drink in, at the monuments of art and of science, the genius and inspiration he seeks for in vain in his own country. He feels, only too keenly, that railroads and telegraphs, steamships and power-looms, banking-houses and stock companies, though good and useful institutions, are not the mothers of genius, nor the schools of inspiration; and therefore he leaves his country, and goes to Rome, and there feasts on the fruits gathered by the hands of St. Peter's successors, and then returns home with a name which will live for ages in the memory of those who have learned to appreciate the true and the beautiful.

It is thus that the Catholic Church has accomplished the great work of enlightening society. She has shed the light of Faith over the East and the West, over the North and the South, and with the faith she has established the principles of true science on their natural bases. She has imparted education to the masses, wherever she was left free to adopt her own, and untrammelled by civil interference. She has fostered and protected the arts and the sciences, and to-day, if all the libraries, and all the museums, and all the galleries of art in the world were destroyed, Rome alone would possess quite enough to supply the want, as it did in former ages, when others supplied themselves by plundering Rome.

The depravity of man shows itself in the constant endeavor to shake off the restraint placed by law and duty upon his will; and to this we must ascribe the licentiousness which has at all times afflicted society. Passion acknowledges no law, and spares neither rights nor conventions; where it has the power, it exercises it to the advantage of self, and to the detriment of social order. The Church is by its very constitution Catholic, and hence looks upon all men as brothers of the same family. She acknowledges not the natural right of one man over another, and hence her Catholicity lays a heavy restraint upon all the efforts of self-love, and curbs with a mighty hand the temerity of those who would destroy the harmony of life implied in the idea of Catholicity.

One of the first principles of all social happiness is, that before the law of nature, and before the face of God, all men are equal. This principle is based on the unity of the human race, the origin of all men from one common father. If we study the History of Paganism, we find that all heathen nations overturned this great principle, since we find among all heathen nations the evil of *Slavery*. Prior to the coming of Christ, the great majority of men were looked upon as a higher development of the animal, as animated instruments which might be bought and sold, given away and pawned; which might be tormented, maltreated, or murdered; as beings, in a word, for whom the idea of right, duty, pity, mercy, and law had no existence. Who can read, without a feeling of intense horror, the accounts left us of the treatment of their slaves by the Romans? There was no law that could restrain in the least the wantonness, the cruelty, the licentious excess of the master, who, as master, possessed the absolute right to do with his slaves whatsoever he pleased. To remove this stain of slavery has ever been the aim of the Catholic Church. "Since the Saviour and Creator of the world," says Pope Gregory I., in his celebrated decree, "wished to become man, in order, by grace and liberty, to break the chains of our slavery, it is right and good to bestow again upon man, whom nature has permitted to be born free, but whom the law of nations has brought under the yoke of slavery, the blessing of their original liberty." Through all the middle ages—called by Protestants the *dark ages of the world*—the echo of these words of Gregory I. is heard; and in the thirteenth century Pope Pius II. could say, "Thanks to God, and the Apostolic See, the yoke of slavery does no longer disgrace any European nation." Since then slavery was again introduced into Africa, and the newly-discovered regions of America, and again the Popes raised their voices in the interests of liberty,—from Pius II. to Pius VII., who, even at the time Napoleon had robbed him of his liberty, and held him captive in a foreign land, became the defender of the negro, to Gregory XVI., who, on the third of November, 1839, insisted in a special Bull on the abolition of the slave trade, and who spoke in a strain as if he had lived and sat side by side with Gregory I., thirteen hundred years before. But here let us observe, that not only the vindication of liberty for all, not only the abolition of slavery, but the very mode of action followed in this matter by the Popes, has gained for them immortal honor, and the esteem of all good men. When the Church abolished slavery in any country where it existed, the Popes did not compel masters, by harshness or threats, to manumit their slaves; they did not bring into action the base intrigues, the low chicanery, the canting hypocrisy of modern statesmen; they did not raise armies, and send them into the lands of their masters to burn and to pillage, to lay waste and to destroy; they did not slaughter, by their schemes, over a million of free men and another million of slaves; they did not make widows and orphans without numbers; they did not impoverish the land, and lay upon their subjects burdens which would crush them into very dust. Nothing of all this. That is not the way in which the Church abolished slavery. The Popes sent bishops and priests into those countries where slavery existed, to enlighten the minds of the masters, and convince them that slaves were men, and consequently had souls, like other people, too. The Popes, bishops and priests infused into the hearts of masters a deep love for Jesus Christ, and consequently a deep love for souls. The Popes, bishops and priests taught masters to look upon their slaves as created by the same God, redeemed by the same Jesus Christ, destined for the same glory. The consequence was, that the relations of slave and master became the relations of brother to brother; the master began to love his slave, and to ameliorate his condition, till at last, forced by his own acknowledged principles, he granted to him his liberty. Thus it was that slavery was abolished by the preaching of the Popes, bishops and priests. The great barrier to all the healthy, permanent, and free development of nations was thus broken down; the blessings, the privileges of society, were made equally attainable by the masses, and ceased to be the special monopoly of a few, who, for the most part, had nothing to recommend them except their wealth.

If any doubt remain as to the favorable influence of Catholicity on civil liberty, it would be dispelled by the express teaching of the theologians, writing in accordance with the principles and the spirit of the Church. Not to extend this point too much, I will confine myself to the authority of the great St. Thomas Aquinas, who, as a theologian, has perhaps had greater weight in the Catholic Church than any other man. His testimony may also show us what were the general sentiments of the school-men in the thirteenth century, when he wrote.

Speaking of the origin of civil power and the objects of law, he lays down these principles: "The law, strictly speaking, is directed primarily and principally to the common good; and to decree anything for the common benefit *belongs either to the whole body of the people, or to some one acting in their place.*" (Summa Theologiæ, i. 2, I. Quæst. Art. iii., Resp.) He pronounces the following opinion as to the best form of government: "Wherefore the choice of rulers in any state or kingdom is best, when one is *chosen for his merit to preside over all,* and under him are other rulers *chosen for their merit; and the government belongs to all, because the rulers may be chosen from any class of society; and the choice is made by all.*" (Ibid, Quæst. cv. Art. 1.) One would think that he is hearing a Democrat of the modern stamp, and yet it is a monk of the dark ages! Many other testimonies of similar import might be cited, but these will suffice.

And what has Protestantism done for human freedom? The Reformation dawned on the world in the year 1517. What did it do for the cause of freedom from that date down to 1776—when our Republic arose? Did it strike one blow for liberty during these two centuries and a half? Did it originate one republican principle, or found one solitary republic? Not one. In Germany, where it had full sway, it ruthlessly trampled in the dust all the noble franchises of the Catholic middle ages; it established political despotism everywhere; it united church and state; in a word, it brought about that very state of things which continues to exist, with but slight amelioration, even down to the present day. In England, it did the same; it broke down the bulwarks of the British Constitution, derived from the Catholic Magna Charta; it set at naught popular rights, and gave to the king or queen unlimited power in church and state; and it required a bloody struggle and a revolution, one hundred and fifty years afterwards, to restore to something of their former integrity the old chartered rights of the British people.

Protestantism has always boasted much, but it has really done little for the cause of human freedom. As to the liberties which we enjoy in our country, we cheerfully award to our Protestant fellow-citizens the praise which is so justly due them for *their* share in the glorious struggle.

But as to the power of Protestantism to maintain the Republic by checking the great evils that have already sapped its foundations, it has not any at all. How could Protestantism check infidelity, since it leads to it? There are two causes of infidelity that have existed from the beginning of the world. But about three centuries ago Protestantism opened a very wide avenue to infidelity. Protestantism introduced the principle, "There is no divinely-commissioned authority to teach infallibly." Now infidelity exists in this principle of Protestantism, as the oak exists in the acorn, as the consequence is in the premise. On the claim of private judgment, Protestants reject the authority of St. Peter, the Vicar of Christ. The Calvinists, going, as they do, by the same principle, reject the Real Presence of our Lord in the Blessed Sacrament.

The Socinians, following the same principle, reject, to-day, the Divinity of Christ, and therefore abjure Christianity, and fall back into utter incredulity.

The German and French philosophers, rationalists, and pantheists, of all degrees, do not even stop at that; they go farther, and deny the existence of a God Creator, and all by the privilege of free and private judgment.

The individual reason taking, as it does, the place of faith, the Protestant, whether he believes it or not, is an infidel in germ, and the infidel is a Protestant in full bloom; in other words, infidelity is nothing but Protestantism in the highest degree. Hence it is that Edgar Quinet, a great herald of Protestantism, is right in styling the Protestant sects *the thousand gates open to get out of Christianity*. No wonder, then, that thousands of Protestants have ended, and continue to end, in framing their formula of faith thus: "I believe in nothing."

But let us bring this subject home to our country. The disastrous issue of the revolutionary movements which convulsed all Europe in 1848-9, has thrown upon our shores masses of foreign political refugees, most of whom are infidels in religion, and red republicans, or destructionists of all social order in politics. They are men of desperate character and fortune—outlaws from society, with the brand of infidelity upon their brow. It is by this fast-increasing class of men that "Young America" is attracted, and learn from them their anarchical principles. The greatest, and, in fact, the only real danger to the permanency of our republican institutions, is to be apprehended from this class of infidels in our community.

Now what has contributed most towards the enormous increase of these enemies of our republic? It is the godless education given in the Public Schools. And who established these schools, and who robbed the money from the people to support them—to make this source of infidelity flow so abundantly all over the land? You find the answer to this question in Chapter III.

Protestantism was a separation from the source and current of the Divine-human life which exists in the Catholic Church, and which redeems and saves the world; and Protestants are therefore thrown back upon nature, and able to live only the natural life of the race—saving the portion of Christian life they brought away with them at the time of separation, and which, as not renewed from its source, must, in time, be exhausted.

It is therefore evident that Protestantism cannot fight infidelity. It is only the Catholic Church that can take open ground against these men so hostile to our country, and she feels honored by their bitter hostility. It could not be otherwise. Her principles are eminently conservative in all questions of religion and of civil policy; theirs are radical and destructive in both. Theirs is the old war of Satan against Christ; of the sons of Belial against the keepers of the law; of false and anti-social against true and rational liberty—"the liberty of the glory of the children of God."

Let these enemies of the country unfold their banners of "Infidelity," "Socialism," "Free Thought," "Scepticism," "Communism," "No God," "No Christ," "No Pope," "No Church," and a thousand others; let them grind their teeth, let them froth and foam at the mouth, let them tremble with rage, let them shake their heads with an air of majesty, as if they would say to the Church, "We bury you to-morrow, we write your epitaph and chant your De Profundis; our league is mighty, our forces are multitudinous, our weapons are powerful, our bravery is desperate."

The Catholic Church calmly answers, "I know you hate me because I am the palladium of truth and of public and private morality; I am the root and bond of charity and faith; I love justice and hate iniquity. But it is for this very reason that I will remain forever; for truth and justice being, in the end, always victorious, I will not cease to bless and to triumph. All the works of the earth have perished; time has obliterated them. But I remain, because Christ remains, and I will endure until I pass from my earthly exile to my country in heaven.

"Human theories and systems have flitted across my path like birds of night, but they have vanished; numberless sects have, like so many waves, dashed themselves to froth against me, this rock, or, recoiling, have been lost in the vast ocean of forgetfulness. Kingdoms and empires that once existed in inimitable worldly grandeur are no more; dynasties have died out, and have been replaced by others.

"Thrones and sceptres and crowns have withstood me; but, immutable, like God, who laid my foundation, I am the firm, unshaken centre round which the weal and woe of nations move—weal if they adhere to it—woe if they separate from it. If the world takes from me the cross of gold, I will bless the world with one of wood.

"Tear down my Banner of the Cross if you can! Touch a single fold of it if you dare! Sound your battle-cry; rally your hosts—marshal your ranks! Storm these lofty summits. They never yet have been surrendered. The flag that waves above them has never trailed in defeat, and the hearts that guard that flag have never flinched before the foe, and the bravery that shoots through every film of these hearts has never faltered. On with the conflict! Let it rage! Our line of battle reaches back to Calvary. That line has never been broken by wildest onset! These soldiers have never fled! We are the sons of veterans who have marched through a campaign of eighteen hundred years—marched and never halted—marched and always triumphed! We belong to the old Imperial Guard of Faith! We never yet have met a Waterloo!

"I am a queen—but a warrior-queen. You will never find me on a throne here below. Banner in hand, I am ever in the midst of battle. I have never granted a day of truce to my enemies. War against all who war against God—war against all who war against Christ—war against all who war against man—war against all who war against truth—this is my destiny.

"Peace here below, I have never known. Rest here below, I have never found. I am always on the march—my banner ever unfurled—my war-cry ever sounding!

"Therefore, in the storm and shock of my battle of to-day with my enemies, my soldier-children fear not. Around my old chieftain they rally. What though some may desert and leave the lines? The lines close up again—and the deserters are not missed. What though a Judas Iscariot may betray? A brave Matthias takes his place. What though a few of craven spirit may flee? The ranks they left are filled by brave men and true.

"From the hill of Calvary to the hill of the Vatican, from Peter before the Council to Pius before the Sardinian, my history has been one long, uninterrupted battle—and my battle one long and glorious victory."

We cannot but smile when we hear infidels talk of the downfall of the Church. What could hell and its agents do more than they have already done for her destruction? They have employed tortures for the body, but they could not reach the spirit; they have tried heresy, or the denial of revealed truth, to such an extent that we cannot see room for any new heresy; they have, by the hand of schism, torn whole countries from the unity of the Church; but what she lost on one side of the globe, she gained tenfold on the other. All these have ignominiously failed to verify the prophecies of hell, that "the Church shall fall."

Look, for instance, at the tremendous effort of the so-called glorious Reformation, together with its twin sister—the unbelief of the nineteenth century. Whole legions of church reformers, together with armies of philosophers armed with negation, and a thousand and one systems of Paganism, rushed on against the Chair of Peter, and swore that the Papacy would fall, and with it the whole Church. Three hundred years are over, and the Catholic Church is still alive, and, to all appearances, more vigorous than ever. The nations have proved that they can get along very well without reformers, but not without the Catholic Church. Men are foolish enough to dream of the destruction of the Papacy. Napoleon tried the game, and, from the summit of his empire, walked into exile, whilst his victim, Pius VII., leaving his prison, entered Rome in triumph. A great statesman of France said, not long ago, that those who tried to swallow the Papacy, and with it the whole Church, always died of indigestion. Let the enemies of the Catholic Church beware! If they dash their heads against this rock, they must not be astonished to find them broken.

And what power has Protestantism to check the National Crime—the murder of helpless innocents? Everybody knows, who knows anything about the subject, that among the Roman Catholic population this crime is hardly known. The reason for the rare occurrence of this crime among Catholics, is their religion. The doctrine of the Catholic Church, her canons, her pontifical constitutions, her theologians, without exception, teach, and always have taught, that even the intention of preventing or destroying human life, at any period from the first instant of conception, is a heinous crime, equal at least in guilt to the crime of murder.

Now as to the power of Protestantism to check this crime, Dr. Storer, the distinguished Protestant physician of Boston, says: "We are compelled to admit that *Protestantism* has failed to check the increase of criminal abortion." (Criminal Abortion, p. 55.) "There can be no doubt that the Romish ordinance, flanked, on the one hand, by the confessional, and by denouncement and excommunications on the other, has saved to the world *thousands of infant lives*." (Ibid. p. 74.) "During the ten years which have passed since the preceding sentence was written, we have had ample verification of its truth. *Several hundreds of Protestant women* have personally acknowledged to us their guilt, against whom only seven Catholics, and of these we found, upon further inquiry, that all but two were only nominally so, not going to the confession."—(Ibid.)

It is, then, not Protestantism, it is the Catholic Church alone that has the power to oppose herself to the propagation of so heinous a crime, and prevent her children from shedding the blood of helpless innocents.

The third great evil which has made the most fearful inroad among us, so as already to have extorted many a warning cry, is *the contempt of the marriage tie.*

The family, as I have said in a previous chapter, is the groundwork of civil society. If the family be Christian, the State will also be Christian; and if the family be corrupt, the State cannot remain long untarnished. It is the holy sacrament of marriage that gives sanctity to the family, and strength to civil society. To reject that sacrament is to sow the seeds of revolution. Revolution in the family begets revolution in the State. When a government, which, by its very nature, should restrain immorality, allows the separation of man and wife, it sanctions the right of revolution in the family, and sooner or later that government will feel the dire effects of its own corrupt doctrine. Now it is a matter of fact that the contempt of the marriage tie, so prevalent in our country, is owing to Protestantism. If any one wishes to learn how the Continental Reformers regarded the Sacrament of Matrimony, let him read Luther's sermon on Marriage (if he can do so without a blush), or, better still, the dogmatical judgment of Luther, Melanchthon, Bucer, and the rest, giving permission! to the innocent Landgrave of Hesse to commit bigamy, pure and simple.

It is the Catholic Church alone, again, that has always regarded the Christian marriage as the corner-stone of society; and at that corner-stone have the Popes stood guard for eighteen centuries, by insisting that Christian marriage is one, holy, and indissoluble. Woman, weak and unprotected, has, as the history of the Church abundantly proves, found at Rome that guaranty which was refused her by him who had sworn at the altar of God to love her and to cherish her till death. Whilst, in the nations whom the Reformation of the sixteenth century tore from the bosom of the Church, the sacred laws of matrimony are trampled in the dust, whilst the statistics of these nations hold up to the world the sad spectacle of divorces as numerous as marriages, of separations of husband from wife, and wife from husband, for the most trivial causes, thus granting to lust the widest margin of license, and legalizing concubinage and adultery; whilst the nineteenth century records in its annals the existence of a community of licentious polygamists within the borders of one of the most civilized countries of the earth, we must yet see the decree emanating from Rome that would permit even a beggar to repudiate his lawful wife, in order to give his affections to an adulteress.

The female portion of our race would always have sunk back into a new slavery, had not the Popes entered the breach for the protection of the Unity, the sanctity, the Indissolubility of matrimony. In the midst of the barbarous ages, during which the conqueror and warrior swayed the sceptre of empire, and kings and petty tyrants acknowledged no other right but that of force, it was the Popes that opposed their authority, like a wall of brass, to the sensuality and the passions of the mighty ones of the earth, and stood forth as the protectors of innocence and outraged virtue, as the champions of the rights of women, against the wanton excesses of tyrannical husbands, by enforcing, in their full severity, the laws of Christian marriage. If Christian Europe is not covered with harems, if polygamy has never gained a foothold in Europe, if, with the indissolubility and sanctity of matrimony, the palladium of European civilization has been saved from destruction, it is all owing to the Popes. "If the Popes"—says the Protestant Von Müller—"if the Popes could hold up no other merit than that which they gained by protecting monogamy against the brutal lusts of those in power, notwithstanding bribes, threats, and persecutions, that alone would render them immortal for all future ages."

And how had they to battle till they had gained this merit? What sufferings had they to endure, what trials to undergo? When King Lothair, in the ninth century, repudiated his lawful wife in order to live with a concubine, Pope Nicholas I. at once took upon himself the defence of the rights and of the honor of the unhappy wife. All the arts of an intriguing policy were plied, but Nicholas remained unshaken; threats were used, but Nicholas remained firm. At last the king's brother, Louis II., appears with an army before the walls of Rome, in order to compel the Pope to yield. It is useless—Nicholas swerves not from the line of duty. Rome is besieged; the priests and people are maltreated and plundered; sanctuaries are desecrated; the cross is torn down and trampled under foot, and, in the midst of these scenes of blood and sacrilege, Nicholas flies to the Church of St. Peter; there he is besieged by the army of the Emperor for two days and two nights; left without food or drink, he is willing to die of starvation on the tomb of St. Peter, rather than yield to a brutal tyrant, and sacrifice the sanctity of Christian marriage, the law of life of Christian society. And the perseverance of Nicholas I. was crowned with victory. He had to contend against a licentious king, who was tired of restraint; against an emperor, who, with an army at his heels, came to enforce his brother's unjust demands; against two councils of venal bishops, the one at Metz, the other at Aix-la-Chapelle, who had sanctioned the scandals of the adulterous monarch. Yet, with all this opposition, and the suffering it cost him, the Pope succeeded in procuring the acknowledgment of the rights of an injured woman. And during succeeding ages we find Gregory V. carrying on a similar combat against King Robert, and Urban II. against King Philip of France. In the thirteenth century, Philip Augustus, mightier than his predecessors, set to work all the levers of power, in order to move the Pope to divorce him from his wife Ingelburgis. Hear the noble answer of the great Innocent III.:

"Since, by the grace of God, we have the firm and unshaken will never to separate ourselves from Justice and Truth, neither moved by petitions, nor bribed by presents, neither induced by love, nor intimidated by hate, we will continue to go on in the royal path, turning neither to the right nor to the left; and we judge without any respect to persons, since God Himself does not respect persons."

After the death of his first wife, Isabella, Philip Augustus wished to gain the favor of Denmark by marrying Ingelburgis. The union had hardly been solemnized, when he wished to be divorced from her. A council of venal bishops assembled at Compiegne, and annulled his lawful marriage. The queen, poor woman, was summoned before her Judges, and the sentence was read and translated to her. She could not speak the language of France, so her only cry was "Rome!" And Rome heard her cry of distress, and came to her rescue. Innocent III. needed the alliance of France in the troubles in which he was engaged with Germany; Innocent III. needed the assistance of France for the Crusade; yet Innocent III. sent Peter of Capua as Legate to France; a Council is convoked by the Legate of the Pope; Philip refuses to appear, in spite of the summons, and the whole of the kingdom of Philip is placed under interdict. Philip's rage knows no bounds: bishops are banished, his lawful wife is imprisoned, and the king vents his rage on the clergy of France. The barons, at last, appeal against Philip to the sword. The king complains to the Pope of the harshness of the Legate, and when Innocent only confirms the sentence of the Legate, the king exclaims, "Happy Saladin; he had no Pope!" Yet the king was forced to obey. When he asked the barons assembled in council, "What must I do?" their answer was: "Obey the Pope; put away Agnes and restore Ingelburgis." And, thanks to the severity of Innocent III., Philip repudiated the concubine, and restored Ingelburgis to her rights, as wife and queen. Hear what the Protestant Hurter says, in his life of Innocent: "If Christianity has not been thrown aside, as a worthless creed, into some isolated corner of the world; if it has not, like the sects of India, been reduced to a mere theory; if its European vitality has outlived the voluptuous effeminacy of the East, it is due to the watchful severity of the Roman Pontiffs—to their increasing care to maintain the principles of authority in the Church."

As often as we look to England, that land of perfidy and deceit, we are reminded of the words of Innocent III. to Philip Augustus. We see Clement using them as his principles in his conduct towards the royal brute Henry VIII. Catherine of Aragon, the lawful wife of Henry, had been repudiated by her disgraceful husband, and it was again to Rome she appealed for protection. Clement remonstrates with Henry. The monarch calls the Pope hard names. Clement repeats, "Thou shalt not commit adultery!" Henry threatens to tear England from the Church; he does it; still Clement insists, "Thou shalt not commit adultery!" Fisher and More go to bleed out their life at Tyburn; still the Pope repeats, "Thou shalt not commit adultery!" Henry had two wives at the same time, and, after *them,* took a new wife, and killed off his old wife, whenever his beastly passion prompted. The enslavement of the people followed. Henry made himself head of the Church, and bade the English nation recognize him as such. The penalty of disobeying the tyrant was death. The mass of the English yielded. This adulterous beast—this ferocious monster—they accepted as their pope; and their children, following in their steps, accepted his bastard brood—of either sex—as their popes; while the only and true Pope, the successor of St. Peter, the Vicar of Jesus Christ, was rejected by them. To such depths of servility and degradation do apostate nations fall. The firmness of the Pope cost England's loss to the Church. It cost the Pope bitter tears, and he prayed to Heaven not to visit on the people of England the crimes of the despot; he prayed for the conversion of the nation; but sacrifice the sanctity, the indissolubility of matrimony, that he could never do—abandon helpless women to the brutality of men who were tired of the restraints of morality—no, that the Pope could never permit. If the Court, if the palace of the domestic hearth refused a shelter, Rome was always open, a refuge to injured and downtrodden innocence.

"One must obey God more than man." This has ever been the language of the Popes, whenever there was question of defending the laws of God against the powers of the earth; and in thus defending the laws of God, they protected against outrage the personal dignity, the moral liberty and the intellectual freedom of man. "Because there was a Pope," says a Protestant historian, "there could not any longer be a Tiberius in Europe, and the direction of the religious and spiritual welfare of man was withdrawn from the hands of royalty." Because there were Popes, the will of Cæsar could not any longer be substituted for law; for the Popes made the Gospel the law-book of the nations. Now the Gospel teaches that all power comes from God; that from God the sovereign derives his power, to rule in justice and equity for the welfare of his subjects, and that the subjects are bound to obey their rules, for conscience sake. Hence, adopting the great principal of action, the Popes have at all times condemned the spirit of rebellion, and have anathematized those principles, those factions, those organizations whose aim is, and has always been, to overturn lawful authority and to substitute anarchy in the place of the harmony of legitimate government. In conformity with this rule of action the Popes Clement XII., Benedict XIV., Pius VII., Leo XII., Gregory XVI., and Pius IX. have condemned secret societies, whose object is the overthrow of civil and religious government. But at the same time that the Popes required from subjects obedience to their lawful governments, they have ever defended subjects against the abuse of power, or against the tyranny of unjust rulers. In Pagan times it had the appearance as if the people existed for the sovereign, and not the sovereign for the people; but in the days and in the countries where the spiritual supremacy of the Pope was acknowledged by rulers, the Pagan idea had necessarily to disappear, for the Popes gave the princes to understand that they existed for the people, and not the people for them.

Viewed in this light, what a magnificent spectacle does the Catholic Church present to our admiration, and how does the honest heart of downtrodden nationality yearn that these happy days may once more return! Taken mostly from the middle classes, sometimes even from the most humble ranks of society, the Popes ascended the Chair of Peter; and these men, who had been the sons of artisans and mechanics, but who had, by their virtue and talent, gained a merit which neither wealth nor a noble pedigree could bestow, became the arbiters between nation and nation, between prince and people, always prepared to weld together the chain of broken friendship, and to protect, by their power and authority, the rights of subjects oppressed by tyrannical rulers. It was indeed a blessing for Europe that Nicholas I. could curb, with an iron hand, the tyranny of kings and nobles. It was indeed a blessing, not for Europe alone, but for the world, that there lived a genius on earth in the person of Gregory VII., who knew how to protect the Saxons against the wanton lawlessness of Henry, King of Germany, a monster who ground his subjects remorselessly in the dust, and respected neither the sanctity of virginity nor the sacredness of marriage; neither the rights of the Church, nor those of the State; whose very existence seemed to have no other aim but that of the leech, to draw out the blood from the hearts of his unhappy subjects. What would have become of Germany had there not been a power superior to that of this godless prince? It was Gregory VII. who hurled him from his throne, and restored to the noble Saxons and Thuringians their independence, not by the power of the sword, but by the scathing power of his anathema. The same I may say of Boniface VIII., and of Innocent III. There was, happily for Europe, a Court of Appeal, to which even monarchs were forced to bow; and that court was Rome. It was to Rome that the nations appealed, when their independence was at stake or their rights were trampled upon. And Rome was never deaf to the cry of distress, whether it came from Germany or from France, from England or from Poland, from Spain or from the shores of the Bosphorus.

And when the liberty of a nation was on the verge of destruction, and when emperors, and kings, and barons rode rough-shod over the rights, natural and vested, of their subjects, forgetting the sacred trust confided to them, became tyrants, when neither prosperity nor undivided liberty were secure from that rapacious grasp; when even the rights of conscience were set aside with impunity; it was the Popes of Rome who buckled on the armor of Justice, and humbled the pride of princes—even if, as a consequence, they had to say, with a Gregory VII., "Dilexi Justitiam et odivi iniquitatem; ideo morior in exilio"—"I die in exile because I have loved justice and hated iniquity."

The influence of Catholicity tends strongly to break down all barriers of separate nationalities, and to bring about a brotherhood of citizens, in which the love of our common country and of one another would absorb every sectional feeling.

Catholicity is of no nation, of no language, of no people; she knows no geographical bounds; she breaks down all the walls of separation between race and race, and she looks alike upon every people, and tribe, and caste. Her views are as enlarged as the territory which she inhabits; and this is as wide as the world. Jew and Gentile, Greek and barbarian, Irish, German, French, English, and American, are all alike to her. The evident tendency of this principle is to level all sectional feelings and local prejudices, by enlarging the views of mankind, and thus to bring about harmony in society, based upon mutual forbearance and charity. And, in fact, so far as the influence of the Catholic Church could be brought to bear upon the anomalous condition of society in America, it has been exercised for securing the desirable result of causing all its heterogeneous elements to be merged in the one variegated but homogeneous nationality. Protestantism isolates and divides; Catholicity brings together and unites.

The Catholic Church is a grand fact in history—a fact so great that there would be no history without it—a fact permanent, repeating itself perpetually, entering into the concerns of all the nations on the face of the earth, appearing again and again on the records of time, and benefiting, perceived or unperceived, directly or indirectly, socially, morally, and supernaturally, every individual who forms part of the great organism of human society.

Around this Church human society moves like a wheel around its axle; it is on this Church that society depends for its support, its life, its energy, like the planetary system on the sun. Show me an age, a country, a nation deprived of the influence of Catholicity, and I will show you an age, a country, a nation without morals, without virtue. Yes, if "Religion and Science, Liberty and Justice, Principle and Right," are not empty sounds—if they have a meaning—they owe their energetic existence in the world to the Catholic Church.

Such is the power and such is the influence of Catholicity. Yet I do not pretend that our Catholic population is perfect, or that in them you will find no shortcomings, nothing to be censured or regretted. Certainly in our cities and large towns may be found, I am sorry to say, many so-called liberal or *nominal* Catholics, who are no credit to their religion, to the land of their birth, or to that of their adoption. Subjected at home, as they were, to the restraints imposed by Protestant or quasi-Protestant governments, they feel, on coming here, that they are loosed from all restraints, and forgetting the obedience they owe to their pastors, to the prelates whom the Holy Ghost has placed over them, they become insubordinate, and live more as non-Catholics than as Catholics. The children of these are, to a great extent, shamefully neglected, and suffered to grow up without the simplest moral and religious instruction, and to become recruits to our vicious population, our rowdies and our criminals. This is certainly to be deplored, but can easily be explained without prejudice to the influence of Catholicity, by adverting to the condition to which those individuals were reduced before coming here; to their disappointments and discouragements in a strange land; to their exposure to new and unlooked-for temptations; to the fact that they were by no means the best of Catholics even in their native countries; to their poverty, destitution, ignorance, insufficient culture, and a certain natural shiftlessness and recklessness, and to our *great lack of schools, churches, and priests*. The proportion, however, that these bear to our whole Catholic population, is far less than is commonly supposed, and they are not so habitually depraved as they appear, for they seldom or never consult appearances, and have little skill in concealing their vices. As low and degraded as this class of our Catholic population may be, they never are so low or so vicious as the corresponding class of non-Catholics in every nation. A non-Catholic vicious class is always worse than it appears; a Catholic vicious class is less bad. In the worst there is always some germ that, with proper care, may be nursed into life, that may blossom and bear fruit. Yet, if we look at the Catholic population as it is, and is every year becoming, we cannot but be struck with its marvellous energy and progress. We will find that population more intellectual, more cultivated, more moral, more active, living, and energetic than any other.

The Catholic population of this country, taken as a body, have a personal freedom, an independence, a self-respect, a conscientiousness, a love of truth, and a devotion to principle, not to be found in any other class of American citizens. Their moral tone, as well as their moral standard, is far higher, and they act more uniformly under a sense of deep responsibility to God and their country. They are the most law-loving and law-abiding people. The men of that population are the most vigorous, and the hardiest; their virgins are the chastest; their matrons the most faithful. Catholics do, as to the great majority, act from honest principle, from sincere and earnest conviction, and are prepared to die sooner than in any grave matters swerve from what they regard as truth and justice. They have the principle and the firmness to stand by what they believe true and just, in good report and evil report, whether the world be with them or be against them. Among Catholics you will not find the flunkeyism which Carlyle so unmercifully ridicules in the middling classes of Great Britain, or that respect to mere wealth, that worship of the money-bag, or that base servility to the mob, or public opinion, so common and so ruinous to public and private virtue in the United States.

The mental activity of Catholics, all things considered, is far more remarkable than that of our non-Catholic countrymen; and, in proportion to their numbers and means, they contribute far more than any other class of American citizens to the purposes of education, both common and liberal, for they receive little or nothing from the public treasury; and in addition to supporting numerous schools of their own, they are forced to contribute their quota to the support of those of the State. Thus, to take a single illustration, the public school-tax in Cincinnati for last year amounted to $810,000. Of this the Catholics—such is their proportion in that community—contributed $230,000, or more than one-third of the whole rate. This large sum—£162,000—goes to the management and formation of schools which the Catholics of Cincinnati are debarred, by their consciences, from entering. They have therefore their own schools, which they have built, and support entirely at their own expense, without any assistance whatever from the State. The education which they give is known to be excellent; but it is based on religion, and is not controlled by the State and paid officials. The consequence is, that not only are they not encouraged, but they are actually taxed by the State.

Thus, for instance, the Cathedral School is obliged to pay to the State an annual tax of £120, and the schools of another parish £200. The Catholics of the Cathedral Parish have not only to pay the State school-tax, and the heavy tax laid on their school-buildings, but they have to find $3,500 annually to meet the current school expenses. All this has to be collected by the clergy as best they can.

The non-Catholic has no conception of the treasure the Union possesses in these thirteen millions of Catholics, humble in their outward circumstances as the majority of them may be. A true, high-toned, chivalric national character will be formed, and a true, generous, and lofty patriotism will be generated and sustained in proportion as the force of Catholicity is brought to bear upon our American people, and the life of practical Catholics falls into the current of American life. Catholics have their faults and shortcomings, yet they are the salt of the American community, and the really conservative element in the American population. In a few years they will be the Americans of the Americans, and on them will rest the performance of the glorious work of sustaining American civilization, and realizing the hopes of the founders of our great and growing Republic.

It must, then, be evident to every true lover of the Republic, that the State, were it at liberty to favor any particular portion of the community, should favor its conservative element—the Catholics—instead of robbing Catholics of millions of dollars, to continue, by godless education, the impious work for the increase of the number of enemies of the Republic; it should rather supply Catholics with the means to bring up their children in the spirit of true freedom—in the spirit of devotedness to republican institutions. But as the State is neither Catholic nor Protestant, it should at least act justly and impartially; it should not favor its own enemies; it should not make a lie or a farce of our glorious Constitution; it should no longer play the usurper and the robber; it should no longer continue digging its own grave; it should not tax Catholics any longer to support infidel institutions—nurseries of all kinds of crimes—and thus continue to violate most atrociously the very letter and spirit of the Constitution, and to commit a direct outrage on the most sacred convictions of Catholics.

It is the well-instructed practical Catholic that is alone capable of appreciating and realizing true freedom. Ever foremost to concede the rights of God, ever careful to trench on the rights of his fellow-creatures, he is, for all this (and precisely *because* of this), well aware of his own rights and dignity as a man, as a citizen, and as a baptized Christian—a regenerated son of God—and, knowing his rights and dignity, he dares maintain them! He protests against godless education as a volcano that is destined to bury law and authority, and bring about universal anarchy, and prepare and establish the reign of antichrist. We must, then, have separate schools to educate our rising generation in a religious atmosphere, and imbue them with the principles of Christianity. All those who oppose any longer the denominational system, in any manner whatsoever, are traitors to the Republic and the worst enemies of the country, and from henceforth the vengeance of God will not be slow to overtake them. On the contrary, he who will be first and foremost in promoting this noblest of objects—the establishment of denominational schools—may truly be called the *saviour* of the Republic,—the *father of his country*; he will be as great, nay, even greater, than Washington himself. Upon him the blessings of heaven will descend in superabundance, and his name will be blessed from generation to generation.

CHAPTER XIII.

THE CATHOLIC PRIEST ON THE PUBLIC SCHOOL SYSTEM.

So far I have spoken as an American citizen. I have shown to all my fellow-citizens the tree with its fruits—the Public School system in broad daylight. All who call themselves Christians, or who consider themselves men of common sense, and warm promoters of the happiness of their fellow-citizens, will agree with me in saying that the Public School system is a tree of which we must say what God said to Adam of the tree standing in the middle of paradise: "Of the tree of knowledge of good and evil thou shalt not eat. For in what day soever thou *shalt eat of it thou shalt die the death.*"—(Gen ii. 17.) It is now time for me to speak as a priest of the Roman Catholic Church. It is the duty of the Catholic priest to teach the children of the Catholic Church the language of their spiritual Mother—the Church. This language is no other than that of the Supreme Head of the Church—the Pope. Now the language of the Vicar of Christ in regard to godless education is very plain and unmistakable.

Jesus Christ, our Divine Saviour, has said: "What doth it profit a man if he gain the whole world, and suffer the loss of his own soul?"—(Matt. xvi. 26.) What will it profit you or your children to gain all knowledge, and to attain the greatest success in this world, if, through your fault, and through your exposing them to the danger of evil education, they suffer the loss of that faith, without which "it is impossible to please God"?—(Heb. xi.)

Teaching of the Syllabus.

Guided by this principle, our Holy Father, Pope Pius IX., has declared that Catholics cannot *"approve of a system of educating youth unconnected with the Catholic Faith and the power of the Church, and which regards the knowledge of merely natural things, and only, or at least primarily, the ends of earthly social life."*[8] Catholic parents cannot approve of an education which fits their children only for this life, and ignores that life in which the soul is to live forever. As faith is the foundation of all our hopes for eternity, and as faith without good works is dead, we cannot choose for our children an education which would endanger their faith and morals, and consequently imperil their eternal welfare.

---

[8] "Hant propositionem auctoritate Nostra Apostolica reprobamus, proscribimus atque damnamus eamque ab omnibus Catholicæ Ecclesiæ filiis veluti reprobatam, proscriptam atque damnatam omnino haberi volumus et mandamus."—Syllabus, Prop. xlviii.

Teaching of Pope Pius VII.

This is no novel doctrine, as some assert. In the beginning of the century, the illustrious Pius VII., in an Encyclical letter addressed to the Bishops of the Catholic world, July 10th, 1800, thus writes:—

"It is your duty to take care of the whole flock over which the Holy Ghost has placed you as Bishops, but in particular to watch over children and young men. They ought to be the special object of your paternal love, of your vigilant solicitude, of your zeal, of all your care. They who have tried to subvert society and families, to destroy authority, divine and human, have spared no pains to infect and corrupt youth, hoping thus the more easily to execute their infamous projects. They know that the mind and heart of young persons, like soft wax, to which one may give what form he pleases, are very susceptible of every sort of impression; that they keep tenaciously, when age has now hardened them, those which they had early received, and reject others. Thence the well-known proverb taken from the Scripture, 'A young man according to his way, even when he is old he will not depart from it.' Suffer not, then, venerable brethren, the children of this world to be more prudent in this respect than the children of light. Examine, therefore, with the greatest attention, to what manner of persons is confided the education of children, and of young men in the colleges and seminaries; of what sort are the instructions given them; what sort of schools exist among you; of what sort are the teachers in the lyceums. Examine into all this with the greatest care, sound everything, let nothing escape your vigilant eye; keep off, repulse the ravening wolves that seek to devour these innocent lambs; drive out of the sheepfold those which have gotten in; remove them as soon as can be, for such is the power which has been given to you by the Lord for the edification of your sheep."

Rescripts of His Present Holiness Condemning the Queen's Colleges of England.

Our Holy Father Pope Pius IX., consulting for the special wants of the Catholics of Ireland, has not ceased, almost from the very beginning of his glorious pontificate, to repeat similar instructions in his apostolic letters to the Irish Bishops. Hence, by his rescripts of October 1847, and October 1848, he condemned, from their first institution, the Queen's Colleges, on account of their "grievous and intrinsic dangers to faith and morals"; and since then he has frequently repeated his sacred admonitions, warning the bishops and the faithful people to beware of evil systems of public instruction; and to secure, by every means in their power, the blessings of Catholic education for the rising generation.

Resolutions of Irish Bishops in 1824 and 1826.

Nor have the Irish prelates been unmindful of their duty in this respect. In 1824, that is to say, five years before Catholic emancipation, and in the midst of the struggle for that recognition of the existence of their people as citizens, they presented to Parliament a petition, from which I make the following extract, which clearly shows their conviction of the necessity of religious education:

"That in the Roman Catholic Church the literary and religious instruction of youth are universally combined, and that no system of education which separates them can be acceptable to the members of her communion; that the religious instruction of youth in Catholic schools is always conveyed by means of catachetical instruction, daily prayer, and the reading of religious books, wherein the Gospel morality is explained and inculcated; that Roman Catholics have ever considered the reading of the Sacred Scriptures by children as an inadequate means of imparting to them religious instruction, as a usage whereby the Word of God is made liable to irreverence, youth exposed to misunderstand its meaning, and thereby not unfrequently to receive in early life impressions which may afterwards prove injurious to their own best interests, as well as to those of the society which they are destined to form. That schools whereof the master professes a religion different from that of his pupils, or from which such religious instruction as the Catholic Church prescribes for youth is excluded, or in which books and tracts not sanctioned by it are read or commented on, cannot be resorted to by the children of Roman Catholics; and that threats and rewards have been found equally unavailing as a means of inducing Catholic parents to procure education for their children from such persons or in such schools; that any system of education incompatible with the discipline of the Catholic Church, or superintended exclusively by persons professing a religion different from that of the vast majority of the poor of Ireland, cannot possibly be acceptable to the latter, and must, in its progress, be slow and embarrassed, generating often distrust and discord as well as a want of that mutual good faith and perfect confidence which should prevail between those who receive benefits and those who dispense them."

The Irish Bishops again expressed the like sentiments in 1826.* * * * *

Address of the National Synod of Thurles.

A National Synod met in Thurles in August, 1860, and again the Prelates spoke words of instruction, of which recent sad events in France have furnished a new and most melancholy confirmation.

"As rulers of the Church of Christ, chief pastors of His flock, religiously responsible to the Prince of Pastors for every soul committed to our charge, it forms, as is obvious, our first and paramount duty to attend to the pastures in which they feed—the doctrines with which they are nourished. And surely if ever there was a period which called for the unsleeping vigilance, the prudent foresight, the intrepid and self-sacrificing zeal of our august ministry—that period is the present. The alarming spectacle which the Christian world exhibits at the present day, the novel but formidable forms in which error presents itself, and the manifold evils and perils by which the Church is encompassed, must be evident to the most superficial observer. It is no longer a single heresy or an eccentric fanaticism, the denial of some revealed truth, or the excesses of some extravagant error, but a comprehensive, all-pervading, well-digested system of unbelief, suited to every capacity and reaching every intellect, that corrupts and desolates the moral world. Is not such the calamitous spectacle which the continent of Europe offers to us at this moment? Education, the source of all intellectual life, by which the mind of man is nurtured and disciplined, his principles determined, his feelings regulated, his judgments fixed, his character formed, has been forcibly dissevered from every connection with religion, and made the vehicle of that cold scepticism and heartless indifferentism which have seduced and corrupted youth, and by a necessary consequence shaken to its centre the whole fabric of social life. Separated from her heavenly monitor, learning is no longer the organ of that wisdom which cometh from above, which, according to St. James, is 'chaste, peaceable, modest, easy to be persuaded, consenting to the good, full of mercy and good fruits, without judging, without dissimulation,' but rather of that wisdom which he describes as 'earthly, sensual, and devilish.'—(James iii. 15-17.)

"It is, we feel assured, unnecessary to observe to you, that of all modes of propagating error, education is the most subtle and dangerous, furnishing, as it does, the aliment by which the social body is sustained, which circulates through every vein, and reaches every member; and that if this aliment should prove to be corrupt or deleterious, it will not fail to carry moral disease and death to the entire system. Hence the awful obligations we are under, at the peril of our souls, of watching over the education of the people whom God has intrusted to our charge.

"Listen to the emphatic words in which the present illustrious Pontiff sets forth the dangers to which youth is exposed at the present time, and the duties which are placed upon the pastors of the people in this regard. 'It is incumbent upon you,' he says, 'and upon ourselves, to labor with all diligence and energy, and with great firmness of purpose, and to be vigilant in everything that regards schools, and the instruction and education of children and youths of both sexes. For you well know that the modern enemies of religion and human society, with a most diabolical spirit, direct all their artifices to pervert the minds and hearts of youth from their earliest years. Wherefore, they leave nothing untried; they shrink from no attempt to withdraw schools, and every institution destined for the education of youth, from the authority of the Church and the vigilance of her holy pastors.'—*Encycl. Letter of Pius IX., eighth December, 1849.*

"Such are the words of the Vicar of Jesus Christ, which show the responsibility under which we are placed, and point out our duty to protect from the insidious snares laid for their destruction the lambs of the fold—that most helpless but precious portion of the flock of Jesus Christ which the prophet represents as carried in His bosom."

Mixed System again Condemned.

Again, in 1859, 1862, 1863, 1867, and 1869, the Irish Bishops renewed their condemnation of the godless system, and demanded for their children the advantage of truly Catholic education.

Unanimity of Catholic Bishops throughout the World on this Point.

The Bishops of Prussia, of Austria, of Belgium, of Holland, of Canada, and of the United States, in their pastorals, their synodical addresses, and in their other publications, condemn with one accord the mixed system, and declare that education based upon our holy religion is alone suitable for Catholic children. Not to multiply quotations, it will suffice to cite the following extract from the address of the Plenary Synod of the Church of the United States, held at Baltimore, in the year 1866. That Council was one of the most numerous assemblies held after the Council of Trent, until the meeting of the General Council of the Vatican. Its decrees were signed by seven Archbishops, thirty-seven Bishops, two procurators of absent Bishops, and two Abbots.

"ADDRESS OF THE PLENARY SYNOD OF BALTIMORE, UNITED STATES.

"The experience of every day shows more and more plainly what serious evils and great dangers are entailed upon Catholic youth by their frequentation of Public Schools in this country. Such is the nature of the system of teaching therein employed, that it is not possible to prevent young Catholics from incurring, through its influence, danger to their faith and morals; nor can we ascribe to any other cause that destructive spirit of indifferentism which has made, and is now making, such rapid strides in this country, and that corruption of morals which we have to deplore in those of tender years. Familiar intercourse with those of false religions, or of no religion; the daily use of authors who assail with calumny and sarcasm our holy religion, its practices, and even its saints—these gradually impair, in the minds of Catholic children, the vigor and influence of the true religion. Besides, the morals and examples of their fellow-scholars are generally so corrupt, and so great their license in word and deed, that through continual contact with them the modesty and piety of our children, even of those who have been best trained at home, disappear like wax before the fire. These evils and dangers did not escape the knowledge of our predecessors, as we learn from the following decrees:

"'(*a*) Whereas many Catholic children, especially those born of poor parents, have been, and are still, exposed in several places of this province, to great danger of losing their faith and morals, owing to the want of good masters to whom their education may safely be intrusted, we consider it absolutely necessary that schools should be established in which the young may be imbued with the principles of faith and morality, and at the same receive instruction in letters.'"—*Council of Baltimore, No. 33.*

Teachings of the Supreme Pontiff, Pius IX.

In fine, to show the union of the Bishops throughout the world with the Apostolic See in their teaching respecting education, I add the words of the Supreme Pontiff Pope Pius IX., in which, replying to the Archbishop of Freiburg, in Germany, His Holiness clearly expounds, as the Infallible Teacher of the faithful, the truth I am now developing for the instruction of Catholics:

"It is not wonderful that these unhappy efforts (to spread irreligious and revolutionary principles) should be directed chiefly to corrupt the training and education of youth; and there is no doubt that the greatest injury is inflicted on society, when the directing authority and salutary power of the Church are withdrawn from public and private education, on which the happiness of the Church and of the Commonwealth depends so much. For thus society is, little by little, deprived of that truly Christian spirit which alone can permanently secure the foundation of peace and public order, and promote and direct the true and useful progress of civilization, and give man those helps which are necessary for him in order to attain, after this life, his last end hereafter—eternal happiness. And in truth a system of teaching, which not only is limited to the knowledge of natural things, and does not pass beyond the bounds of our life on earth, but also departs from the truth revealed by God, must necessarily be guided by the spirit of error and lies; and education, which, without the aid of the Christian doctrine and of its salutary moral precepts, instructs the minds and moulds the tender heart of youth, which is so prone to evil, must infallibly produce a generation which will have no guide but its own wicked passions and wild conceits, and which will be a source of the greatest misfortunes to the Commonwealth and their own families.

"But if this detestable system of education, so far removed from Catholic faith and ecclesiastical authority, becomes a source of evils, both to individuals and to society, when it is employed in the higher teaching, and in schools frequented by the better class, who does not see that the same system will give rise to still greater evils, if it be introduced into primary schools? For it is in these schools, above all, that the children of the people ought to be carefully taught from their tender years the mysteries and precepts of our holy religion, and to be trained with diligence to piety, good morals, religion and civilization. In such schools religious teaching ought to have so leading a place in all that concerns education and instruction, that whatever else the children may learn should appear subsidiary to it. The young, therefore, are exposed to the greatest perils whenever, in the schools, education is not closely united with religious teaching. Wherefore, since primary schools are established chiefly to give the people a religious education, and to lead them to piety and Christian morality, they have justly attracted to themselves, in a greater degree than other educational institutions, all the care, solicitude, and vigilance of the Church. The design of withdrawing primary schools from the control of the Church, and the exertions made to carry this design into effect, are therefore inspired by a spirit of hostility towards her, and by the desire of extinguishing among the people the divine light of our holy faith. The Church, which has founded these schools, has ever regarded them with the greatest care and interest, and looked upon them as the chief object of her ecclesiastical authority and government; and whatsoever removed them from her, inflicted serious injury both on her and on the schools. Those who pretend that the Church ought to abdicate or suspend her control and her salutary action upon the primary schools, in reality ask her to disobey the commands of her Divine Author, and to be false to the charge she has received from God, of guiding all men to salvation; and in whatever country this pernicious design of removing the schools from the ecclesiastical authority should be entertained and carried into execution, and the young thereby exposed to the danger of losing their faith, there the Church would be in duty bound not only to use her best efforts, and to employ every means to secure for them the necessary Christian education and instruction, but, moreover, would feel herself obliged to warn all the faithful, and to declare that no one can in conscience frequent such schools, as being adverse to the Catholic Church."

I exclaim with the great St. Augustine: "Securus judicat orbis terrarum." The Bishops of the universal world, united to the Vicar of Christ, speak with authority; their judgment cannot be gainsaid. Peter has spoken through Pius; the question is settled; would that the error, too, were at an end!

Testimonies of Enemies of the Catholic Church.

However, it is not from the Bishops alone that we learn the dangers of bad education. Our opponents, too, the enemies of our holy religion, deem no other means more efficacious for alienating our children from our mother, the Catholic Church.

One of the greatest enemies of the Catholic faith in the first half of the last century, Primate Boulter, who took a chief part in founding the notorious "Charter Schools," writing to the Bishop of London on the fifteenth of May, 1730, said:

"I can assure you the Papists here are so numerous, that it highly concerns us in point of interest, as well as out of concern for the salvation of these poor creatures who are our fellow-subjects, to try all possible means to bring them and theirs to the true religion; and one of the most likely methods we can think of is, if possible, *instructing and converting the young generation*; for instead of converting these that are adults, we are daily losing many of our meaner people, who go off to Popery."

And with respect to mixed education in particular, we have the opinion of another Anglican prelate, who, in despite of his professions of liberality, may be fittingly classed with Primate Boulter in his contempt for our people, and desire to subvert our holy religion by the means of education—the late Protestant Archbishop of Dublin, Dr. Whately. We are informed by his daughter, that on one occasion he said: "The education supplied by the National Board is gradually undermining the vast fabric of the Irish Roman Catholic Church.". (*Life of Dr. Whately*, pp. 244, first edition.) Again: "I believe, as I said the other day, that *mixed education* is gradually enlightening the mass of the people, and that if we give it up, we give the only hope of weaning the Irish from the abuses of Popery. But I cannot venture openly to profess this opinion, I cannot openly support the Educational Board as an instrument of conversion. I have to fight its battles with one hand, and that my best, tied behind me." (p. 246.)

The language of the Church, then, and even that of the enemies of our religion, is quite plain on the subject of godless education. The good Catholic understands this language of his spiritual mother; he listens to it; he repeats it to himself and others, and he goes by it. Not long ago the Catholics of Ireland presented a requisition to the English Government to show their unanimity, and their determination to secure a Catholic education for Catholic children. What a glorious array of signatures is attached to it! There we find the honored names of the only Catholic lords that the operation of penal laws has left in that land ever faithful to the Church. There we read the names of the Lord Mayor, and the aldermen and town councillors of the great City of Dublin, of many baronets and deputy lieutenants, of several members of Parliament, magistrates, high sheriffs, clergymen, wealthy merchants, and land-owners; of men distinguished in the various scientific and literary professions or pursuits; of country gentlemen, traders, artisans, and of all the classes that constitute the bone and sinew of the country. In a word, the requisition is signed by more than 30,000 Catholics of every degree. May it not be considered as a great plebiscite? Is it not a proof that the laity and clergy are all of one mind? Is it not a solid refutation of the foolish assertion of some Presbyterians, that the Catholic laity take no interest in the education question, and that, were it not for the priests, the laity would be perfectly satisfied to accept godless instruction for their children? Those who attribute this baneful indifference to the laity, misrepresent and calumniate them, and show their ignorance of their real feelings, and of the efforts which Catholics in Ireland, in Belgium, in Germany, and in other countries, have made to have and to preserve a good Christian education for their children. The principal Catholic gentlemen in Ireland some time ago published an important declaration, presented afterwards to Parliament, in which they proclaimed their adhesion to the principles held by the true Church in regard to education.

As for the Catholic laity of Ireland in general, feeling, as they do in a special manner, the signal blessing they enjoy in possessing the true faith, and knowing that it is a priceless treasure with which, far more precious than worldly substance, they can enrich their children, their love for Catholic education is proved to evidence by the multitudes of their sons and daughters who throng every Catholic school, and especially every school in which the presence of Christian Brothers or of Nuns gives a guarantee that religion shall have the first place, and shall impregnate the whole atmosphere which their little ones are to breathe for so many hours of the day. They have proved, also, their dislike and fear of mixed education, by turning their faces away from schools in which no expense had been spared, on which thousands of pounds of the public money had been squandered, but against which their Bishops deemed it their duty to warn them. Hence, in several Model Schools erected in populous cities and towns, where the great majority of the inhabitants are Catholics, sometimes not ten, sometimes not two of their children are found within the unhallowed precincts of those mixed institutions.

In fine, the opinion of all the Irish Catholics on this subject of education is so well known, that nearly all of the Liberal candidates who sought their votes at the last elections for the House of Commons, declared in their electioneering addresses their adhesion to the principle of denominational education, and their determination to uphold it, and push it forward in Parliament.

And with good reason are they steadfast in those principles, for they know the necessary connection between good education and the maintenance of religion in their country. And they are determined to struggle for the establishment, in Ireland, of a sound Catholic system of public education, and never to relax their efforts till they obtain the recognition of this, their own and their children's right, even as they wrung Catholic emancipation from a hostile Parliament.

Thus the Catholic laity practise what their pastors teach; and in Ireland and other countries, both pastors and people are united in holding that nothing so effectually destroys religion in a country as a godless system of instruction, whilst they believe, at the same time, that a good Christian education contributes to preserve true religion, and to spread the practice of every virtue and of good works through the land.

Though the Catholic Church and her children are so anxious for the progress of knowledge, and have made such sacrifices for the civilization and enlightenment of the world, yet they do not indiscriminately approve of every system of education. Every one knows how much is done in our days, by the enemies of religion, to poison the sources of knowledge, and to undermine religion, under the pretext of promoting the liberal arts and sciences. In order to give a proper impulse to study, by securing protection for it, some insist that the full control of public instruction should be given to the government of each country, to be carried on by Ministers of State, or public boards; others attach so much importance to the development of the intellectual faculties, that they call for compulsory and gratuitous education, in order to give a great degree of culture to all classes; and others, in fine, demand an unsectarian education, pretending that God should be banished from the school, and children brought up without being subjected to any religious influences. The Catholic Church and her pastors, being charged to feed the flock of Christ with the food of truth and life, and to preserve the lambs of the fold from the contagion of error, cannot approve such systems, which seem to have been invented by the fashion of the day, a desire of innovation, or a spirit of hostility to religion.

It was to His Church, and not to the State, that Jesus Christ gave the command, "Go and teach all nations."—(Matt. xxviii.) "As the Father hath sent Me, so do I send you also."—(John xx.) "Feed My lambs, feed My sheep."—(John xxi.)

The office of the Church is to teach and sanctify all men. She receives the child on its first entrance into the world, and, by means of holy baptism, makes it a child of God. Like her Divine Bridegroom, she says: "Suffer the little children to come to me."

Now the Christian school is the place and the provision made for the training of those who are baptized into the Christian faith. They have been made children of God, and as such they have a right to four things belonging to them by a right of inheritance, to which all other rights are secondary. They have a right to the knowledge of their faith; to the training of their conscience by the knowledge of God's commandments; to the Sacraments of grace; and to a moral formation, founded on the precepts and example of our Divine Saviour. These four things belong, by a Divine right, to the child of the poorest working man; by a right more sacred than that which guards the inheritance of lands and titles to the child of the rich. A child of God, and an heir to the kingdom of heaven, holds these four things by a higher title; and his claim is under the jurisdiction of a Divine Judge. But the school is the place and the provision for the insuring of these four vital parts of his right to the Christian child. They cannot be taught or learned elsewhere; there is no other place of systematic and sufficient formation. And if so, then the school becomes the depository of the rights of parents, and of the inheritance of their children. The school is strictly a court of the Temple, a porch outside the Sanctuary. It cannot be separated from the Church. It was created by the Church, and the Church created it for its own mission to its children. As the Church cannot surrender to any power on earth the formation of its own children, so it cannot surrender to any the direction of its own schools.

It was the Church, as I have shown in the second chapter, that gave life and being to Christian education; and education must remain under the guardianship of the Church, if it will not cease to be Christian. History shows us that it is the Church that has civilized the nations, and it is the Church that keeps them from falling back into their former degradation. Learning was not diffused among mankind until the Church removed the veil of sin and ignorance, made man really free, and widened the narrow limits of human thought by showing to man the infinite, the eternal destiny that awaited him. This supernatural light—this "freedom of the children of God"—is the very foundation, the very lifespring of civilization. The Catholic Church, then, far from being opposed to education, is its great and most zealous promoter. But she cannot help being opposed to the Pagan system of education adopted in the Public Schools of this country.

It is clear that this plan takes away the right of parents, whom God has charged with the care of their children, and it must necessarily interfere with the proper management of families. In the second place, it ignores the rights of the Church, to whom Christ gave the commission to teach all nations. In the third place, since governments, as constituted at present, have no religion, the teaching they give must tend to infidelity. In the fourth place, if governments take into their hands the management of things which do not appertain to them, the probability is that they will neglect, or carry on badly, the great temporal affairs which it is their duty to attend to. In the last place, experience shows that education carried on by the State is most expensive, and that it opens the way to intrigues and frauds. To confirm all these observations, it is sufficient to refer to France, where State influence has been supreme for the last seventy years in university education, and where the Government has exercised an exorbitant control over every branch of public instruction. What has been the result? Literature has fallen away, the number of schools has decreased, the French language has decayed, whilst moral corruption has penetrated the heart of the country, and infidelity of the worst kind has been patronized and encouraged among the teachers of youth, and the highest honors have been decreed to Littres and Renans, and other decided enemies of Jesus Christ. May we not read the condemnation of all such proceedings in the lurid flames of the burning Capital of modern civilization? Now, is it not clear that the primary object of education must be frustrated in the mixed system which proposes to unite children of all religions in the same school, and to treat of nothing in the class hours that could offend any of these discordant elements? If there be a Jew in the school, you cannot speak of the Gospel; if there be a Mahometan, nothing could be said against polygamy, and other degrading doctrines of the Koran; due respect must also be paid to the teaching of Arians and Socinians, who deny the Trinity of persons in God, and the Divinity of Christ; and to the opinions of Calvinists and Lutherans, of Methodists and other sectaries, who assail almost every point of revealed religion. In this case, how can the atmosphere of the school be religious; and must not children living in it grow up in ignorance both of the dogmas and practices of religion?

This result may not be unacceptable to those who are outside the Catholic Church, because, not acknowledging any Divine authority to guide or rule them, they have no certainty in doctrinal matters, and they do not attach any importance to external discipline. But how different is the case with Catholics! We have many distinctive doctrines, such as the Real Presence in the Blessed Eucharist, the power of remitting sin, the Divine origin of the Church, and the primacy and infallibity of the Pope, all which it is our duty to learn and to believe. We are also bound to observe many precepts, to hear Mass, to pray and make the sign of the Cross, to go to confession, to fast and abstain, and to obey other commandments of the Church. If these doctrines, so sublime, and so far above the intelligence of man, be not continually inculcated on the mind of a child, how can he know them, or believe them as he ought? And if the practices referred to be not frequently urged on his attention, will he not ignore or neglect them because they are hard to flesh and blood? And what will be the case where the Protestant pupils in a school are in a considerable majority, and the teacher of the same religion? Will not the Protestant children turn the doctrines and practices of the Catholics into ridicule? And will not the example, and the words, and the gestures of the heterodox master, especially if he be kind and friendly, produce impressions dangerous to belief on the youthful Catholic mind? Is it not probable that a Catholic boy, observing how his master, to whom he looks up with respect, is accustomed to act, will easily persuade himself that there is no necessity of going to confession, or fasting, or making the sign of the cross, or performing works of mortification? Indeed, the probability is that Catholics educated in such circumstances, if they do not abandon their religion altogether, will be only lukewarm, indifferent, or dangerous members of the Church.

And here let me direct your attention to another dangerous tendency of godless education. In this system all religions, true or false, are treated with equal respect; not only Anglicans and Presbyterians, but Wesleyans and Plymouth Brothers, and the followers of every other small and miserable sect that has started into existence in modern times, are put on a footing of equality with the true Catholic Church, which traces its origin back to its Divine Founder, has existed in every age, defied the fury of persecution and the ravages of time, and numbers under its sceptre two hundred millions of faithful children spread over the world. And is not this to proclaim that there is no difference between light and darkness, no preference to be given to Christ over Belial, to truth over heresy, and error and infidelity? In a word, is not this to teach indifference to religion, or, what is equivalent, that no religion is necessary? What shall I now say of books so compiled as to meet the exigencies of godless education? Have they not the same tendency to promote ignorance of, or indifference to, religion? No religious dogmatical teaching, no inculcation of pious practices, no mention of the great and sublime mysteries of Catholicity can be admitted in them, lest some things should be said offensive to any sect that sends children to the school. This suppression of Catholic truth is most detrimental to our poor Catholic children, many of whom never read any books except those which they use in school, and learn nothing except what they meet with in those books, or hear from their master. Is not this a serious loss? Is it not a great evil for Catholics to be brought up in ignorance, not only of the doctrines, but also of the history of the Church to which they belong, and of the life and deeds of so many Christian heroes whose virtues illustrated the world?

How far superior is the system of the Christian Brothers, and other Catholic educational institutions! Their books make continual reference to the mysteries of religion, they depict the glories of the Church, the majesties of the Apostolic See, and continually inflame the youthful mind to the practice of good works, by proposing to them the lives and virtues of holy men, and by continually reminding them of their religious duties, of the end of man, and of other great motives calculated to induce them to serve God. In regard to this matter, I shall merely add that the common school-books have been generally compiled by Protestants, that scarcely any extract from Catholic authors is admitted in them, that they contain many Methodistical stories, that their language is that of the Protestant Bible, and that they contain many things offensive to our love of religion.

Do you want to see what man without God—without religion—can do? Read the history of the last eighty years in Paris. You have there one simple phenomenon—generation rising after generation, without God in the world. And why? Because, without Christian education. First, an atheistical revolution; next, an empire penetrated through with a masking philosophy and a reckless indifferentism; afterwards came governments changed in name and in form, but not in practice, nor in spirit. The Church, trammelled by protection, her spiritual action faint and paralyzed, could not penetrate the masses of the people, and bring her salutary influence to bear upon them. She labored fervently; her sons fought nobly for Christian freedom; thousands were saved; but for eighty years the mass of men has grown up without God and without Christ in the world. These outbursts of horror, strife, outrage, sacrilege, bloodshed, are the harvest reaped from the rank soil in which such seed was cast. All this is true. But how did souls created to the image of God grow up in such a state? They were robbed: robbed before they were born; robbed of their inheritance, and reared up in an education without Christianity. Let this be a warning to ourselves! We are told that a child may be taught to read, and to write, and to spell, and to sum, without Christianity. Who denies it? But what does this make of them? To what do they grow up? The formation of the will and heart and character, the formation of a man, is education, and not the reading, and the writing, and the spelling, and the summing. Physiology, astronomy, chemistry, anatomy, and all other sciences with sounding names, and of Greek etymology, will not teach our children the respect, love, and obedience due to parents. They will not teach them modesty, which is the brightest ornament of woman, and renders the relation of man with his fellow-man harmonious and pleasant. They will not teach them industry and purity, which insure peace and happiness in the family circle. They will not teach them the fidelity which the espoused owe to each other, nor the obligations contracted by parents towards their children, nor will they teach them to know, love, and serve God in this world, in order to be happy with Him forever in the next.

For fifteen hundred years Christians served God and loved man, before, as yet, they received this cultivation of our age; and we, because we have it so profusely, are forgetting the deeper and diviner lessons. The tradition of Christian education in this country is, as yet, unbroken. It has, however, been greatly undermined. It will be completely broken if we Catholics do not strive, to the best of our power, to preserve it. We Catholics, therefore, believe that it is our most sacred duty to bring up our children in "the discipline and correction of the Lord." We hold that it is our most conscientious obligation to bequeath to our children the most valuable of all legacies—good religious impressions, and a sound religious education. We hold that religious education is the most essential part of instruction.

Now we know that religious education *is not*, and cannot, be given in our present school system. Our present system of common-school education either ignores religion altogether, or teaches principles which are false and dangerous; and if it gives any religious education, it consists merely in certain vague, unmeaning generalities, and is often worse than no education at all. Instruction without religion, is like a ship without a compass. Ignorance is, indeed, a great evil; but of the two evils, it is even better, in some respects, for our children to remain ignorant, than to acquire mere worldly knowledge without any religious training; for without religion they grow up a burden to themselves, and a pest to society.

Human nature is prone to evil; and the rising passions, especially in youth, need religious influence to check them. There is a vast difference between teaching the child's *head* and forming his *heart*. Mere instruction in reading, writing, and arithmetic will never teach a young man to control his passions, and to practise virtue. Such instruction may do for Pagans, but it will never do for Catholics.

We can say that, so far as our Catholic children are concerned, the workings of our Public School system have proved, and do prove, highly detrimental to their faith and morals. So strongly has the conviction of this been impressed upon the minds both of the pastors and parents, that most strenuous efforts, and even enormous sacrifices have been made, and continue to be made, in order to establish and support Catholic parochial schools. In many cities of the Union there is, at the present moment, in daily attendance at these schools, an average number of between eighteen and twenty thousand children. The annual expense for the maintenance of these schools does not fall short of one hundred thousand dollars; while the amount expended for the purchase of lots, and the erection of proper school buildings, etc., considerably exceeds a million.

The Catholics of New York subscribed, in 1868, $132,000 for the support of their own school, and, besides, they had contributed a million and a quarter of dollars for the sites and the buildings of Catholic schools.

Nothing but the deepest sense of the many dangers to which the religious and moral principles of the children are exposed, could prompt Catholic parents to make such pecuniary sacrifices, or assume such onerous burdens; for it has to be borne in mind that, while they are thus obliged, through conscientious motives, to support their own schools, they have, at the same time, to bear their share of the taxation imposed for the support of the Public Schools.

All this is true; yet I can scarcely refrain from expressing my surprise at the extremely abnormal lethargy manifested by so many Catholics, both in high and low places, regarding a duty, the chief one incumbent upon them as members of the family, as citizens, as Christians and as Catholics.

Now the cause for the indifference existing among our people on the question of Catholic education, may be attributed to a false process of reasoning. They argue: it will cost money. True; but it is not by *State* aid, or *City* aid, that the work of Catholic daily instruction and education in parochial schools is to be carried on. These schools are to be supported, as our *churches* are, by the alms of the faithful.

The Catholics of other countries have their duties to perform, different, in part, from ours, but demanding great self-sacrifice. We, too, except we be "bastards, and not sons," must make our great sacrifices. The first, the most pressing, is that of supporting a good Catholic education. In neglecting Catholic education, we lose that which money cannot buy. Can we conceive of a parent, a Catholic parent, so cruel, so depraved, and so God-forsaken as to sacrifice his child, both body and soul, and devote him to eternal destruction, through eagerness to spare the paltry pence that a proper education might cost? It seems quite certain that if we wait for just appropriations from the State before we shoulder the burden ourselves, wait for it to compel us to accept of Catholic education, we shall find ourselves in a very unfit condition to appreciate the favor; and from present indications, this generation, at least, is likely to pass away before such interest will be manifested in our behalf.

Now we must be persuaded that if we allow one generation to be brought up in unbelief, and the course of tradition to be once interrupted, the following generations will fall into a darkness and ignorance worse than that of Paganism; living here without a God, and quitting this world without any consoling hope of a blessed immortality.

So it proved, not long ago, with an unhappy wretch, the child of parents that had forgotten the law of their God, and sent her to one of the Public Schools in a town on the North River. She played the harlot, when she grew old enough, and then sought to add to this the crime of a horrible *murder*—the murder of the child that was of her own flesh and blood. In procuring its murder, she lost her own life. In the den of the monster-abortionist, and finding herself dying, one of the vile attendants now declares that she shrieked and begged for a Catholic priest. The Jew into whose murderous gripe she had put herself, found some means to quiet her cry, and she died without seeing a priest. God will keep His word! He has said, "Because *thou* hast forgotten the law of thy God, I will *forget thy children*!"

I do not say that Catholic parents are obliged, under the pain of mortal sin, to have *any* secular education given to their children. But I do say that they *are forbidden*, by the law of the Catholic Church, to send their children to *any* schools where the Catholic religion is not *practised and taught*.

If neglect to comply with the law of God and of His Church, neglect to receive the sacraments at certain times, and under certain circumstances, is a mortal sin, is it much less a sin to neglect the proper education of our youth, upon which, to a great extent, their entire future depends? And if the sacraments are refused to persons persisting in sin, should not a sin of this great character be also considered in the conditions requisite for the worthy reception of the sacraments? I hesitate not to pronounce this matter of education a matter of conscience, and it should be treated accordingly by those who have the charge of souls. We see ecclesiastical edifices of great magnitude, splendor, and expense, erected everywhere by Catholics, but for what purpose? To attract non-Catholics? Bosh! A Catholic can hear Mass in caverns, in catacombs, or under hedges, as they have often been obliged to do; but if we lose our children there will be none to hear it anywhere, nor any to offer the Holy Sacrifice, even in our most gorgeous cathedrals. Where will be our Catholics? Scandal and disgrace will be the order of the day.

I do not wish it to be understood here that I entertain any, even the least, doubt of the indefectibility of the Church, or of the faithful fulfilment of the promises of Christ; for the Church will exist in spite of man. But again I say that Catholics are violating a most sacred duty in not providing facilities for Catholic education.

This, O Catholics! is what the money you are making so rapidly ought, in generous part, to be devoted to. So *you* will think, at a day fast coming, when your bodies will be buried sumptuously, your souls forgotten by the living, and the estates you have hoarded with so much industry shall have become, perhaps, the objects of disgraceful law-suits among your heirs.

Dear Catholics, let us cast off our lethargy; let us be unitedly active in this matter; let us discard the flimsy arguments of "*liberal*" Catholics who would discourage the enterprise, regarding every such as our most dangerous foe. Let us make our voice heard and our actions felt, and bring up our children in a manner creditable to ourselves, an honor and consolation to their parents, a blessing to society, worthy members of the Church of God, and candidates for the kingdom of heaven.

CHAPTER XIV.

ANSWERS TO OBJECTIONS.

There are some who assert that "there is no sectarian teaching in the Public Schools, and consequently a Catholic may send his children to them without exposing them to any danger." Now even supposing there really were no sectarian teaching in the common schools, even then a Catholic parent cannot send his children to such a school without exposing them to the greatest danger. Those who approve of the Public Schools because nothing sectarian is taught there, act like a certain husbandman who wished to transplant a fine young tree to a certain part of his garden. On examining the new place, however, he found that the ground was filled with poisonous ingredients, which would greatly endanger the life of the tree. He therefore transplanted the tree to a sandy hill, where there were, indeed, no poisonous ingredients, but where there was also no nourishment for the tree. Now will any one assert that the young tree was not in danger of perishing in this new place? And will any one assert that the faith and soul of a child are not in danger of being ruined in those godless common schools? Even if Protestantism is not taught there, infidelity is taught and practised there, and infidelity is even worse than Protestantism.

But is it really true that Protestantism is not taught in many of our Public Schools? This is unfortunately far from being the case. Napoleon I. introduced the Public School system into France, in order, as he honestly declared, "to possess the means of controlling political and moral opinions." Puritans and Freemasons, in this country, have clearly the same end in view in upholding the present system of Public Schools.

In the early days of New England, and even of several of the other American States, the Puritans always used the Public Schools as a powerful means of spreading their peculiar doctrines. When they were stripped of this power by the liberal founders of American independence, they still struggled for many years to accomplish, by indirect means, the injustice which they dared not *maintain* openly. We all remember how the poor Catholic boys and girls of the Public Schools were harassed by colporteurs and proselytizers, who carried baskets filled, not with bread for the poor hungry children, no, but with oily tracts, cunningly devised to weaken, or even destroy, the religious faith of those poor little ones. In some schools even, Catholic children were urged and enticed to go to the sectarian Sunday-schools, and pictures, cakes, and sweetmeats were liberally promised, in order to induce them to go. Teachers were selected with special regard to their bitter hatred of the Catholic Church, and their zeal for "evangelical" propagandism.

Some years ago, in New Orleans, when the school-board was composed of bigoted sectarians, many of them sectarian preachers, all the Catholic teachers, male and female, were turned out of the schools, merely because they were Catholics.

And even if Catholic children are not always expressly taught doctrines opposed to their religion, nevertheless the school-books which they use are, as I have said, frequently tainted with anti-Catholic prejudices and misrepresentations. Nothing can be more evident than the decidedly anti-Catholic spirit of English literature in all its departments. It has grown up, ever since England's apostasy, in an anti-Catholic soil, in an anti-Catholic atmosphere, and from an anti-Catholic stem. It is essentially anti-Catholic, and tends, wherever it comes in contact with Catholic feelings and principles, to sully, infect, and utterly corrupt them. *Sound knowledge*, a *sound head, strong faith*, and *great grace*—all these combined—may indeed preserve one whom the necessity of his position may lead into un-Catholic schools; but no one will deny that this anti-Catholic literature must exercise a most baneful influence over all those who, without sufficient preparation from nature or grace, plunge into it, in the pursuit of amusement or knowledge. Protestant ideas will not make the Catholic turn Protestant, there is not much danger of that, but they will tend to make him an infidel; they will destroy his principles without putting others in their place; they will relax and deaden the whole spiritual man.

In these schools, Catholic children are taught that the Catholic Church is the nursery of ignorance and vice; they are taught that all the knowledge, civilization, and virtue which the world now possesses, are the offspring of the so-called "Reformation." They learn nothing of the true history of Spain, Portugal, Italy, France, Ireland, Austria, and the other Catholic countries of Europe; they learn nothing of the true history of Mexico, and the various Catholic countries of North and South America. They never hear of the vast libraries of Catholic learning, the rich endowments of Catholic education all over the world, for ages; they never hear of the countless universities, colleges, academies, and free schools established by the Catholic Church, and by Catholic governments, throughout Christendom. Where is the common school book whose author has manly honesty enough to acknowledge that even the famous universities of Oxford and Cambridge were founded by Catholics, and plundered from their lawful possessors by an apostate government?

Moreover, Catholic children are often singled out by their school-companions, and sometimes even by their teachers, as objects of ridicule. Now what is the result of all this training? The consequence is, that either the Catholic children become ashamed of their holy religion, and despise their parents, or, if they have the courage to hold out, their tender minds are subject to numberless petty annoyances; they must endure a species of martyrdom. This is no exaggeration; I have it from good authority. Practically speaking, the present common school system is but a gigantic scheme for proselytism and for infidelity.

Now we intend that our children shall be taught to love and revere their holy Church. We wish to teach them that that Church has been, for over eighteen hundred years, the faithful guardian of that very Bible of which Protestants prate so loudly, and which they dishonor so much. We wish our children to learn that the

Catholic Church has been, in all ages, the friend and supporter of true liberty; *i.e.*, liberty united to order and justice. We wish them to know that the Catholic Church has ever been the jealous guardian of the sanctity of marriage; that she has always defended it against brutal lust, and heathen divorce courts. We wish our children to know, moreover, that the Catholic Church holds the sword of vengeance uplifted above the heads of the child-murderers, and the perpetrators of unnatural crimes. We wish our children, in fine, to regard the Church as the only hope of society, the only salvation of their country, the only means of preserving intact all the blessings of freedom.

The Public Schools are not only seminaries of infidelity, they are, moreover, in many cases, hot-beds of immorality. In these schools every child is received, no matter how vicious or corrupt he or his parents may be. "One mangy sheep," as the homely proverb says, "infects the whole flock." So one corrupt child in a school is capable of corrupting and ruining all the others. And, in fact, where have our young people learned the shameful habit of self-abuse, and many other foul, unnatural crimes, that are bringing so many thousands to an early grave? Ask those unhappy victims, ask our physicians throughout the country, and they will tell you that, in almost every instance, it was from the evil companions with whom they associated in the common schools. Ah! you will see, only on the Day of Judgment, how many unnatural crimes have been taught and propagated, from generation to generation, in these very hot-beds of iniquity.

"But, Father," some one will say, "what harm can there be in sending children to Public Schools? for many of the teachers are professing Christians, and exert a continual Christian influence."

But many more are non-professors, and exert an anti-Christian influence. Go and visit those schools, and you will soon be able to tell the religious *status* of the teachers in charge, by the general tone of the exercises. One presided over by a zealous Methodist resembles a Methodist Sunday-school, or conference meeting. Another, under the care of a "smart young man," delighting in love songs, boating songs, etc., has the general tone of a young folks' glee-club. In another, in which one of the professors is an atheist, it is a matter of common remark among the boys that Prof. — — said there was no God. In another, one of the teachers is overheard sneering at a child because she believes in our Lord Jesus Christ, and has a reverence for religious things.

What I have just said is true. I have it from good authority. It is therefore no recommendation at all for the Public School system to say that many of the teachers are professing Christians. Even the very fact that many of the teachers in the Public Schools are good Catholics, is no recommendation whatever for these schools, for it matters nothing, absolutely nothing, whether the teacher be Catholic or not; according to *law*, no teacher is allowed to explain a single dogma of Catholic faith. Now the dogmas of our holy faith have been *revealed*, and, in order to be known, *they must be taught*. Ordinarily speaking, education is necessary to learn and preserve the faith. The Catholics of Ireland, indeed, by the special assistance of God, preserved their holy faith, though they were not permitted, by a bigoted government, to receive the education they needed and desired. But in this country, where there is no such prohibition, where parents are free to send their children to Catholic schools, it is presumption in them, it is a rash defiance to the ordinary laws of God's providence, to neglect the daily systematic training of the minds and hearts of their children, in conformity with Catholic discipline. Julian the Apostate forbade Catholics to be educated in their holy faith, for he knew very well that there is no more certain means of destroying the faith than by not suffering it to be taught.

It is almost certain that wherever there are no Catholic schools, wherever the Catholic religion is not taught and practised in school, there the Catholic religion will practically die out, as soon as immigration from Catholic countries ceases.

Bishop England has asserted that the Catholic Church loses more, in this country, by apostasy, than it gains by conversions. Archbishop Spalding, of Baltimore, asserted one day that, in one body of Methodist ministers, he observed seven or eight who were children of Catholics, and they were the smartest preachers among them.

Neglected children of Catholic parents become the worst enemies of the Catholic Church. The young man who set fire to St. Augustine's Church, in Philadelphia, Pa., was a Catholic, and he gloried in being able to burn his name out of the baptismal record. By a just punishment of God, these neglected Catholic children will become our persecutors.

It is not sufficient to teach the Catechism in church or at home. No! it is not the *knowledge* of the faith, but the *daily practice* of it, that produces Catholic life. Nothing but the constant practice of our holy religion can train our youth to withstand the dangers of this age, and this country. It is not necessary to argue this point. Look at the tens of thousands of Catholics who never think of going to Mass on a week-day, and who often neglect it even on Sundays and holy days. Look at all those who never think of visiting our Lord in the Blessed Sacrament; who never go to confession more than once or twice a year, and sometimes not even that. Do they not prove, beyond a doubt, that the practical *habit* of devotion was not taught them in their youth?

Look, on the other hand, at those congregations who, in the tender, susceptible time of youth, were in the habit of going to Mass every day before the opening of the school. See how, when the bell rings, a goodly number of them find time, even on week-days, to assist at the most holy Sacrifice of the Mass. In such congregations there is indeed Catholic life. These pious Catholics carry the blessing of heaven with them wherever they go. Amid all the cares and troubles of life they are gay and cheerful, whilst others grumble and are sad. The religious doctrines and practices learned in youth, can seldom or never be blotted out. The question of Catholic schools is a question of making the country Catholic. If this means be neglected, all other means will avail but little.

There are others, again, who assert "that the discussion of the education question should be put off for the present as yet, under the pretence that our adversaries are as yet too numerous, and that it is well for us to do nothing until their feelings are more in our favor." If we are to wait until it will please them to say that our claims are just, the day will never dawn when our rights shall be admitted; darkness cannot coalesce with light, vice with virtue, or Belial with Christ. Will those who deny the Divine authority of the Church, assail her doctrines, and seek her destruction, ever cordially assist us in obtaining from our rulers a system of public instruction not dangerous or destructive to our faith? If we consent to defer the education question until the torrent of bigotry will be dried up, we shall be laughed at, and compared to the simple peasant who determined to sit on the bank of a great river and not to attempt to pass it until all its waters should have rolled by; or we shall be compared to the careless farmer who allows rank weeds to grow up in his garden, together with the good plants, till at last the good plants are dwarfed and smothered by the noxious weeds. In my opinion, our own policy with those in authority should be to insist on our rights in season and out of season; and even when our claims may have been slighted or rejected, to continue our demands until every grievance shall be removed.

We must make great exertions to obtain the object of our desires, and display great energy in our proceedings. We have numerous and active enemies to contend with—men as enthusiastic in a bad cause as the Pharisees of the Gospel, who compassed earth and sea to make a proselyte, but who cared very little for his moral progress, once they had secured his adherence to their views. However, we are not left alone in our struggle for religious education. With us we have the sympathy of the Catholics of the world, who are fighting the same battle as we ourselves, and cheer us on by their example. We have with us the blessing of the successor of St. Peter, who has repeatedly approved of the justice of our cause, and we have the sanction of Christ Himself for the safety of the lambs of whose folds we are laboring. But omitting all this, I believe that the most influential and distinguished members, lay and clerical, of the Anglican body, are with us, and that the principal liberal and enlightened Protestants of the Union wish us success.

The State does not interfere with the free exercise of our religion, neither should it interfere with our system of education;—two measures of great importance, well calculated gradually to promote the public welfare of the country. If the State seriously wishes to check the growth of revolution, or to stem the growing torrent of communism and infidelity, they ought to discountenance infidel institutions, and give schools to Catholics, in which they may uphold the true principles of authority, human and Divine, in accordance with the traditions of the Catholic Church of America, and thus strengthen the foundations not only of religion, but of society in general.

Again, some will say, "I do not see why people can object so much to Public Schools; I myself went there, and I think I am as good a Catholic as any one of those who were educated at Catholic schools and institutions."

If you really have tried to be a good Catholic, if you have complied faithfully with all your religious duties, you will have to avow that it is all owing to the beneficial Catholic influence under which you were placed during the time of your scholarship, and afterwards. If you escaped the general contagion of unbelief and vice, remember that it is owing to a kind of miracle of Divine Protection. But what I have said in reference to Public Schools shows sufficiently that such a protection is extended to but few children—it is an exception to the ordinary course of Divine Providence, and God is not bound to grant it to any one.

A certain friend of mine—a man of great learning and experience—wrote to me one day, that "he himself had been, in his youth, subjected to college training; that, be it by nature or by grace, or both combined, he resisted and escaped. But," he adds, "from my observation and experience, I would say it did require a miracle for Catholic youth to escape the damnable effects of a non-Catholic school education." I have had opportunities, in this line, that many a priest has never had. I assert that a Catholic boy of tender years, and perhaps careless training, can be preserved from moral contamination, in public and mixed schools, by nothing less than a miracle. I will not chop logic with any one about it. It is a matter of fact. I therefore assert it as of ascertained result, that in *most* cases—*especially* in those cases where there are enough of Catholics together to have a school of their own—their frequenting a school without religion will land *most* of them in utter carelessness of their religion.

Grace does not destroy *nature*. And it is *nature* that—

"... as the twig is bent, the tree inclines."

But let me ask you, How can you think that you are as good a Catholic as others; you who object to the teaching of the Church, to the persuasion of all sensible men? Indeed, your language betrays you. Your very language convinces me still more of the necessity of having Catholic schools where our children learn the language and imbibe the spirit of their spiritual mother—the Catholic Church. The Public Schools are none the better for your having frequented them. Let us suppose a father wishes to send his children across the ocean. Now he knows for certain that the vessel which is about to leave for the old country will be wrecked; he also knows that a few of the passengers will be saved, as it were, by a miracle, but he knows not who they are. Will he send his children by that vessel?

Now the Public Schools are like a large vessel. The greater part of those who have embarked in it have suffered shipwreck in their faith and good morals. What father, then, will be mad enough to send his children by this vessel, across the ocean of time, to their heavenly fatherland?

There are others, again, who assert "that we must not attempt to have Catholic schools until we can afford to conduct them so as to compete with the Public Schools."

The point in question is godless schools, which are condemned on account of being infidel in principle. Even with all their faults, our schools are, it must be conceded, not infidel, but Christian schools. We are at liberty, there, to teach our children our holy religion whenever we wish. We can give them good books, and bring them up in a religious atmosphere. If we do for the establishment and organization of Catholic schools what we can, God will not hold us responsible for the loss of those of our children who did not profit by their religious education, while, on the contrary, we remain accountable to God for those who, for want of a Catholic education, suffer shipwreck in their faith and morals, and are lost forever. In the sight of God, the above excuse will avail us nothing.

Some, even most of our schools, may have been more or less defective in the beginning. Well, what was the Church at the time of the Apostles? There were then no gorgeous cathedrals as nowadays. The Christians were instructed and sanctified in the Catacombs, and in poor private dwellings. So, in a country like ours, the kingdom of heaven is compared to a mustard seed. Churches and schools are insignificant in the beginning; but, by degrees, more life and splendor is infused into them, and they grow up to perfection.

We honor and venerate the Apostles as the corner-stones of Christianity. Happy, thrice happy, those pastors who lay solid foundations for future Catholic life by establishing nurseries—Catholic schools—for its maintenance and propagation. Their reward will be like unto that of the Apostles. Our successors will bring our feeble beginnings to perfection. This is the natural course of things. We may not have the happiness to witness a plentiful harvest from the seed that we have sown with so much toil and labor; but we should nevertheless bear in mind that those bishops and priests who have the happiness of laying the foundations of future Catholic life in our country, resemble our Lord Jesus Christ, Who suffered His Apostles to perform even greater miracles than He Himself had wrought.

I know the above objection is more frequently made in the New England States than anywhere else. Now it is a well-known fact that the Yankee race is fast dying out. They have either no children at all, or only one or two. Hence it is that the larger portion of the Public School children are the children of Catholic parents. These States foresee that were the Catholic children to leave their schools, their Public School buildings would soon be empty, and stand there as eloquent monuments to tell on the folly of the States for having erected them. Now in order to keep the Catholic children at their schools, and thus keep up their fine lucrative establishments, they have, in several places, taken in the Catholic priests as members of the School Boards. Truly, "the children of this world are wiser in their generation than the children of light." These priests, by accepting the honor! of membership! of the School Board, give, thereby, at least a *tacit approbation* of the godless Public Schools. Thus the State, by conferring this privilege! throws dust into the eyes of the people. It is, therefore, quite evident that were this *tacit approbation* of the Catholic clergy withdrawn, were they to erect Catholic schools, the godless schools would soon be emptied and suspended, and there would hardly be other but Catholic schools. The Catholic teachers of the Public Schools would follow our children, and would be too happy in teaching on Catholic ground, and according to Catholic principles.

Should a sufficient number of children be left for the Public Schools, this would be no reason whatever to fear that our Catholic schools could not compete with the Public Schools; for, generally speaking, Catholic children are more talented than those of Protestants or infidels. The reason of this is easily to be seen: they have been baptized; the veil of sin has been raised from their souls, and the Catholic life which they lead makes their minds brighter, more quick to perceive, and to understand what is difficult. About six months ago the priests of St. James's Church, in New York, exhorted the parents to take their children out of the Public Schools, and send them to Catholic schools. What happened? Three of the Public

School teachers came and complained to the priests that the brightest gems of their school had left, and that, on that account, they could not have the exhibition which they intended soon to give. A short time ago, at an exhibition in Boston, it was a Catholic young lady that took the prize medal.

And after all, the principal object for getting up Catholic schools is not to show off their superiority to, or their equality with, infidel schools—this is not even a secondary end—we want Catholic schools to preserve our Catholic religion, our Catholic traditions, our Catholic spirit and morals; we want them to raise in them children for heaven, not for hell; children for God, not for the devil; children for a happy eternity, not for everlasting damnation. That's all. Hence Jesus Christ, on the Day of Judgment, will not ask parents and pastors of souls whether their schools could compete with infidel schools, but whether they did all in their power to secure the eternal welfare of their children by a good Catholic education.

Father John de Starchia, Provincial of the Friars Minor, made regulations more favorable to worldly science than to the spirit of piety and religion, attaching, as he did, more importance to the education of the mind than to that of the heart. St. Francis of Assisium upbraided him for it, but in vain. So the great servant of God cursed the Provincial, and deposed him at the ensuing chapter. The saint was entreated, by some of his brethren in religion, to withdraw this curse from the Provincial, a learned noble man, and to give him his blessing. But neither the learning nor the noble extraction of the Provincial could prevail upon St. Francis to comply with their request. "I cannot," said he, "bless him whom the Lord has cursed"—a dreadful reply, which soon after was verified. This unfortunate man died exclaiming: "I am damned and cursed for all eternity!" Some frightful circumstances which followed after his death, confirmed his awful prediction. (Life of St. Francis of Assisium.) Such a malediction should strike terror into the hearts of all those who attach more importance to the cultivation of the mind than to that of the heart, and on that account prefer godless Public Schools to Catholic schools.

Again, one may object: "The religious development does not necessarily suppose a literary development too. A person may be illiterate, and yet learned in the science of the saints, and a man may be learned in science, and ignorant of his duty towards God and his fellow-creatures. There were, are, and will be members of the Catholic Church, who, ignorant of science, of book-learning, did not become infidels, but exhibited a practical faith throughout life, and died in the odor of sanctity. Divine faith does not require as a companion, in the individual Catholic, a knowledge of profane literature, but humility, compunction, self-denial, and a contempt of the world. Schools are therefore not absolutely necessary for our children."

As far as the little profit is concerned that mere book-learning does towards enabling the masses of mankind to accomplish the great end of their being—the salvation of their souls—I am disposed to go all lengths with him in this. But he and I must both acknowledge that the whole current of Catholic influence and practice has set in favor of book-learning and of schools. The Popes have been constant in this line, and Catholic Bishops have acted in the same direction.

But grant that *school learning* is of little account. Something even harder is said of *riches*. There is no *woe* on those that spend their time on book-learning; there *is* a "woe to them that are rich"! Nevertheless, Catholics, as others, strive to acquire wealth. So that they do it honestly, the Catholic Church does not condemn it. Book education, like riches, is a means of advancement in the world. The instructed are, on the whole, of greater consideration than the uninstructed. The business of the Catholic Church is to see that this source of power is not turned to the destruction of those that acquire it.

Besides, I fully agree that, as a universal proposition, school-learning, or book-learning, is not necessary to the salvation of souls—which is the *great* end of human life. So far, the objection is correct in saying that *Catholic* schools are not, as a universal proposition, necessary for Catholics.

But, *in hac providentia;* in a condition in which Catholics, like others, are striving that their children may obtain the mastery, *book*-learning is, like money, a grand element of strength and of consideration. This is what those in care of souls must look to. Book-learning and wealth are neither of them against faith. They are simple elements of power—*physical paraphernalia*. The great thing is, how they may be *used*!

Again mark! I do not say that it is of strict obligation for Catholics to send their children to *any* school. For the comparatively few that have at once the means and the disposition, I hold that there is *no* education like that received under the parental roof. *There* is the true home of sturdy independence in men, and of affectionate and chaste devotion in women. Moreover, it is a great good fortune for conscientious parents, with growing childhood around them, to have the charge and responsibility of these children. It is education for parents as well as children. It brings the strong element of parental affection, in aid of all other motives for living a good life, as an example to beloved young ones. We mourn that Catholics, at least, so seldom, when they have the means, make their own houses the schools for their own children. But this can be done by few, comparatively. Nor can select and private schools, with few scholars, and those picked ones, be had. As a matter of fact, the children of most Catholics must receive whatever *school* instruction they get, in large and general schools.

God may, by a miracle, preserve the faith in a whole nation, as He really did in the Irish, because they were *forbidden* to use the ordinary means whereby Catholics bring up their offspring in the faith. But, when Irish men and women come to this country, where there is *no* prohibition of their having Catholic schools, and having their children educated in them, it is, as I have said, a rash defiance of the ordinary laws of God's Providence, to neglect the daily and systematic training of the intellects of their children in conformity with Catholic discipline.

There are some who say "they pay taxes, and they, of course, would like to profit as well as others by their contribution to the school fund." It is nothing but right that they should; but they cannot, and ought not, to do so upon the conditions imposed on them. The Christians of the first centuries paid taxes to the Roman Empire, for they had been taught by their Divine Master to render unto

Cæsar what belonged to Cæsar; but rather than refuse to render to God what belonged to God, rather than give up their faith, or expose themselves to the danger of losing it, they went to the lions.

At a later period, the Irish, so much taunted for their ignorance in reading and writing, paid heavy taxes to the British Government, and, be it said to their honor, they, for a time, deprived themselves of the most useful knowledge, not on account of their opposition to schools, but because when the teachers of their choice were hunted down by government officials, and shot like wild beasts, if caught in the act of teaching, they refused to go to the State schools, which they could not attend without betraying the faith of their ancestors.

We also pay taxes, and will continue to do so in submission to a most unjust law; but, thanks be to God! we are at liberty to seek legal redress, and our exertions should increase until it is obtained by those very means which were used to establish godless schools, viz.: the press, lecturing, preaching, etc., to form, again, *public opinion* in favor of Christian schools, and electing such men to legislatures as are down upon godless schools, and advocate the establishment of Christian schools for the well-being of our country. In the meantime, in order to preserve the true faith, and save the world from the deadly indifference into which it is falling, Catholic schools must be got up, and kept up, at any cost.

Finally, there are some of the clergy who say, "It is so much trouble to get up schools, and to support them—where to get the teachers, and the money to pay them." True, it is troublesome to establish schools; but we have to live on troubles. Our very troubles become our ladder to heaven, if borne for the sake of Jesus Christ. If we do not wish to undergo troubles and trials of every kind for the sake of Jesus, and for the salvation of those for whom He shed His heart's blood, we should not have become priests. Our right and claim to heaven can be established only by following our Lord, and by carrying our cross after Him.

As to the fear of not getting money for building and supporting schools, let us look at those magnificent school-buildings in every city and town of the country. Where did those priests who built them get the money? It was no angel from heaven that brought it. The parents of the children that are educated in these schools gave it. Let us rest assured that money will not be wanting to a priest if his zeal is great enough to show to parents the absolute necessity of Catholic schools, in order to save their children from becoming scourges for society in this life, and from becoming victims of hell in the next. Let a priest unite great charity and affection for children, and he will at once lay hold on the hearts and money of their parents. Those parents who have no money to offer, will most willingly offer their labor for so noble a work. This has been our experience for years in every place where we took charge of a congregation. Let every child—the poor excepted—pay from thirty to forty cents a month. The money thus collected will cover all the expenses for teachers, and for the books of the poor children. Parents are but too happy to have a priest who takes a lively interest in the temporal and eternal happiness of their children. For the promotion of this happiness, parents will give to the priest the last cent they have got—nay, their own hearts' blood, if necessary. This we have witnessed many times. We have established schools in country places, where the people made very little money; yet they were but too happy to give us money for the building and support of schools. There are hundreds of priests who can say the same of themselves. And should there be refractory characters who do not care about a good Catholic education, let us refuse them absolution, as penitents who are not disposed for the worthy reception of the sacraments. We cannot scruple to do this.

The voice of common sense, the voice of sad experience, the voice of Catholic bishops, and especially the voice of the Holy Father, is raised against, and condemns, the Public School system as a huge humbug, injuring, not promoting, personal virtue and good citizenship, and as being most pernicious to Catholic faith, and life, and all good morals. A pastor, therefore, cannot maintain the contrary opinion without incurring great guilt before God and the Church. He cannot allow parents to send their children to such schools of infidelity and immorality. He cannot give them absolution, and say, "Innocens sum!" For he must know and understand that parents are bound before the Almighty to raise their children good Catholics, to plant in their hearts the seed of godliness and parental obedience; this was their promise at the baptismal font. They are bound in conscience to redeem this promise; but they cannot do this, so long as their children go to the Public Schools; for it must be conceded that children attending these godless Public Schools are in *proximate occasion of sin*, and this occasion is in esse for them. This being so, parents cannot receive absolution unless they remove from their children this occasion of sin. "I do not see," says the Archbishop of Cincinnati—and many other bishops say the same—"I do not see how parents can be absolved, if they are not disposed to support Catholic schools, and send their children thereto."

"Duty compels us"—says the Bishop of Vincennes, Ind., in his Pastoral Letter of 1872—"duty compels us to instruct the pastors of our churches to refuse absolution to parents who, having the facilities and means of educating their children in a Christian manner, do, from worldly motives, expose them to the danger of losing their faith. This measure, however, being very rigorous, we intend that it shall be recurred to in extreme cases only, and when all means of persuasion have been exhausted."

As for teachers, there are everywhere many young ladies who have received a splendid education, and who would feel but too happy to become teachers for our children, and bring them up in such a manner as to fit them for business in this life, and for heaven hereafter.

But why so many objections? It was in the following manner that two bishops silenced all such objections, and made Catholic schools spring up all over their dioceses in a short time: they told their priests "that, were they not to have schools within a certain limited time, they would dismiss them from their dioceses; and that, should their parishioners not be willing to provide the means for establishing and supporting Catholic schools, they would withdraw from them their priests." This looks like believing in the Catholic Church. From the moment that the priests saw this determination of their bishop—the people were overjoyed at it—*Catholic schools*, and, with them, *Catholic life*, sprang up, and diffused itself at once all over the two dioceses.

Let, then, everyone of our clergy take courage, and the Lord will dispose the hearts of the rich and the poor in his favor;—the hearts of the rich to provide him with means, the hearts of the poor to aid him, by their prayers, in the promotion of so noble a work as is the establishment of good Catholic schools.

CHAPTER XV.

ZEAL OF THE PRIEST FOR THE CATHOLIC EDUCATION OF OUR CHILDREN.

It is a matter of fact that the Protestant movement was chiefly directed against the Papacy, and that it involved a hundred years of so-called religious wars. This movement gave the princes who took the side of the Church an opportunity, of which they were not slow to avail themselves, to extend and consolidate their power over their Catholic subjects, and to establish in their dominions monarchical absolutism, or what we may choose to call modern Cæsarism.

Under plea of serving religion, they extended their power over matters which had hitherto either been left free, or subject only to the jurisdiction of the spiritual authority. They were defenders of the faith against armed heretics; and they pretended that this excess of power was necessary, in order to succeed in their undertaking. A habit of depending on them as the external defenders of religion and her altars, of the freedom of conscience, and of the Catholic civilization itself, was generated; the king took the place in the thoughts and affections of the people that was due to the Soverign Pontiff, and by giving the direction to the schools and universities in all things not absolutely of faith, they gradually became the lords of men's minds as well as bodies. In France, Spain, Portugal, and a large part of Italy, all through the seventeenth century, the youth were trained in the maxim—the Prince is the State, and his pleasure is law. Bossuet, in his politics, did only faithfully express the political sentiments and convictions of his age, shared by the great body of Catholics as well as of non-Catholics. Rational liberty had few defenders, and they were excluded, like Fenelon, from the Court. The politics of Philip II. of Spain, of Richelieu, Mazarin, and Louis XIV. in France, which were the politics of Catholic Europe, scarcely opposed by any one, except by the Popes, through the greater part of the sixteenth and the whole of the seventeenth centuries, tended directly to enslave the people, and to restrict the freedom and influence of the Church.

Trained under despotic influences by the skilful hand of despotism, extending to all matters not absolutely of the sanctuary, and sometimes daring, with sacrilegious foot, to invade the sanctuary itself, the people were gradually formed interiorly, as well as exteriorly, to the purposes of the despot. They grew up with the habits and beliefs which Cæsarism, when not resisted, is sure to generate.

The clergy, sympathizing, as is the case with every national clergy, with the sentiments of their age and nation in all things not strictly of faith, had little disposition to labor to keep alive the spirit of freedom in the hearts of the people, and would not have been permitted to do it, even if they had been so disposed. Schools were sustained, but, affected by the prevailing despotism, education declined; free thought was prohibited; and it is hard to find a literature tamer, less original and living, than that of Catholic Europe all through the eighteenth century, down almost to our own times.

As the Catholic religion was professedly patronized by the sovereigns, the Church, in superficial minds, seemed to sanction the prevailing Cæsarism. The clergy, because they preached peace, and thought to fulfil their mission without disturbing the State, came, for the first time in history, to be regarded as the chief supporters of the despot.

They who retained some reminiscences of the liberties once enjoyed by Catholic Europe, and the noble principles of freedom, asserted in the Middle Ages by the monks in their cells, and the most eminent Doctors of the Church from their chairs, became alienated from Catholicity in proportion as they cherished the spirit of resistance, and, unhappily, imbibed the fatal conviction that to overthrow the despot's throne they must break down the altar. Rightly interpreted, the old French Revolution, although bitterly anti-Catholic and infidel, was not so much hatred of religion, and impatience of her salutary restraints, as the indignant uprising of a misgoverned people against a civil despotism that affected injuriously all orders, ranks and conditions of society. The sovereigns had taken good care that an attack on them should involve an attack on religion, and to have it deeply impressed on their subjects that resistance to them was rebellion against God. The priest, who should have labored publicly to correct the issue made up by the sovereigns in accord with unbelievers, would have promoted sedition, and done more harm than good; besides, he would have been at once reduced to silence, in some one of the many ways despotism has usually at its command.

The horrors of the French Revolution, the universal breaking up of society it involved, the persecution of the Church and of her clergy, and her religious, which it shamelessly introduced in the name of liberty, the ruthless war it waged upon religion, virtue, all that wise and good men hold sacred, not unnaturally, to say the least, tended to create in the minds of the clergy and the people, who remained firm in their faith, and justly regarded religion as the first want of man and society, a deeper distrust of the practicability of liberty, and a deeper horror of all movements attempted in its name. This, again, as naturally tended to alienate the party clamoring for political and social reform still more from Catholicity; which, in its turn, has reacted with new force on the Catholic party, and made them still more determined in their anti-liberal convictions and efforts. These tendencies, on both sides, have been aggravated by the European revolutions and repressions, till now almost everywhere the lines are well defined, and the so-called Liberals are, almost to a man, bitterly anti-Catholic, and the sovereigns seem to have succeeded in forcing the issue: The Church and Cæsarism, or Liberty and Infidelity.

Certainly, as religion is of the highest necessity to man and society, infinitely more important than political freedom and social well-being, I am unable to conceive how the Catholic party, under the circumstances, could well have acted differently. Their error was in their want of vigilance and sagacity in the beginning, in suffering the political Cæsarism to revive and consolidate itself in the State, or the sovereigns, in the outset, to force upon the Catholic world so false an issue, or to place them in so unnatural and so embarrassing a position. The truth is, the Catholic party, yielding to the sovereigns, lost, to some extent, for the eighteenth century, the control of the mind of the age, and failed to lead its intelligence—they who should always be first and foremost in every department of human thought and activity.

That the struggles in Europe have an influence on the Catholic clergy and laity in this country, cannot be denied. As yet many of our Catholics, whether foreign-born or native-born, seem scarcely to realize the fact that they are freemen, and possess, in this land of freedom, equal rights with their fellow-citizens of every other denomination. They have so long been an oppressed people, that their freedom here seems hardly real. And unhappily even some of the clergy seem to be too timid and backward in defending boldly and publicly those doctrines of our holy faith which are opposed to the popular errors of our infidel age. So far we have, thank God, been enjoying full religious liberty; but it will depend mainly on the Catholic clergy to maintain this liberty, by upholding the religious principles upon which all true liberty is based. In order to maintain these principles they must defend liberty of education to the utmost, and must not cease to remind the State that it is its solemn duty to govern a free Christian people in a Christian manner, and according to the Constitution of the Republic; and that, under no pretence whatever, can it violate this Constitution in so vital a point as is the education of our children; and that it is a constant and crying injustice to tax Catholics for the support of godless schools. We must not yield any of our constitutional rights; if we do, the Church will be implicated, by degrees, in the same kind of struggle which is now becoming so serious in Europe.

Now in order to meet with success, let us take up the press. In our country, unfortunately, an unchristian press is guaranteed the fullest liberty, and the evils that flow from that liberty are widely spread. It is certain that this unrestricted freedom of the press, which every one is ready to abuse, and which allows every one to constitute himself a teacher of the public, can be defended neither on principles of reason nor of faith. It becomes, therefore, not only our privilege, but our solemn duty, to combat the unchristian by a really Christian press—a matter on which the Church, and the Head of the Church, have spoken in an unmistakable manner. If Catholics have not thorough Catholic papers, they will take periodicals which are not Catholic. To have even one good paper, through which we can give expression to our thoughts, is a great blessing and a great gain; but that certainly does not enable us to give our voice that weight in the questions of the day to which it is entitled. A great deal has, of late years, been done for the establishment of Catholic journals, and much good has been accomplished by them. But far more might have been done had the Catholic press received more support both from the clergy and laity. It is so easy for the clergy to give this support by encouraging the Catholics in general, but especially the members of so many excellent Catholic associations, to subscribe to such periodicals. One word from the priest on the usefulness of having a good Catholic paper and magazine in the family, will induce a hundred times more Catholics to become subscribers, than the longest appeal of a newspaper editor. The stronger the Catholic press becomes, the more the attention of the nation is called to it, the more shall we secure their respect for us and our religion. Yes, it is absolutely necessary in a country like ours, where religious tracts from Protestant societies, and pamphlets and periodicals of the most obscene character, are flying over the land like leaves before the autumn wind, that Catholic journals should be called into existence on every hand, and that no sacrifice should be spared to do so, and to encourage those already in existence. If the clergy only take the matter in hand, they will find those willing and able to carry the matter through. Let us use our talents, as God shall grant us grace and ability, that we may, by so powerful a means as is the press, disseminate the principles of truth, in order to contend with error. The light of truth is far more calculated to dispel the darkness of error, than the light of the sun is to disperse the darkness of the night. Why are there so many talents lying idle among us? Why so many pens that move not, when they should be burning with love for God, and for the welfare of their fellow-men? Why so many tongues that are ever silent, when they might, day after day, preach the good tidings of the Gospel of Christ? Let us rest assured God has given to us, to every man his vocation, his sphere of action and holy influence, wherein he can proclaim to those around him that faith which maketh wise unto salvation. Let us not be cowards,—let us show as much determination and courage, let us sacrifice as much for the propagation of truth as its enemies do for the dissemination of error; bearing, however, always in mind that the manner in which we must combat error ought to be charitable; for otherwise it is not calculated to command respect, and make a salutary impression. It is thus that our fellow-citizens of other denominations will come to understand that we appreciate our liberty, and know how to use it for the benefit of the public.

But all rights and liberties avail nothing, in the end, if Catholic education itself is not what it ought to be. And the great battle that is waging, that education may not be deprived of its Christian character, can be won by us only on condition that teachers, and educators themselves, as well as parents and the clergy, understand precisely the full bearing of the question.

To-day, more than ever, we need a thorough Catholic education. The enemies of our religion are now making war upon its dogmas more generally and craftily than at any former period. Their attacks, for being wily and concealed, are all the more pernicious. The impious rage of a Voltaire, or the "solemn sneer" of a Gibbon, would be less dangerous than this insidious warfare. They disguise their designs under the appearance of devotion to progressive ideas, and hatred of superstition and intolerance, all the better to instil the slow but deadly poison. By honeyed words, a studied candor, a dazzle of erudition, they have spread their "gossamer nets of seduction" over the world. The press teems with books and journals in which doctrines subversive of religion and morality are so elegantly set forth, that the unguarded reader is very apt to be deceived by the fascination of false charms, and to mistake a most hideous and dangerous object for the very type of beauty. The serpent stealthily glides under the silken verdure of a polished style. Nothing is omitted. The passions are fed, and the morbid sensibilities pandered to; firmness in the cause of truth or virtue is called obstinacy; and strength of soul, a refractory blindness. The bases of morality are sapped in the name of liberty; the discipline of the Church, when not branded as sheer "mummery," is held up as hostile to personal freedom; and her dogmas, with one or two exceptions, are treated as opinions which may be received or rejected with like indifference.

Nor is this irreligious tendency confined to literary publications; it finds numerous and powerful advocates in men of scientific pursuits, who strive to make the worse appear the better cause. The chemist has never found in his crucible that intangible something which men call spirit; so, in the name of science, he pronounces it a myth. The anatomist has dissected the human frame; but, failing to meet the immaterial substance—the soul—he denies its existence. The physicist has weighed the conflicting theories of his predecessors in the scale of criticism, and finally decides that bodies are nothing more than the accidental assemblage of atoms, and rejects the very idea of a Creator. The geologist, after investigating the secrets of the earth, triumphantly tells us that he has accumulated an overwhelming mass of facts to refute the biblical cosmogony, and thus subvert the authority of the inspired record. The astronomer flatters himself that he has discovered natural and necessary laws, which do away with the necessity of admitting that a Divine Hand once launched the heavenly bodies into space, and still guides them in their courses; the stenographer has studied the peculiarities of the races; he has met with widely-different conformations, and believes himself sufficiently authorized to deny the unity of the human family; in a word, they conclude that nothing exists but matter, that God is a myth, and the soul "the dream of a dream."

Thus do men attack these sacred truths, which cannot be shaken without greatly injuring, and finally destroying, the social edifice.

Now, when we see the snares so cunningly laid to entrap our youth, can we wonder that so many of our Catholic young men, even after they have been educated at Catholic colleges, are caught in them, and fall into infidelity? A short time ago, a gentleman of great learning, and a celebrated convert to our Church, told me that he had the greatest trouble to keep his son from falling into infidelity, though he was naturally inclined to piety. He said that he had him educated at one of the best colleges in the country, and that he felt surprised at the fact that so many of the young men educated there had become infidels. "I cannot," he said, "account for this, otherwise than by presuming that the religious training there is not solid enough; that the heathen world is too much read and studied; that principles somewhat too lax are in vogue; that the truths of our religion are taught too superficially; that the principles which underlie the dogmas are not sufficiently explained, inculcated, and impressed upon the minds of the young men, and that their educators fail in giving them a correct idea of the spirit and essence of our religion, which is based on divine revelation, and invested in a Body divinely commissioned to teach all men, authoritatively and infallibly, all its sacred and immutable truths—truths which we are consequently bound in conscience to receive without hesitation.

"Now what I have said of certain colleges applies also, unhappily, to many of our female academies; they are by no means what they should be, according to the spirit of the Church; they conform too much to the spirit of the world; they have too many human considerations; they make too many allowances for Protestant pupils at the expense of the Catholic spirit and training of our young Catholic ladies; they yield too much to the spirit of the age; in a word, they attend more to the intellectual than to the spiritual culture of their pupils.

"But what is even more surprising than all this is, that some of our Catholic clergy, and among them some even of those who should be first and foremost in fighting for sound religious principles, and seeing that our youth are carefully brought up in them, are too much inclined to yield to the godless spirit of the age—to the so-called liberal views on Catholic education, which have been clearly and solemnly condemned by the Holy See. They tell us poor people in the world, that, if we are careless in bringing up our children as good Catholics, we are worse than heathens, and have denied our faith! that, if our children are lost through our neglect, we also shall be lost. I would like to know whether God will show Himself more merciful to those of our clergy who take so little interest in the religious instruction of our youth; who make little or no exertions to establish Catholic schools, where we could have our children properly educated; who, when they condescend to instruct them, do so in bombastic language, in scholastic terms which the poor children cannot understand, taking no pains to give their instructions in plain words, and in a manner attractive for children.

"As the pastor is, so is the flock. We enjoy full religious liberty in our country. All we need is good, courageous pastors—standard-bearers in the cause of God and the people. We would be only too happy to follow them, and to support and encourage them by every means in our power. What an immense amount of good could thus be achieved in a short time! Our religion never loses anything of its efficacy upon the minds and hearts of men; it can only lose in as far as it is not brought to bear upon them. What is most wanted is not argument, but instruction and explanation.

"I can hardly account for this want of zeal for true Catholic education in so many of our clergy, who are otherwise models of every virtue, than by supposing the fact that their ecclesiastical training must have been deficient in many respects, or that they must have spent their youth in our godless Public Schools, where they were never thoroughly imbued with the true spirit of the Catholic Church—the spirit of God.

"I have quietly, for some time, studied, as far as I was able, the prevailing spirit of our people; noted the remarks and efforts of a few ecclesiastics, laics, and Catholic periodicals (and, alas! how very few) made in behalf of the sacred obligation of education, and endeavored to compare the results with the efforts, and the observation *made* is sadly disheartening.

"Examine the Catholic almanacs, the census of the various States, or those of the United States, and ascertain, first, the number of Catholics in the country; second, the number of those between the ages of six and twenty-one years; then divide this last number by the number of Catholic schools, including colleges, academies, convents, parochial and private schools, and the *quotient* will be what? *Indifference to Catholic education!* In other words, this simple operation in vulgar arithmetic demonstrates that in no country claiming to be enlightened can be found *thirteen millions* of Catholics with such an inadequate number of schools as we have, or are likely to have, if a policy widely different from that which prevails at present be not *early* inaugurated and steadily pursued. It is, indeed, true—and I willingly, cheerfully admit the fact—that most of our priests, and nearly all our bishops, are exerting themselves zealously, strenuously, and with marked success, in the cause of education. But *not all* the priests; *not all* the bishops are enlisted in the cause; nor are all in *positive* sympathy with it. All may be, perhaps are, agreed in believing that Catholic education is necessary; but *all are not* agreed as to the necessity of Catholic schools in which it may be secured. Unanimity exists as to the *end*, but not as to the *means* to that end. And this lack or absence of unanimity, especially among those whose peculiar province it is to shape and direct Catholic sentiment, has produced, and continues to produce, the most injurious consequences.

"Many of the clergy are *not* opposed to the Public Schools, nor do they feel reluctant to publicly make known the "faith which is in them," when an opportunity presents itself. Many are opposed to these schools, but theirs is a *negative* opposition; that is, they are not in favor of them. They believe that Catholic schools are better and safer, but they do not consider it a duty incumbent on themselves to undertake the labor and trouble inseparable from the establishment and direction of parochial schools. These reverend gentlemen are simply neutrals; that is, *if men may, or can, be neutral on such a subject*.

"Thought is free, and it may, perhaps, be impossible to have entire unanimity in matters of opinion only; but if one of the ends sought to be attained by the Church be the securing to each child a Catholic education, it is very evident that the establishment of schools should not be left to the discretion or whim of the several pastors. Upon subjects far less important than that of schools, the statutes in many dioceses are clear, explicit, binding. Is there any reason for their silence on the subject of education? Our bishops have not only the power, but the will, to enforce such matters of discipline as they deem necessary. This granted—because too clear to be denied—does it not follow that the establishment of schools maybe made obligatory upon pastors? Let discipline be made uniform, and we will not witness such an anomalous condition of things as exist at present. Duties are never in collision; obligations never clash. There is but one right thing to be done, but one right cause to pursue, all things considered; and whatever is in conflict with this cannot be a duty, whatever may seem to be its claim. In some parts of this country, the sacraments are refused to those who decline to have their children attend Catholic schools where such are convenient; but there is not, so far as I am informed, in those parts, any *rule* making it obligatory upon pastors to establish such schools. In other sections, to withhold the sacraments for such a cause is unthought of. The consequence is that many Catholics are at a loss to understand why it is that an act which subjects them to such severe punishment in one diocese should in another not call forth even a mild reproof—pass unnoticed. In actions indifferent in themselves, it may be wise, "when in Rome, to do as the Romans do";

but where *principle* is involved, such an easy adaptability cannot be encouraged.

"In this laxity of discipline, and in this want of uniformity, in this wide difference of opinion among those who give direction to Catholic sentiment, and who speak, as it were, *ex cathedra,* may be found some of the causes for the indifference existing among our people on the question of Catholic education.

"But it is so convenient to allow things to go on in the old way, and so hard to establish anything new. Yet a thing which, in the great struggle between the Church and antichrist, is one of the most powerful means of victory, is really worth the highest sacrifice. Indeed, the establishment of thorough Catholic schools is the most important step that can be taken by our clergy to solve certain social questions, and which can be solved only on Catholic principles. The greatest social danger of the age, is the dechristianization and demoralization of the rising generation. This dechristianization and demoralization are, to a great extent, the cause of the wretchedness of society, and make that wretchedness almost incurable. What enormous dimensions has this evil assumed under the present godless system of education in the Public Schools! But even the evils resulting from this system might, to a great extent, be healed, if the clergy labor, with the zeal and fire of apostolic times, to have good schools, and imbue our children therein with thorough Christian knowledge, with fervent piety and earnest devotion. Oh! if the children of light were only as wise as the children of the world, we should witness wonders. It is true that evil makes its way in this world better than goodness does, but it is also true that goodness does not prosper, because those who represent it take the matter too lightly, or do not go about it as they should. More is often done for the worst cause than men are willing to do or to sacrifice for the best. A great deal has of late years been done for the establishment and maintenance of Catholic schools. Let us sincerely hope that a great deal more will be done, and more universally; and need requires us not only to pray, but to work with all our strength, with inexhaustible patience and devotion, at the establishment of Catholic schools, and make, for this noblest of objects, sacrifices not less generous than those made by infidels in behalf of godless education."

It was thus that the good old gentleman spoke to me. He uttered great truths. His language is that of all good Catholics in the country. I have often heard it. It is no exaggeration to assert that the salvation of those of our clergy who have charge of congregations depends, in a great measure, on the solicitude with which they promote the thorough Catholic education of those children who are confided to their care.

"Therefore, ye shepherds, hear the word of the Lord: Thus saith the Lord God: Behold I Myself come upon the shepherds, I will require My flock at their hand."—(Ezek. xxxiv. 9, 10.)

If our Lord will require His flock at the hands of their pastors, He will undoubtedly require from them a stricter account of that part of his flock for which he has always shown a particular predilection, that is, for children. It was to children that He gave the special honor of being the first to shed their blood for His name's sake. He has given them to us as a model of humility, which we should imitate: "Unless you become like little children, you shall not enter the kingdom of heaven." He wishes that every one should hold them in great honor: "See that you despise not one of these little ones." Why not? "For I say to you, that their angels always see the face of My Father who is in heaven."—(Matt. xviii. 10.)

He wishes every one to be on his guard, lest he should scandalize a little child: "It were better for him that a mill-stone were put about his neck, and he cast into the sea, than that he should scandalize one of these little ones."—(Matt. xviii. 6.)

He says that the love, attention, and respect paid to a child, is paid to Himself. "And Jesus took a child and said to them: Whosoever shall receive this child in My name, receiveth Me."—(Luke ix. 48.)

He rebuked those who tried to prevent little children from being presented to Him, that He might bless them: "And they brought to Him young children, that he might touch them. And the disciples rebuked those who brought them; whom, when Jesus saw, He was much displeased, and saith to them: Suffer the little ones to come unto Me, and forbid them not: for of such is the kingdom of God. Amen I say to you, whosoever shall not receive the kingdom of God as a *little child*, shall not enter into it. And embracing them, and laying His hands upon them, He blessed them."—(Mark x. 13-16.)

The motives, then, that should induce every priest to devote himself zealously to the spiritual welfare of youth, are: First, the great interest which Jesus Christ takes in children; and second, the more abundant fruits reaped from the care bestowed upon the young.

The Son of God came into the world to redeem all who were lost. But do children profit by His abundant redemption? Do they draw from the source of graces that are open to all? Will they be marked with the seal of Divine Adoption, and be nourished with His own Flesh in the Sacrament of His love? Will they be counted, in the course of their career, among the number of His faithful disciples, or among the enemies of His law? Will they one day be admitted into His kingdom? Will they be excluded? Is it heaven or hell that will be their lot for all eternity? It is we priests, and almost we only, that are expected to solve these problems. Children are the noblest portion of the flock that is confided to our care. Their fate is in our hands. If our zeal is not active in their salvation, Jesus will lose, in them, the fruit of His sufferings and death. How many are deprived forever of the sight and possession of God, because they have not received a good Catholic education. Who is to blame? Has the pastor sufficiently instructed, warned, and watched over them? How many lose their baptismal innocence almost as soon as they are capable of losing it, grow up in vicious habits, grow old in sin, and die impenitent at last, because they were neglected in early youth, were not subjected to the amiable yoke of virtue! "Bonum est viro, cum portaverit jugum ab adolescentia suâ."—(Thren. iii. 27.) If the first years of life are pure, they often sanctify all the after life; but if the roots of the tree are rotten and dead, the branches will not be more healthy. "Adolescentes, cum semel à malitiâ fuerint occupati, quasi incaptivitatem essent adducti, quoquo diabolus jusserit eunt."—(S. Chrys. Hom. 19 in Gen.) Education is the mould in which a man's moral, intellectual, and religious character is formed. Man will become, in his old age, what education made him in his youth. "Adolescens juxta viam suam, etiam cum senuerit, non recedet ab ea."—(Prov. xxii. 6.) All is a snare and seduction for youth. If the fear of God, the horror of evil, the maxims of religion, are not profoundly engraven in the soul, what is to protect young people from their passions? What can be expected of a young man who has never heard of the happiness of virtue, the hopes of the future life, and the blessings or the woes of eternity? Now who will give the Christian education, if not the pastor? Can we rely on the parents? on Sunday-school teachers? Oh, priests! we are almost the only resource of these poor children. Can we, knowing, as we do, how much Jesus Christ loves them, can we, I say, resign ourselves to leaving them in their misery? "The kings of the earth have their favorites," said St. Augustine. The favorites of Jesus Christ are innocent souls. What is more innocent than the heart of a child whom baptism has purified from original stain, and who has not, as yet, contracted the stain of actual sin? This heart is the sanctuary of the Holy Ghost. Who can tell with what delight He makes of it His abode? Deliciæ meæ esse cum filiis hominum. Look at the mothers who penetrated the crowd that surrounded the Saviour, in order to beg Him to bless their children. . . . They are at first repulsed; but soon after, what is their joy when they hear the good Master approve their desires, and justify what a zeal, little enlightened, taxed with indiscretion! Ah! let us understand the desires of the Son of God. "Suffer," says He to us, "suffer little children to come to me." What! You banish those who are dearest to Me? They who resemble them belong to the kingdom of heaven. If you love Me, take care of My sheep, but neglect not My lambs. Pasce agnos meos. Despise not one of My little ones. "Videte ne contemnatis unum ex his pusillis."—(Matt. xviii. 10.) I regard as done to Myself, all that is done to them. "Qui susceperit unum parvulum talem, in nomine meo, me suscipit."—(Ibid. 5.) O Saviour of the world! the desire to be beloved by Thee, and to prove my love for Thee, urges me to devote myself to the Catholic education of our children.

How great and consoling are not the fruits of zeal, when it has youth for its object! The good pastor never despairs of the salvation of his sheep, whatever may be their wanderings; he knows the power of grace, and the infinite mercy of the Lord. But what difficulties does he not encounter when he undertakes to bring back to God persons advanced in age! Children, on the contrary, oppose but one obstacle to his zeal—levity. All he needs with them is patience. Their souls are like new earth, which waits only culture to produce a quadruple. They are flexible plants, which take the form and direction given to them. Their hearts, pure from criminal affections, are susceptible of happy impressions and tendencies. They believe in authority. A religious instinct leads them to the priest. They adopt with confidence the faith and the sentiments of those who instruct them. Oh, how easy to soften that age, in speaking of a God Who has made Himself a child, and Who died for us! to awaken the fear of the Lord, compassion for those who suffer, gratitude, divine love, in souls predisposed, by the grace of baptism, to all the Christian virtues! Ask the most zealous pastors, and all will tell you that no part of their ministry is more consoling than that which is exercised for youth, because the fruits are incomparably more abundant. Although all my efforts for the sanctification of an old man, ever unfaithful to his duties, should be crowned with success, they could not help his long life being frightfully void of merits, and a permanent revolt against heaven. But if there be a child in question, my zeal sanctifies his whole life; I deposit in his soul the germ of all the good that he will do, and I shall participate in all the good works with which his career will be filled. All believers have come out of one single Abraham. From one child, well brought up, a whole generation of true Christians can proceed. In this little flock that surrounds me, God sees, perhaps, elect souls on whom His Providence has formed great designs—pious instructors, holy priests, who will carry far the knowledge of His name, and aid Him in saving millions of souls. In what astonishment would the first catechists of a St. Vincent de Paul, of a Francis Xavier, be thrown, had they been told what would become of those children, and what they would one day accomplish! But even supposing that all those confided to me follow the common way, I have in them the surest means of renewing my parish. To-day they receive the movement, in fifteen years they will give it. They will transmit good principles, happy inclinations to their own children, who will transmit them in their turn. Behold, it is thus that holy traditions are established, and a chain of solid virtues perpetuated; ages will reap what I have sown in a few days. It is by these considerations that the greatest saints, and the finest geniuses of Christianity, became so much attached to the education of youth. St. Jerome, St. Gregory Pope, St. Augustine, St. Vincent Ferrier, St. Charles Borromeo, St. Francis de Sales, St. Joseph Calasanctius, Gerson, Bellarmin, Bossuet, Fenelon, M. Olier, etc., believed they could never better employ their time and talents than in consecrating them to the education of the young. "It is considered honorable and useful to educate the son of a monarch, presumptive heir to his crown. . . . But the child that I form to virtue, is he not the child of God, inheritor of the kingdom of heaven?"—(Gerson.) "Believe me," said St. Francis de Sales, "the angels of little children love those with a particular love who bring them up in the fear of God, and who plant in their tender souls holy devotion." Have we always comprehended all the good that we can do to children by our humble functions?

But if we wish for the end, we must also wish for the means—for Catholic schools. They are the nurseries of the Church, as novitiates are the nurseries of religious orders. The chief pastoral work of the Church is to be done in the school. The school must be the chief solicitude of the priest. He must consider no trouble too great, no sacrifice of time and convenience too much, in order to secure good attendance and efficiency in the school. Neither sick calls, nor any other ecclesiastical duties, should be allowed to interfere with the school. He must be the life and character of the school, and it is principally he who must administer correction. The authority of the priest, his interest in the school, and his relation towards the parents, are far more persuasive and effectual as corrections, than scoldings and penances inflicted by the master and mistress.

It seems to me that we cannot insist too much upon the vital importance of the Catholic school. A priest's time is never better employed than when three or four hours of it are daily spent in school—and that so regularly, that his presence in the school is looked for alike by teachers, children, and parents—and when he then occupies another portion of his day in looking after the defaulters, and in talking with parents over the school duties, and the future prospects of their children.

Thus the parents feel that in sending their children to be educated there, they are not turning them over to a number of paid teachers, nor even to Brothers and Sisters, but to the clergy themselves, for their education. This personal interest and solicitude of the priest reacts upon the parents as well as upon the children.

A pastor, then, wishing to secure the salvation of the best part of the flock of Jesus Christ, must do all in his power to establish good Catholic schools, and oblige parents to send their children to them, and not to Public Schools—to the grave of Catholicity. It is *then*, also, and not till then, that we shall see more young people called to the priesthood, and to such religious orders as devote themselves especially to the education of youth. In Europe, the bishops and priests, together with the laity, fight for the liberty of educating the children according to Catholic principles and customs. In this country, our religious liberty is as great as it possibly can be. Now not to profit by this liberty, is for the shepherds of the flock of Jesus Christ to incur the greatest guilt; it is to be like that ungodly Bishop of Burgos, who, on being told by Las Casas that seven thousand children had perished in three months, said: "Look you, what a queer fool! what is this to me, and what is that to the King?" To which Las Casas replied: "Is it nothing to your Lordship that all these souls should perish? Oh, great and eternal God! And to whom, then, is it of any concern?"—(Life of Las Casas, by Arthur Helps.)

To be destitute of ardent zeal for the spiritual welfare of children, is to see, with indifferent eyes, the Blood of Jesus Christ trodden under foot; it is to see the image and likeness of God lie in the mire, and not care for it; it is to despise the Blessed Trinity; the Father, who created them; the Son, who redeemed them; the Holy Ghost, who sanctified them; it is to belong to that class of shepherds, of whom the Lord commanded Ezekiel to prophesy as follows: "Son of man, prophesy concerning the shepherds of Israel: prophesy and say to the shepherds: Thus saith the Lord God: Wo to the shepherds of Israel. . . . My flock you did not feed. The weak you have not strengthened; and that which was sick, you have not healed: that which was broken, you have not bound up; and that which was driven away, you have not brought again; neither have you sought that which was lost:. . . and My sheep were scattered, because there was no shepherd: and they became the prey of all the beasts of the field, and were scattered. My sheep have wandered in every mountain, and in every high hill: and there was none, I say, that sought them. Therefore, ye shepherds, hear the word of the Lord: Behold, I Myself come upon the shepherds. I will require My flock at their hands."—(Ezek. xxxiv. 2-10.) To be destitute of this zeal for the Catholic education of our children, is to hide the five talents which the Lord has given us, instead of gaining other five talents. Surely the Lord will say: "And the unprofitable servant cast ye out into the exterior darkness. There shall be weeping and gnashing of teeth."—(Matt. xxv. 30.)

What a shame for pastors of souls to know that the devil, in alliance with the wicked, is at work, day and night, for the ruin and destruction of youth, and to be so little concerned about their eternal loss; just as if it was not true what the holy Fathers say, that the salvation of one soul is worth more than the whole visible world! Since when is it, then, that the price of the souls of little children has been lessened? Ah, as long as the price of the Blood of Jesus Christ remains of an infinite value, so long the price of souls will remain the same also! Heaven and earth will pass away, but this truth will not. The devil knows and understands it but too well. Oh! how he delights in a priest who is called, by Jesus Christ, "the hireling, because he has no care for the sheep, and who seeth the wolf coming and leaveth the sheep and flieth."—(John x. 12.)

On the Day of Judgment, such a priest will be confounded by that poor man of whom we read, in the life of St. Francis de Sales, as follows: One day this holy and zealous pastor, on a visit of his diocese, had reached the top of one of those dreadful mountains, overwhelmed with fatigue and cold, his hands and feet completely benumbed, in order to visit a single parish in that dreary situation; while he was viewing, with astonishment, those immense blocks of ice of an uncommon thickness, the inhabitants, who had approached to meet him, related that some days before a shepherd, running after a strayed sheep, had fallen into one of these tremendous precipices. They added that his fate would never have been known if his companion, who was in search of him, had not discovered his hat on the edge of the precipice. The poor man, therefore, imagined that the shepherd might be still relieved, or, if he should have perished, that he might be honored with a Christian burial.

With this view he descended, by the means of ropes, this icy precipice, whence he was drawn up, pierced through with cold, and holding in his arms his companion, who was dead, and almost frozen into a block of ice. Francis, hearing this account, turned to his attendants, who were disheartened with the extreme fatigues which they had every day to encounter, and availing himself of this circumstance to encourage them, he said: "Some persons imagine that we do too much, and we certainly do far less than these poor people. You have heard in what manner one has lost his life in an attempt to find a strayed animal; and how another has exposed himself to the danger of perishing, in order to procure for his friend a burial, which, under these circumstances, might have been dispensed with. These examples speak to us in forcible language; by this charity we are confounded, we who perform much less for the salvation of souls intrusted to our care, than those poor people do for the security of animals confided to their charge." Then the holy Prelate heaved a deep sigh, saying: "My God, what a beautiful lesson for bishops and pastors! This poor shepherd has sacrificed his life to save a strayed sheep, and I, alas! have so little zeal for the salvation of souls. The least obstacle suffices to deter me, and make me calculate my every step and trouble. Great God, give me true zeal, and the genuine spirit of a good shepherd! Ah, how many shepherds of souls will not this herdsman judge!" Alas! how just and how true is this remark. If we saw our very enemies surrounded by fire, we would think of means to rescue them from the danger; and now we see thousands of little children, redeemed at the price of the blood of Jesus Christ, on the point of losing their faith, and with it their souls; and shall we be less concerned and less active for these images and likenesses of God than for their frames, their bodies?

We hear a little child weeping, and we at once try to console it; we hear a little dog whining at the door, and we open it; a poor beggar asks for a piece of bread, and we give it; and we hear the Mother of our Catholic children—the Catholic

Church—cry in lamentable accents: "Let my little ones have the bread of life—a good Christian education"—and we do not heed her voice. We hear Jesus Christ cry, "Suffer the little ones to come unto Me," by means of a Catholic education; we hear him say: "Woe to him who scandalizes a little child"—who makes it lose his innocence—his faith—his soul, by sending it to godless schools; we see Him weep over Jerusalem, over the loss of so many Catholic children, and we hear Him say: "Weep not over me, but for *your children*"; and neither His voice nor His tears make any impression. We say with the man in the Gospel, "Trouble me not, the door (of our heart) is now shut, I cannot rise and give thee."—(Luke xi.) If an ass, says our Lord, falls into a pit, you will pull him out even on a Sabbath-day; and an innocent soul, nay, thousands of innocent children, fall away from Me and pass over to the army of the apostate angels, and become My and your adversaries, and you do not care. Oh, what great cruelty, what hardness of heart, nay, what great impiety! If we were blind, we should not have sin; but as Jesus Christ has spoken to us on the subject of education through His Vicar on earth, through so many zealous bishops, through sad experience, nay, even through many of those who are outside the Church, we have no excuse for our sin of suffering devilish wolves to devour our youth in our country. "My watchmen," says the Lord, "are all *dumb dogs*, not able to bark, seeing vain things, *sleeping*, and loving dreams."—(Isa. lvi. 10.) Truly the curses and maledictions of all those who led a bad life, and were damned for want of a good Christian education, which we neglected to give them, will come down upon us! What shall we answer? "And he was silent."—Matt. xxii.

Marvellous, indeed, have been God's gracious dealings with this poor land of ours, so very far above what we could have dreamed or hoped for some years ago, that we may say in all truth that the finger of God has touched us. That touch has quickened Catholic life in our land to a wonderful extent; not, indeed, as yet, with the great exuberance of Catholic European countries, but nevertheless with almost exulting gladness; for to-day there are few indeed of our cities and towns in which at least the pulse of Catholic life does not beat strongly.

But why have these great things been done for us? Why has our Catholic life been increased and strengthened so wonderfully, except to win more souls to Christ, to bring more of the American people into closer union with God? If this be so, then we must not leave our Lord to work alone; we must be fellow-workers with Him, by helping forward the growth of holiness, the progress of the spiritual life, the poverty of the Cross, the spreading of His Spirit in opposition to the formal and self-indulgent spirit of the age, and this by every means in our power; and, above all, by multiplying amongst us Catholic schools and institutions. What the future may have in store for the Church in America we cannot tell; whether, when more of God's Spirit has been poured out upon us, our sons and our daughters shall prophesy, and our young men shall see visions, and our old men shall dream dreams, as in the days of old; but of this we may be sure, that in exact proportion as our clergy exert that mighty energy which springs from the living faith that overcomes the world, in order to leaven the mass of the American people, and to build up, throughout the length and breadth of the land, temples and schools to God's holy name, and altars to His honor, will be the manifestation of the kingdom of God with power and majesty in the midst of this American land, and the grasp of God's Church upon the hearts and minds of this American people!

I have now only to add that I submit this, and whatever else I have written, to the better judgment of our Bishops, but especially to the Holy See, anxiously desirous to think nothing, to say nothing, to teach nothing but what is approved of by those to whom the sacred deposit of Faith has been committed—those who watch over us as being *to render an account to God for our souls*.

Now, should the Prelates of the Church deem this publication ever so little calculated to promote the great cause for which it has been written, the compiler will believe himself amply rewarded for his labor, and he will feel extremely grateful if they encourage its circulation by giving it their special approbation and recommendation.

9 789361 381096

Printed by Libri Plureos GmbH in Hamburg,
Germany